THE ESSENCE OF HUMAN

CW00816062

THE ESSENCE OF HUMAN FREEDOM

An Introduction to Philosophy

Martin Heidegger

Translated by Ted Sadler

continuum
LONDON • NEW YORK

Continuum

The Tower Building
11 York Road
London SE1 7NX

15 East 26th Street
New York
NY 10010

www.continuumbooks.com

This English translation © Continuum 2002

This edition 2005
Originally published as *Vom Wesen der menschlichen Freiheit*
© Vittorio Klostermann GmbH, Frankfurt am Main, 1982

Die Herausgabe dieses Werkes wurde aus Mitteln von INTER NATIONES, Bonn gefördert

British Library Cataloguing in Publication Data
A catalogue record for this book is available
from the British Library.

Library of Congress Cataloging in Publication Data
A catalog record for this book is available from the Library of Congress

ISBN 0–8264–7936–7

Typeset by RefineCatch Limited, Bungay, Suffolk
Printed and bound in Great Britain by Antony Rowe, Chippenham, Wiltshire

Contents

PART ONE

POSITIVE DEFINITION OF PHILOSOPHY FROM THE CONTENT OF THE PROBLEM OF FREEDOM

THE PROBLEM OF HUMAN FREEDOM AND THE FUNDAMENTAL QUESTION OF PHILOSOPHY

CHAPTER THREE

PART TWO

CAUSALITY AND FREEDOM

TRANSCENDENTAL AND PRACTICAL
FREEDOM IN KANT

CHAPTER ONE

CONCLUSION

Translator's Foreword

This book is a translation of *Vom Wesen der menschlichen Freiheit: Einleitung in die Philosophie*, first published in 1982 (2nd edn 1994) as Volume 31 of Martin Heidegger's *Gesamtausgabe*. The text is based on a lecture course delivered by Heidegger at the University of Freiburg in the summer semester of 1930. As the title indicates, the fundamental theme of the course as a whole is the essence of human freedom. However, after a preliminary discussion of the problem of freedom and its relationship to philosophy in general, Heidegger devotes Part One of the course primarily to the problem of being in Greek metaphysics, this providing the framework for his interpretation of *Kant's* treatment of freedom and causality in Part Two. In no other work by Heidegger do we find a comparably detailed consideration of Kant's practical philosophy as that given in the present text. Further, in no other work is Heidegger's interpretation of the key Chapter 10 of Aristotle's *Metaphysics* Θ presented with comparable thoroughness.

Information on the origin of the German text as printed in the *Gesamtausgabe* can be found in Hartmut Tietjen's Afterword to the original edition (pp. 209–11 of this volume). The reader of the present translation should bear in mind that Heidegger did not originally intend, nor at any time did he prepare, this lecture course for publication. As is also the case in respect of other posthumously published lecture courses by Heidegger, the German text does not have the character of a polished work, often exhibiting a roughness and stylistic irregularity indicative of oral presentation. My translation attempts to remain as close as possible to Heidegger's actual words, remaining faithful to the unfinished nature of the text while giving due attention to readability.

It is well-known that Heidegger's language poses formidable difficulties for the translator, difficulties that are compounded when one is dealing with texts derived from lecture manuscripts and transcripts. Insertion of the original German in square brackets within the translation is one way of drawing attention to specific problems, but this practice, if carried out extensively, could easily overburden an already complex text. Accordingly I have sought to minimize such insertions, for the most part restricting them to especially significant occurrences of operational terms and to words whose etymological interrelations Heidegger is seeking to highlight. However, I have provided an extensive English–German Glossary, which, while not an infallible guide, should answer most queries as to what German word is being translated at any particular point. I have also attached a short Greek–English Glossary.

One translational decision requires specific comment, especially as it is reflected in the title of this volume. In line with most previous translations of Heidegger and other German philosophers I have rendered 'Wesen' as 'essence'. It should be kept in mind, however, that when Heidegger uses 'Wesen' in connection with freedom, truth, and the human being, he does not mean the same thing as the Latin 'essentia', which refers to the 'what-ness' or 'essential nature' of something. Instead, in such contexts Heidegger wants to convey the original *verbal* meaning of 'Wesen'. For example, since freedom is not a 'thing', the 'essence of freedom' does not refer to anything fixed and static, but rather to an 'occurrence' wherein the human being actively 'appropriates' its proper being.

The frequent passages of Greek, particularly in Part One, are usually translated or paraphrased by Heidegger himself. Where this is not the case, I have given standard English translations in the endnotes. Other endnotes are from the editor of the German edition, who as well as giving bibliographical references sometimes puts supplementary material from Heidegger there also.

References to and quotations from Kant's writings have been given according to standard English translations (occasionally modified), with the approximate pagination of the German 'Akademie' edition in brackets; however, references to the *Critique of Pure Reason* (abbreviated CPR) follow the standard numbering system of this particular work.

The Kant translations used are as follows:

Kritik der reinen Vernunft: *Immanuel Kant's Critique of Pure Reason*, trans. Norman Kemp Smith, London: Macmillan, 1933.

Grundlegung zur Metaphysik der Sitten: *Foundations of the Metaphysics of Morals*.
Kritik der praktischen Vernunft: *Critique of Practical Reason*.
Both translated by Lewis White Beck in *Immanuel Kant: Critique of Practical Reason and Other Writings in Moral Philosophy*, trans. and edited by Beck, Chicago: University of Chicago Press, 1949.

Kritik der Urteilskraft: *Critique of Judgement*, trans. Werner S. Pluhar, Indianapolis: Hackett Publishing Company, 1987.

De mundi sensibilis atque intelligibilis forma et principiis: *Dissertation on the Form and Principles of the Sensible and Intelligible World*, trans. John Handyside in *Kant's Inaugural Dissertation and Early Writings on Space*, London: Open Court, 1928.

Prolegomena zu einer jeden künftigen Metaphysik: *Prolegomena to Any Future Metaphysics*, trans. Paul Caurus (extensively revised by James W. Ellington), in *Kant's Philosophy of Material Nature*, Indianapolis: Hackett Publishing Company, 1985.

For assistance in the preparation of this translation I would like to thank Dr Marnie Hanlon. Valuable comments have also been received from Prof. Parvis Emad and Prof. F.-W. von Hermann.

Ted Sadler
August 2001

Preliminary Considerations

§ 1. The Apparent Contradiction between the 'Particular' Question Concerning the Essence of Human Freedom and the 'General' Task of an Introduction to Philosophy

The theme of this introduction to philosophy is already signalled in the title of the lecture course. It is the essence of human freedom. We are to treat of freedom, more specifically, of human freedom. We are to treat of man.

So we shall be considering man and not animals: not plants, not material bodies, not the products of craft and technology, not works of art, not God, but man and his freedom.

Those things just listed as outside or alongside man are as familiar to us as man himself. All these things are spread out before us and we can distinguish various items one from another. Yet we are also acquainted with that in which, despite every distinction and difference, all things agree. Everything we know is known as something that *is*, and everything that *is* we call a being [*ein Seiendes*]. To be a being [*Seiendes zu sein*] is what everything we have mentioned, primarily and in the last instance, has in common.

The human being, whose freedom we are going to consider, is *one* being among all the others. The totality of beings is what we usually call world, and the ground of world is what we commonly call God.[1] If we bring to mind, however indefinitely, the totality of known and unknown beings, at the same time thinking specifically of man, it becomes clear that human beings occupy only a small corner within the totality. Set before the forces of nature and cosmic processes this tiny being exhibits a hopeless fragility, before history with its fates and fortunes an ineluctable powerlessness, before the immeasurable duration of cosmic processes and of history itself an inexorable transitoriness. And it is this tiny, fragile, powerless, and transitory being, the human being, of whom we are to treat.

Further, we shall examine just one of this being's properties – its freedom – and not its other faculties, accomplishments, and characteristics. With the topic 'the essence of human freedom' we strictly bind ourselves to the examination of one *particular question* (freedom) which for its part is related to one *particular being* (man) within the totality.

Yet treating this topic is supposed to be an *introduction to philosophy*. From such an introduction we expect to gain a view of *philosophy* in general, i.e. of the *totality of its questions*. In this way we want to gain an overview of the entire field of philosophy. An introduction to philosophy must provide an orientation to the most general features of philosophy; it must avoid the danger of losing itself too much in particular questions and thereby distorting the view of the whole. To be sure, there may be particular questions within philosophy. But an introduction to philosophy must from the very beginning attempt to bring the whole into view as such.

To attempt an introduction to philosophy by way of the question of human freedom, to seek an understanding of *philosophy in general* by immediately diverting into a *particular question*: this is clearly an impossible undertaking. For the intention, and the means of its realization, are opposed to one another.

a) The 'Particularity' of the Topic and the 'Generality' of an Introduction to Philosophy

The particular is indeed different to the general. The theory of differential equations is not mathematics *as such*. The morphology and physiology of fungus and moss is not botany *as such*. The interpretation of Sophocles' *Antigone* is not classical philology *as such*. The history of Frederick the Second is not medieval history *as such*. Likewise, the treatment of the problem of human freedom is not philosophy *as such*.

And yet how do we begin, for example in mathematics? We do not start with the theory of differential equations but with the calculation of differentials, i.e. we treat this topic in particular and not mathematics as a whole, never the mathematical as such. In philology we begin by reading and interpreting specific individual literary works and not with philology as such or with the literary work as such. So in all the sciences: we begin with the particular and concrete, not in order to remain and get lost at this level, but so that we can proceed to the essential and universal. The particular is different to the universal but this difference does not imply contradiction or mutual exclusion. On the contrary, the particular is always the particularity of one thing, namely of the universal contained within it, and the universal is always the universality of the various particulars determined by it. We must therefore always look to the particular if we wish to discover the universal. To press forward from a treatment of a particular problem – in this case human freedom – to the universality of philosophical knowledge is in no way an impossible undertaking. Instead, this is the only fruitful and scientific method for an introduction to philosophy. It is the method that every science naturally adopts. So the task of these lectures is quite in order.

Such is the situation, provided that philosophy *too* is a science and as such remains bound by the guiding principles of scientific method. But this assumption is erroneous. To be sure, many people strongly insist upon it, and not by accident. Why this presupposition of the scientific character of philosophy is unjustified we cannot now discuss.

We shall consider this one thing only. Originally the totality of beings was called material nature, living nature, etc. Science divides all these beings – the totality of world and God – into different domains, which are then distributed among the particular sciences. Nature is the concern of mathematical physical theory. History (man) is the concern of historical systematic cultural science. God is the concern of theology. Since no specific domain of beings is left over for philosophy, the latter can only concern itself with all beings, and indeed precisely as a whole. If every science is necessarily restricted to one and only one particular domain then philosophy clearly cannot be a science and has no right to call itself one. This consideration is not meant to decide the issue of whether philosophy is or can be scientific but only to show that there are reasonable grounds for at least questioning and disputing this assumption.

From the possibility of thus disputing the scientific character of philosophy we conclude only that it is not so certain that in philosophy we should follow the scientific procedure of setting out from a *particular question* – the problem of freedom – in order to achieve the desired 'introductory' *general orientation to philosophy*.

The view that this latter procedure, owing to its scientific character, is also suitable and necessary for philosophy, rests on another presupposition, namely that the question concerning the essence of human freedom is a special or particular question. Such an opinion has common sense on its side. We ourselves began by indicating that freedom is a particular property of man and that man is a particular being within the totality of beings. Perhaps that is correct. The question concerning the essence of human freedom is nevertheless not a particular question. But if this is so, if the topic of these lectures is not a particular question, then we are not at all in a position to set out from a particular question in order to arrive at something universal.

b) Broadening the Question Concerning the Essence of Human Freedom towards the Totality of Beings (World and God) in the Preliminary Discussion of 'Negative' Freedom. Specific Character of Philosophical as Distinct from Scientific Questioning

But why is the *problem of freedom not a particular question*? At this point it can only be *roughly* indicated why the problem of freedom, from the very outset, cannot be treated as a particular question. Among the definitions of the essence of freedom one has always come to the fore. According to this, freedom primarily refers to autonomy. Freedom is freedom from . . . *Daz dinc ist vrî daz dà an nihte hanget und an deme ouch niht enhanget.*[2] This definition of the essence of freedom as independence, the absence of dependence, involves the denial of dependence on something else. One speaks, therefore, of the negative concept of freedom, more succinctly of *'negative freedom'*. Clearly then, this negative freedom of man is fully defined by specifying what man is independent from, and how such independence is to be conceived. In earlier interpretations of freedom this 'from what' of independence has been experienced and problematized in *two essential directions*.

1. Freedom from . . . is *independence from nature*. By this we mean that human action as such is not primarily caused by natural processes; it is not bound by the lawfulness of natural processes and their necessity. This independence from nature can be grasped in a more essential way by reflecting that the inner decision and resolve of man is in a certain respect independent of the necessity which resides in human fortunes. From what was said above we could call this independence from nature and history an independence from the 'world', where the latter is understood

as the unitary totality of history and nature. Not always, but precisely where a primordial consciousness of freedom has been awakened, a *second* negative concept of freedom goes together with the first.

2. According to this, freedom means *independence from God*, autonomy in relation to God. For only if there is such autonomy can man take up a relationship to God. Only then can *he* seek and acknowledge God, hold to God and take upon *himself* the demands of God. All such being toward God would be in principle impossible if man did not possess the possibility of turning away from God. But the possibility of turning toward or turning away from already presupposes a certain independence and freedom in relation to God. So the *full concept of negative freedom* amounts to *independence of man from world and God.*

So when we treat of the essence of human freedom, albeit as understood only in this negative way, i.e. when we really reflect upon this double independence, we must necessarily keep in mind that *from which* man is independent. *World and God* are not just accidentally or contingently represented in the *negative concept of freedom*, but are *essentially included* in it. If negative freedom is the topic, then world and God necessarily belong to the topic as the 'from what' of independence. But world and God together constitute the totality of what is. If freedom becomes a problem, albeit initially only as negative freedom, then we are *necessarily inquiring into the totality of what is.* The problem of freedom, accordingly, is not a particular problem but clearly a universal problem! It does not concern any particular thing, but rather something quite general? Let us see.

Not only does the question concerning the essence of human freedom not limit our considerations to a particular domain, it *removes limits*; instead of limiting the inquiry it *broadens* it. But in this way we are not setting out from a particular to arrive at its universality. For world and God are not the universal over against man as a particular. Man is not a particular instance of God in the way that the alpine rose is a particular instance of the essence of plant or Aeschylus' *Prometheus* a particular instance of tragedy.

The removal of limits leads us into the totality of beings, i.e. world and God, in the midst of which man himself is situated, and in such a way that he stands in a relationship to world and God. It thus becomes completely clear: *the question concerning the essence of human freedom relates neither to a particular nor to a universal*. This question is completely different to every kind of *scientific* question, which is always confined to a particular domain and inquires into the particularity of a universal. With the question of freedom we leave behind us, or better, we do not at all enter into, everything and anything of a regional character. This difference and distinctiveness of the question concerning human freedom, namely that it leads into the totality of beings, marks it out as a specifically *philosophical* question.

If every scientific question and every science as such are in their essence restricted to a region, and if the question concerning human freedom in its proper meaning forces us into the totality of beings as such, then this question cannot be a scientific one. For not only in a quantitative but also in a qualitative sense, no science has the breadth of horizon to encompass the unitary whole which is intended (albeit unclearly and indefinitely) by the question of freedom.

Awkward as the question might be for us, if we are really intent on asking it we necessarily stand, from the very beginning and from the ground up, somewhere altogether different to the standpoint of every science, whether past, present, or future.

This rough explanation of negative freedom has already shown that the problem of freedom is not a regionally limited particular question. To be sure, it will be replied, it is not a question belonging to any of the particular sciences, but it is still a *particular problem* within philosophy. For philosophy is surely not exhausted by the treatment of this *one* problem. Beside this there are questions concerning the essence of truth, human knowledge, the essence of nature, history, art, and whatever else is commonly listed when one gives an overview of philosophy. The question of human freedom indisputably stands alongside these questions as a particular question in comparison with the still more and most general question concerning the essence of what is as such, whether it be natural, historical, human, or divine.

The question concerning the essence of truth is indeed different to the question concerning the essence of freedom. But both these questions inquire into the totality and thus have a necessary connection with the most general question concerning the essence of beings as such. How the question of freedom opens up the horizon to the totality was indicated already in the discussion of negative freedom. But is this reference to the totality not one-sided and incomplete? Freedom negatively understood as independence from world (nature and history) and God does show a relationship to these, but only a negative one: world and God as what *do not bind* the one who is free. We must always include this 'independent from what', this 'not bound to what', but it does not properly belong to our topic, standing only at the border of it. We must have this in view, but we need not go into it.

If this is the case, then the problem of freedom, despite a material lack of restrictiveness, is subject to thematic restriction. The totality of beings is not as such the topic. So the problem of freedom remains a particular problem within philosophy. Therefore our planned introduction must take a one-sided orientation; its topic may be of exceptional importance, but as an introduction it is necessarily incomplete. This is unfortunate, but its unavoidability can perhaps be justified by referring to the fact that, as a human endeavour, philosophy is always piecemeal, finite, and limited. In addition, philosophy as knowledge of the totality cannot in all modesty conceive the whole in one stroke. Confessing to such limitation and modesty always has a 'sympathetic' effect, indeed many take this as an expression of a critical cast of mind which only inquires into what it can handle and manage.

And yet this banal modesty is not only a licence for the utter super-ficiality and arbitrariness of the common understanding, which takes philosophizing as nothing but the calculation of business expenses. We ourselves have already conceded too much to this superficiality in the above discussion of negative freedom. To begin with, from a consideration of the topic of negative freedom, we concluded that the problem of freedom *does not encompass everything*. We thereby overlooked that, insofar as we rightly speak of *negative* freedom, we *can and must* conceive of positive freedom as well, and that it is just this *positive concept of freedom* which *in the first instance marks out the domain of the problem of freedom*, so that negative freedom must be conceived in unity with positive freedom if we wish to *decide* whether the problem of freedom is a particular question of philosophy among others, or whether it incorporates the whole. Instead, we too hastily decided this either-or in favour of negative freedom. Not only that, but we have also conceived negative freedom inadequately.

c) Deeper Interpretation of 'Negative Freedom' as Freedom-from . . . in Terms of the Essence of Its Relational Character. Beings in the Whole Necessarily Included in the Question Concerning Human Freedom

We interpreted negative freedom as independence from world (nature and history) and God. The 'from which' was included in the concept but not as an explicit topic. The primary topic was freedom, i.e. here 'independence from . . .' as such. What does this mean? If we wish to characterize 'independence from' in a quite general way, we must say it is a relationship, more specifically a relationship of non-dependence of one thing on another. The equivalence of one thing and another is also a relationship, likewise difference as the non-equivalence of one thing and another. In regard to every relationship we distinguish 1. the relatedness of the one to the other as such, and then 2. just this one and another between which this relatedness obtains, the terms of the relationship. The word 'relationship' is generally speaking ambiguous. Sometimes we mean simply relatedness as such, but just as often this relatedness together with the terms of the relationship.

Difference, like independence, is a 'negative' relationship. When e.g., we ascertain the *difference* between this blackboard and this lamp on the ceiling, we are treating of a relationship. In ascertaining such a difference we must not only *co-think* the terms of the relationship (blackboard, lamp) – otherwise the relatedness would hover in mid-air so to speak – but we must *go into* the related terms themselves. We ascertain the so-being of the blackboard and the so-being of the lamp, and from this we grasp their difference. In all ascertaining of relationships the *terms* must themselves be treated. This is obvious. But does it follow that our planned discussion of freedom (say, as independence) must likewise go into the elements of the relationship? Clearly it must, for how otherwise are we to ascertain independence? This relationship does not hover somewhere by itself, but we only discover it by treating man as one element and world as the other element. Do we then want to ascertain independence (freedom)? Can we? We neither want to do this, nor are we able to. We are not treating merely human freedom, but the *essence* of human freedom. The essence of freedom? Three things belong to the clarification of essence: 1. what-being, what it (freedom) as such is. 2. how this what-being is in itself possible. 3. where the ground of this possibility lies.[3]

What we are treating, therefore, is the *essence* of a relationship. We do not seek to establish and prove such a thing as a fact. Even if that were possible we would have to know in advance *what it is* that is to be established. If we consider a relationship in its essence must we enter into the terms of the relationship? If we were to treat of the essence of difference, would we have to discuss *this* blackboard and *this* lamp? Or would we have to consider other cases of difference (house and tree, triangle and moon, etc.)? Clearly not. To ascertain the essence of difference it is irrelevant which specific different things we employ as examples. On the other hand we do need to have the terms of the relationship in view; we cannot dispense with them.

When, therefore, we define the essence of a relationship, we do not, as in the case of establishing a specific factually existing relationship between specific factually given things, have to enter into *these* specific terms of the relationship. We must hold in view the terms of the relationship as such, but whether they are factually constituted in this way or that is beside the point. This irrelevance of the specific content of the respective relational terms does not mean they can be left out of account in clarifying the essence of relatedness. Let us attempt to apply this to our problem.

If we proceed according to the negative concept, then with the question concerning the essence of human freedom we are inquiring into the essence of man's independence from world and God. We do not want to decide whether this or that individual is independent of this or that world, of this or that God, but we seek the essence of the independence of man as such from world and God as such. If we wish to grasp the essence of this relationship, of this independence, we must inquire into the essence of man, and also into the essence of world and God. *Whether*, and *how*, such questioning can be carried through is reserved for later discussion.

From these considerations we conclude only the following: that because independence as a negative relationship so to speak detaches itself and remains removed from that which it is independent of, it does not follow that in examining the essence of independence we can dispense with looking at the 'from which'. Instead the reverse follows. Since 'independence from . . . ' is a relationship to which there belongs as such a relatedness to world and God, precisely for this reason must this 'from what' of independence be brought into consideration, i.e. included in the theme. In brief, what pertains to the essential *content* of the relationship – to be away from . . . – does not pertain to *reflection* on the essence of the relationship.

d) Philosophy as Revealing the Whole by Means of Properly Conceived Particular Problems

Thus, from the very beginning, the question concerning the essence of human freedom thematizes the totality of what is, world and God, and not just the limit or border. While the question concerning the essence of freedom is different from the question concerning the essence of truth, it is not a particular problem, but concerns the whole. And perhaps this also applies to the question concerning the essence of truth. This means, however, that every philosophical question inquires into the whole. Accordingly, taking the question of human freedom as our guideline, we may, indeed we *must*, attempt an actual introduction to philosophy as a whole.

But there remains an inadequacy. Although the problem of freedom lays the whole of philosophy before us, this occurs within a particular perspective, that of freedom, and not, e.g., that of truth. The totality of philosophy is exhibited in *our* introduction with a quite specific emphasis. Were we to choose the problem of truth, as we did in an earlier introductory course,[4] then philosophy as a whole would be shown in a different configuration and constellation of problems. So it would seem that the actual totality of philosophy would be grasped only if we could treat all possible questions and their perspectives.

However we twist and turn, we cannot avoid the fact that an introduction to philosophy guided by the problem of freedom takes on a specific and particular orientation. In the end this is not an inadequacy. Even less does it require any apology, e.g. by appealing to the fragility of all human endeavour. Perhaps the *strength and strike-power of philosophizing* rests precisely on this, that it *reveals the whole only in properly grasped particular problems*. Perhaps the popular procedure of bringing all philosophical questions together in some kind of framework, and then speaking of everything and anything without really *asking*, is the opposite of an introduction to philosophy, i.e. a semblance of philosophy, *sophistry*.[5]

Notes

1 'World' and 'God' are here intended as noncommital words for the totality of beings (the specific totality of nature and history: world) and for the ground of the totality (God).
2 Meister Eckhart, 'Von den 12 nutzen unsers herren lîchames' (*Deutscher Mystiker des vierzehnten Jahrhunderts*, edited by Franz Pfeiffer, Volume Two, 3rd edn, Göttingen, 1914, p. 379, Z. 7/8).
3 See below pp. 125 ff. on analysis of essence and analytics.
4 Heidegger, *Einleitung in die Philosophie* (GA 27: Freiburg lectures 1928/29, edited by Otto Saame and Ina Saame-Speidel, Klostermann, 1996).
5 Cf. Aristotle, *Metaphysics* Γ 2, 1004 b 17 f. and b 26.

PART ONE

Positive Definition of Philosophy from the
Content of the Problem of Freedom

The Problem of Human Freedom and the
Fundamental Question of Philosophy

1

First Breakthrough to the Proper Dimension of the Problem of Freedom in Kant. The Connection of the Problem of Freedom with the Fundamental Problems of Metaphysics

§ 2. Philosophy as Inquiring into the Whole. Going-after-the-Whole as Going-to-the-Roots

Notwithstanding initial doubts, therefore, our intention of providing an introduction to philosophy as a whole by treating the problem of human freedom is quite in order. Unlike the sciences, philosophy from the very beginning aims at the whole, naturally within a specific perspective. We may be confident of being on the right track here. In the course of our preliminary considerations we have already learnt a great deal, albeit in outline, concerning freedom, independence, and the distinctive character of philosophical questioning in its difference to science. The aim of our discussions was obviously to reassure ourselves about the validity of our chosen task. Do we really feel reassured? Should we feel reassured? Doubtless this is necessary if philosophy is to quietly occupy itself with all sorts of interesting questions. However, can the problem of human freedom be simply set before us and demonstrated? Or must we ourselves be led *into* the problem, in order that we subsequently remain firmly within it? We ourselves, not someone else, not some arbitrary other person! Or is philosophy only a higher (because more universal) occupation of the spirit, a luxury and diversion from the often monotonous and arduous procedure of the sciences? Is philosophy an opportunity, of which we occasionally avail ourselves, to widen our view out from the narrow field of the particular sciences for a picture of the whole? For what did we mean when we said that philosophy inquires into the whole? Does this mean that we just create a vantage point for ourselves, so that we can be better placed as observers, better than in the all-too-narrow regions of the particular sciences? Or does philosophy's concern with the whole mean something else? Does it signify that it goes *to our own roots*? And indeed, not by occasionally applying to our own case, in a moral way, philosophical discussions and propositions which we have supposedly understood, thus gaining edification from philosophy. Ultimately we only understand philosophy if the questioning goes to the root of what is questioned. Philosophy is not theoretical knowledge together with practical application, nor is it theoretical and practical at the same time. It is *more primordial* than either, for both of these pertain primarily to the particular sciences.

The character of philosophy as inquiring into the whole remains fundamentally inadequate as long as we do not grasp the 'going-after-the-whole' as a 'going-to-the-roots'. But can philosophizing amount to, and aim at, settling down and being reassured? Do we really begin to philosophize when we begin with a reassurance? Or do we begin in this way in order to turn our backs on philosophy right from the start?

In the end, however, it is not a reassurance if we make it clear to ourselves that our aim and method are quite in order. Perhaps this indicates no more than that we are surely drawing near to a danger-zone – more carefully put, that there is a sure possibility of this. In any case we now know more. The previous definition of philosophy, as concerning the whole, was inadequate. More precisely, this going-after-the-whole must be grasped as a 'going-to-the-root'. Admittedly this is just an assertion. How are we to prove it? Clearly, we can only do so from the content of philosophical questioning itself. How this is to occur must be tried out in actual *philosophizing*. But at the beginning we need an indication of the full sense of philosophy's inquiry into the whole.

There is a particular reason why we could not, in our earlier considerations, press forward to this full sense. While we have distinguished philosophy fundamentally from the particular sciences, we have still oriented philosophy in terms of scientific knowledge. This comparison conveys nothing beyond what philosophy is measured against, i.e. what possibilities there are for distinguishing it from science. So now we must attempt *to understand philosophy in a positive way from itself*, not by empty discussions concerning philosophy in general, but *from the content of the chosen problem*, that of human freedom. In this way the perspectives within which we shall be inquiring concretely during the entire lecture course will open up for us.

§ 3. Formal-Indicative Discussion of 'Positive Freedom' by Reconsideration of 'Transcendental' and 'Practical' Freedom in Kant

Our discussion of the topic and its method of treatment has been restricted to the negative concept of freedom. It is no accident that we have proceeded in this way. Wherever a knowledge of freedom is awakened it is initially comprehended in the negative sense, as 'independence from'. This prominence of *negative* freedom, indeed perhaps of the negative as such, is due to the fact that *being*-free is experienced as *becoming*-free from a bond. Breaking free, casting off fetters, overcoming constrictive forces and powers, must be a fundamental human experience, by which freedom, understood negatively, comes clearly into the light of knowledge. In comparison with this clear and seemingly unambiguous definition of negative freedom, the characterization of positive freedom is obscure and ambiguous. The 'experience' of this wavers and is subject to particular modifications. Not only are individual conceptions of positive freedom different and ambiguous, but the concept of positive freedom as such is indefinite, *especially* if by positive freedom we provisionally understand the *not-negative* freedom. Not-negative freedom can mean: 1. positive freedom as the opposite of the negative; 2. freedom which is not negative, but also not positive, neither the one nor the other. For our preparatory discussion we choose (dispensing with any justification) a quite particular conception of positive freedom.

Negative freedom means freedom from . . . compulsion, a breaking loose, releasement. Freedom in the positive sense does *not* mean the 'away-from . . .', but rather the 'toward-which'; positive freedom means being free for . . ., being open *for* . . ., thus *oneself* being open for . . ., allowing *oneself* to be determined through . . ., determining oneself to . . . This means to determine one's own action purely through *oneself*, to give to oneself the law for one's action. *Kant* conceives positive freedom in this sense of self-determination; further, as absolute self-activity.[1] He calls it the 'power' of man to 'determine himself from himself'.[2]

We make reference precisely to *Kant* in this connection not just to quote a philosophical opinion, but because Kant occupies a distinctive position in the history of the problem of freedom. Kant brings the problem of freedom for the first time explicitly into a radical connection with the fundamental problems of metaphysics. To be sure, as always and necessarily at such decisive moments, this first breakthrough into the proper dimension of the problem leads to a one-sided narrowing which we will have to confront.

We stated that Kant's doctrine of freedom occupies a distinctive position within philosophy. Prior to him, Christian theology had developed the problem in its own way. The theological discussion, from which both positive and negative impulses went into philosophy, was itself (Paul, Augustine, Luther) not uninfluenced by the philosophical discussion. The characterization of *negative* freedom as independence from God already indicates this link between the respective problematics of theology and philosophy. But enough of this. We take up the Kantian conception of freedom (without now entering into an interpretation of this) merely as an example for discussing the positive concept of freedom. We do this to obtain a view of the wider perspectives of the problem of freedom and thus of our own task as such.

We said that Kant conceives freedom as the 'power of self-determination', as 'absolute self-activity'. Neither of these contains anything negative. Certainly, but they *do not mean the same thing*. Kant thus distinguishes a 'cosmological' from a 'practical' concept of freedom.[3] This distinction, however, is by no means identical with that between negative and positive freedom. It falls instead on the side of positive (more precisely, not-negative) freedom.

First, what does Kant understand by cosmological and practical freedom? 'By freedom in its cosmological meaning I understand the power of beginning a state spontaneously. Such causality will not, therefore, itself stand under another cause determining it in time, as required by the law of nature. Freedom in this sense is a pure transcendental idea.'[4] Freedom, therefore, is the *power of the self-origination of a state*. This explains what we quoted above as Kant's concept of freedom: 'absolute self-activity' – originating from oneself, spontaneously, *sua sponte, spons, spondeo, spond,* ΣΠΈΝΔ, σπένδω: to give or freely offer, spontaneously, spontaneity, absolute self-activity. Freedom as absolute spontaneity is freedom in the *cosmological* sense: it is a *transcendental* idea. What this latter refers to will be discussed further on. First we ask about freedom in its 'practical meaning'. 'Freedom in the *practical* sense is the will's independence of coercion through sensuous impulses'.[5] Freedom in the practical sense is *independence*, which is precisely how we characterized negative freedom. But didn't we say that both Kant's concepts of freedom – the transcendental and the practical – are not negative? Indeed. But the definition given of practical freedom undeniably takes this as negative. And, if we look more closely, Kant also explains the practical concept of freedom through precisely those factors we initially referred to upon mentioning the Kantian concept of freedom: 'The human will is ... [free] because sensibility does not necessitate its action. There is in man a power of self-determination, independent of any coercion through sensuous impulses.'[6] *Will* here does not mean arbitrariness and lack of discipline, but the *faculty of will*. Negative freedom is mentioned here, but something else is also mentioned, namely the power of self-determination. But is this not precisely the same thing as *spontaneity*, thus identical with the *cosmological* concept of freedom? Then the latter would be the positive concept of freedom, while practical freedom, independence from sensibility, would be the negative concept.

But this is *not at all* the case. Of course it cannot be denied that Kant, in his definition of practical freedom, refers to *independence* from sensory compulsion. There is a reason for this. The whole discussion takes place in the *Critique of Pure Reason*, i.e. in a work devoted to pure understanding (the theoretical faculty of man) and not to practical understanding (πρᾶξις) in the sense of ethical action. So before we pin Kant down with the quoted definition of practical freedom as independence from sensibility, we must ask how he defines practical freedom in the *Critique of Practical Reason*, where he treats thematically of πρᾶξις, i.e. ethics. More precisely, we must ask how Kant conceives practical (ethical) freedom where he considers ethics as a metaphysical problem, thus in the *Foundations of the Metaphysics of Morals*. At the beginning of the third section of this work, Kant writes: 'As *will* is a kind of causality of living beings so far as they are rational, *freedom* would be that property of this causality by which it can be effective independently of external causes *determining* it, just as *natural necessity* is the property of the causality of all non-rational beings by which they are determined in their activity by the influence of external causes.'[7] Here *again* 'independence' is mentioned. But Kant now speaks more clearly: 'The preceding explanation of freedom is *negative* and therefore affords no insight into its essence. But a positive concept of freedom flows from it which is so much the richer and more fruitful'.[8] Here it is already clear that if a positive concept of freedom is to be obtained it will be a *practical* concept. Kant says: 'What else, then, can the freedom of the will be but *autonomy*, i.e. the property of the will to be *a law to itself*?'[9] The positive concept of freedom means *autonomy* of the will, *giving laws unto oneself*. The practical concept of freedom is not the negation of freedom in its *transcendental* meaning, but *practical* freedom itself divides into negative and positive.

What then is the situation as regards freedom in its transcendental meaning of absolute spontaneity, if it is not the positive practical as opposed to the negative practical? Is absolute spontaneity not the same as autonomy? In both cases it is a matter of the self, of that which has the character of self, the *sua sponte*, αὐτός. But although there is clearly a relationship between the two, they are not the same. Let us look more closely. *Absolute spontaneity* is the faculty of the self-origination of a state; autonomy is the self-legislation of a rational will. Absolute spontaneity (transcendental freedom) is not a matter of will and the law of the will but of the self-origination of a state; autonomy, on the other hand, concerns a particular being to which there belongs willing, πρᾶξις. They are not the same, and yet both pertain to that which has the character of self. How do they belong together? The self-determination of action as self-legislation is a self-origination of a state in the specific domain of the human activity of a rational being. Autonomy is a kind of absolute spontaneity, i.e. the latter delimits the universal essence of the former. Only on the basis of this essence as absolute spontaneity is autonomy possible. Were there no absolute spontaneity there would be no autonomy. The possibility of autonomy is *grounded* in spontaneity, and practical freedom is grounded in transcendental freedom. Accordingly, as Kant says in the *Critique of Pure Reason*: 'It should especially be noted that the practical concept of *freedom* is based on this *transcendental* idea, and that the latter harbours the real source of the difficulty which has always beset the question of the possibility of freedom'.[10]

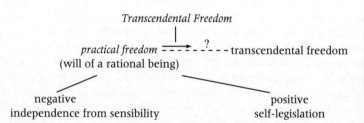

So the transcendental freedom of the practical is not situated *alongside* as the negative, but the *practical* as the condition of its possibility is *prior*. Thus the third section of the *Groundwork of the Metaphysics of Morals* bears the sub-title 'The Concept of Freedom is the Key to the Explanation of the Autonomy of the Will'.[11] The determination of positive freedom as 'autonomy' involves a *specific problem*, with a difficulty it has always borne.

§ 4. Broadening of the Problem of Freedom within the Perspective of the Cosmological Problem as Indicated in the Grounding Character of 'Transcendental Freedom': Freedom – Causality – Movement – Beings as Such

What have we now obtained from our brief discussion of the positive concept of freedom? We wanted to clarify the problem of freedom by giving a preliminary indication of how the substantive problem itself, in going-after-the-whole, also goes-to-the-root. A certain kind of *challenge* is involved in this problem. Thus far, apparently, we have seen little of this. One would think that the challenging character of the problem consists in the fact that freedom is precisely a property of us humans and therefore bears on us. This is true, indeed all too true to capture what we seek. For the trivial opinion just mentioned merely alludes to the practical signifi-cance which freedom possesses precisely as a human property. However, this is already indicated in the negative concept of freedom, perhaps more clearly. If this were the only issue we would have been able to dispense with a discussion of positive freedom. But the issue is something else, namely the *challenging character* of the problem of freedom. This is supposed to emerge from the *innermost essence* of freedom insofar as the latter stands within the horizon of philosophical questioning.

Consequently, in respect of our explanation of positive freedom in terms of the Kantian distinction, we must now ask three things: 1. Does positive freedom bring about a fundamental broadening of the problem-atic? 2. What does this broadening indicate, i.e. what perspective is opened up? 3. Is the broadening of the problem such that we can now see how philosophy as the 'going-after-the-whole' is at the same time a 'going-to-the-root'?

With respect to our *first* question: that positive freedom involves a broadening of the problem, and indeed a fundamental one, can easily be seen. We have already observed that positive freedom, considered in its practical sense, is equivalent to autonomy. Its possibility is grounded in absolute spontaneity (transcendental freedom). This freedom brings us back to another kind of freedom. That besides practical-positive and negative freedom, transcendental freedom also turns up, indicates a broadening, and it is a fundamental one because absolute spontaneity is posited therein as the ground of the practical. Kant asserts this relation between practical and transcendental freedom when he says that 'the denial of transcendental freedom [would] involve the elimination of all practical freedom'.[12] The possibility of the latter depends on the possibility of the former. In this way the first question is answered.

Our *second* question asks about the perspective opened up with this broadening. The perspective is apparently determined by the problem of the enablement of practical freedom (autonomy), i.e. by the problems involved in what Kant calls 'absolute spontaneity'. What does this mean? Where in this is the genuine problem to be found? Once again, spontaneity means the 'from itself', and indeed arising from itself, the beginning of a 'series of events'.[13] Absolute spontaneity means to initiate a series of events 'from itself'; to be the origination of an event, allowing an event to follow on. That which in this way allows something (a thing) to follow on is for Kant the cause. The question of spontaneity, of beginning and letting follow, is the question concerning the cause [*Ursache*]. This, the causation [*Ursachesein*] of a cause (*causa*), is what Kant calls 'causality' [*Kausalität*] (the causality of *causa*). In this sense he speaks pointedly of the 'causality of a cause'.[14] This does not mean 'cause of the cause', but rather the causation of a cause, i.e. *that* and *how* a cause is a cause.

According to Kant, all experience, i.e. all theoretical knowledge of what is present before us as nature, is subject to the law of causality. This law of causation, i.e. the law that a thing given in experience must be caused by another thing, is formulated by Kant[15] in the heading of the Second Analogy (first edition) as follows: 'Everything that happens, that is, begins to be, presupposes something upon which it follows *according to a rule*'.[16] Further, 'the causality of the cause of that which happens or comes into being must itself have come into being, and . . . in accordance with the principle of the understanding it must in its turn require a cause'.[17] Every causation of a cause for its part follows on from a prior cause, i.e. in nature nothing is the cause of itself. Conversely, the *self-origination of a state* (series of events) is an *utterly different causation than the causality of nature*. Kant calls the former *absolute spontaneity*, the *causality of freedom*. From this it is clear that what is genuinely problematical in absolute spontaneity is a problem of *causality*, of *causation*. Accordingly, Kant sees *freedom* as the *power of a specific and distinctive causation*. The *perspective* which is thus opened up by the fundamental broadening brought about by the problem of practical freedom, i.e. by the positing of autonomy as absolute spontaneity, is that of the problem of *causality in general*. Causality in the sense of absolute spontaneity, i.e. causation in the sense of the absolute self-origination of a series of events, is something we do not encounter in experience, i.e. for Kant, in theoretical knowledge of present nature. What we represent through this representation of absolute spontaneity lies outside what is experientially accessible, i.e. it goes beyond this (*transcendere*). *Freedom as absolute spontaneity is transcendental freedom.*

If, as Kant maintains, practical freedom is grounded in transcendental freedom as a distinctive kind of causality, then positive freedom, as grounded in absolute spontaneity (transcendental freedom), harbours within itself the problem of *causality* as such. So the problem of this *distinctive* causality makes it all the more necessary to take up the problem of causality as such.

To be sure, these questions already take us outside the Kantian problem. But we do not regard Kant as the absolute truth, only as the occasion and impetus for the full unfolding of the problem. Proceeding in this way, what was earlier said about the decisive significance of Kant for the problem of freedom remains valid.

Freedom is discussed within the perspective of causation. It was precisely Kant who grasped the problem of freedom in this way. Whether this is the *only* perspective for the problem of freedom, whether there are other and even more radical perspectives, and what they are, are matters we still leave completely open. If we hold to Kant's perspective, this means inquiring into the essence of human freedom, after what freedom is in its inner possibility and ground. Thus to inquire into the essence of human freedom means to make the *essence* of causality, of causation, into a problem. Where does our inquiry take us, if we wish to illuminate the essence of causation in this way? Only by answering this question can we estimate the scope of the problem of freedom.

Causation means, among other things, letting follow on, origination. It belongs in the context of that which runs ahead, relating to processes, events, occurrences, i.e. to what we call *movement in the broader sense*. Further, it turns out that not all movement is the same. For example, what is true of so-called mechanical movement, of the mere shifting of particles of matter, or of the mere running ahead of a process, does not necessarily apply to movement in the sense of growth and degeneration. In each case, causation, letting follow on, origination and outcome, are different. Again, process and growth are different to the behaviour of animals and the comportment of human beings. These in turn can be seen within the events – the movements – of action and transaction. A journey, for example, is not just a mechanical movement with a machine (rail, ship, plane), nor is it a mechanical movement together with a human comportment. It is an occurrence of a nature all its own, whose character is as little known to us as is the essence of the other species of movement.

We know little or nothing of these matters, not because they are in any way inaccessible to us, but because we exist too superficially, i.e. we do not exist in our roots such that we can inquire into these roots and feel this questioning as a burning issue. Thus the philosophical situation in regard to the clarification of movement is miserably inadequate. Since Aristotle, who was the first and last to grasp the *philosophical* problem, philosophy has not taken a single step forward in this area. On the contrary it has gone backward, because the problem is in no way grasped as a problem. Here Kant too completely fails. That the problem of causality was central for him makes this all the more remarkable. It is easy to see that the problem of the essence of movement is the presupposition for even posing, not to speak of solving, the problem of causality.

And the problem of movement, for its part? Movement, i.e. being moved or resting (as a mode of movement), emerges as a fundamental determination of that to which we attribute being, namely beings. The kind of possible movement or non-movement varies with the kind of beings. The problem of movement is grounded in the question concerning the essence of beings as such.

So our view of the problem of freedom broadens out. The individual moments of this broadening can again be indicated: practical freedom (autonomy) – transcendental freedom (absolute spontaneity) – exemplary causality – causality (causation) as such – being moved as such – beings as such. And where are we now?

With this question concerning beings as such, concerning what beings in their breadth and depth actually are, we are asking the very same question which from ancient times has counted as the primary and ultimate question of philosophy – the *leading question of philosophy*: τί τὸ ὄν, what are beings?

§ 5. The Questionable Challenging Character of the Broadened Problem of Freedom and the Traditional Form of the Leading Question of Philosophy. Necessity of a Renewed Interrogation of the Leading Question

The question concerning beings as such emerged by following the specific content of the problem of freedom. It did not emerge as a question upon which the problem of freedom merely borders, nor as a more general question which just hovers over the particular question concerning freedom. Rather, if we really inquire into the essence of freedom, we stand within this question concerning beings as such. Accordingly, the question concerning the essence of human freedom is necessarily built into the question of what beings as such properly are. To stand within this question means to go-after-the-whole, for there can be no broader kind of questioning than that concerning beings as such.

Yet does *this* broadening out of our problem allow us to see how going-after-the-whole means going-to-the-root? We thus come to our *third* question.

We can now pose this question in a more definite way. Is the question concerning the essence of human freedom, as built into the question of beings as such, and as a question concerning the whole, in itself a going-to-the-root? One might answer as follows. Insofar as our inquiry into freedom inquires into beings as such, and insofar as we ourselves, the inquirers, also belong among these beings, the question will also concern us. But merely from the fact that the question of beings also inquires into us as beings, we cannot see in what way it is supposed to go to our root. When we inquire into beings, we also inquire into animals and material nature, for these are likewise beings. Our inquiry into beings also pertains to animals, but in relation to them as to us this co-concern is not at all a going-to-the-root.

How little this is so becomes clear if we look more closely at the question concerning beings. This question of philosophy asks what beings are, just in respect of the fact that they are beings. From here the leading question asks more concisely: what are beings *as such*? This expression 'as such' translates the Latin *ut tale, qua tale*, as employed in the metaphysics of the late Middle Ages, and corresponds to the Greek ἦ. It indicates that that to which it is attached – the table as such – is not to be taken merely as an arbitrary object of conception, opinion, evaluation or possession; instead, the table is to be taken as table, that is to say, in respect of its tablehood. The being-a-table of a table announces *what* a table *is*, its what-being, its essence.

To inquire into a being as such means to inquire into it *hoc ens qua tale*, as precisely this being. The linguistic expression 'as such' is specifically philosophical. It indicates that what is spoken of is intended in the *specific* respect of *its essence*: τί τὸ ὄν ᾗ ὄν. The question concerning beings as such does not just inquire into this or that. The question concerns not just *some* beings as such (animal, man) but *all* beings as such, what beings *are* as beings, irrespective of whether they are plants or humans or animals or God. This question disregards the particular character of beings to embrace all beings whatsoever. It inquires into what pertains most universally to beings in general.

Thus the further we inquire into this question of what beings are as such, the more general, and in respect of particular beings the more indefinite and abstract, the field becomes. To be sure, every particular being falls under the category of beings, but in such a general way that the question concerning beings as such *can no longer be relevant to particular beings*. It is, therefore, no longer just unclear how going-after-the-whole is supposed to mean the same as going-to-the-root, but this equivalence is impossible in principle. For to inquire into beings as such means *dis-regarding* all *particular* beings, including us ourselves as human beings. How can such dis-regarding have the character of a challenge? Going to the roots, as a challenge, must take aim *at us*. The inquiry into beings as such, irrespective of whether they are animal or human, is not directed at us as such, and is therefore anything but a challenge to us. Instead, this dis-regarding generality is much more a flight from ourselves as a specific kind of being, as also from every particular being.

So if we consider our chosen problem, the question of the essence of human freedom, precisely in its full scope and significance, i.e. in respect of the question of beings as such, we can see that this going-after-the-whole does not go-to-the-root, and thus is not at all about *us* as human beings. So our thesis that going-after-the-whole is going-to-the-root remains an arbitrary assertion which can in no way be justified from the substantive content of the question. Indeed, there is still further evidence for this, evidence which cannot be easily dismissed.

We said that the question implicit in the problem of freedom, the question, that is, concerning beings as such, is as old as Western philosophy itself. If we survey the history of philosophy we can see that this question *never and nowhere* leads to grasping philosophy itself as a going-to-the-root, namely to the root of the individual who questions. On the contrary, the concern has always been, especially since the beginning of modern philosophy, to raise philosophy to the rank of science (or absolute science) as theoretical activity, pure contemplation, *speculative knowledge* (Kant), whereby nothing in the nature of a *challenge* can possibly be involved.

What we maintained about the challenging character of the question of beings as such – the question into which is built the problem of freedom – can no more be verified from the history of this question than from its *inner content*. If this is so, then our thesis of the challenging character of philosophy's questioning of the whole is far from self-evident, especially on the usual interpretation of philosophy. It is in no way clear how we are to explain and justify our thesis, and this in spite of the everyday and 'obvious' idea that philosophy must 'be relevant to life'.

Our discussion of the *thesis of the challenging character of philosophy* has brought us before a peculiar dilemma. *On the one hand* our thesis corresponds to the quite *natural* view that philosophy has to do with man himself and should have an influence on his activity. Now this common *interpretation* of philosophy may be confused and erroneous and excite the greatest mistrust, for 'relevance' to life is normally understood as adaptation to the so-called 'demands of today'. Yet the difficulty is precisely that natural pre-philosophical experience and conviction demands what we earlier denied of philosophy. Its so-called 'relevance' to life thus lacks any definite contours. But if philosophy is a primal and ultimate possibility of human existence as such, one will not need to persuade it into relevance but will demand that it demonstrates this *from and through itself*.

On the other hand our unfolding of the full content of the leading question of philosophy has not revealed anything with the character of a challenge. Instead, this questioning interprets itself as θεωρία, *contemplatio*, speculative knowledge. Our thesis conforms to so-called natural and pre-philosophical convictions about the essence of philosophy and is presumably conditioned by these from the start. On the other hand the substantive content of the philosophical question of beings as such says nothing in favour of our thesis, no more than do traditional interpretations of this question. Should we place our trust more in natural convictions about philosophy, or more in philosophy's great tradition, i.e. in previous treatments of its leading problem?

We must mistrust both of these alternatives as they are usually presented to us. We can no more proceed according to common convictions, which would distort philosophy into a world-view doctrine, than we can just accept the traditional leading question as ultimately adequate. Why are we unable to accept it? Is it permissible to dismiss the whole great tradition and maintain the laughable opinion that we can and must begin all over again? Yet if we cannot leap out of the tradition, how and why should we reject the leading question? Is this question – τί τὸ ὄν – perhaps 'wrongly' posed? What could enable us to make such a judgement? What is the proper manner of questioning? How is it at all possible to pose the question wrongly? The totality of beings does indeed demand asking this elementary question as to what beings are as such. *This leading question of Western philosophy is not wrongly posed*, but is *not even posed at all*. At first sight, to be sure, this is an outrageous and presumptuous statement. It also contradicts what we ourselves already indicated, namely that Aristotle poses the question τί τὸ ὄν as the genuine question of philosophy and in so doing saw himself as clarifying what the whole of Greek philosophy before him had been seeking. The question was asked by Plato and Aristotle and can be readily identified in their writings. Indeed, Aristotle and Plato, not so much directly as implicitly throughout their whole work, provided a particular answer to the question, an answer which has since been taken as definitive in the history of Western metaphysics right through to its grand completion in Hegel.

How then can we maintain that this question has not been posed? Plato and Aristotle did, in fact, ask this question. To be sure, but if we merely ascertain that this question, along with a certain answer, occurs in their works, does this mean that they *really and genuinely* pose this question? From the fact that this question, still more their answers and their various implications, occur again and again in the subsequent history of philosophy, can we conclude that this question was genuinely posed? Not at all. To once *again* ask this question of Plato and Aristotle – the question, in brief, of Western philosophy – means something else, namely to ask *more primordially* than they did. In the history of all essential questions, it is our prerogative, and also our responsibility, to become the murderers of our forefathers; indeed, this is even a fateful necessity for us! Only then can we arrive at the problematic in which they *immediately* existed, but precisely for this reason were not able to work through to final *transparency*.

Have we ourselves, in our above considerations, asked this question about what beings are? Not at all: we have only summoned it up. We have only made it clear that the problem of freedom is built into this question, and we have indicated something of the scope of this question, namely that it concerns all beings as such. It emerged that just this question, owing to its general abstract character, does not exhibit anything with the character of a challenge. But can we really maintain this, so long as we have not exhausted the content of this question? Can we exhaust this, indeed can we even bring it into view, so long as we do not really ask the question, but only quote it so to speak, as a question which arises in Greek philosophy? Only when and insofar as we have genuinely asked this traditional leading question of philosophy can we decide whether or not philosophizing necessarily involves a challenge.

Notes

1 CPR A 418, B 446.

2 CPR A 534, B 562.

3 CPR A 533 f., B 561 f.

4 CPR A 533, B 561.

5 CPR A 534, B 562.

6 CPR A 534, B 562.

7 Kant, *Foundations of the Metaphysics of Morals*, pp. 101–2 (IV, 446).

8 *Foundations*, p. 102 (IV, 446).

9 *Foundations*, p. 102 (IV, 446 f.).

10 CPR A 533, B 561.

11 *Foundations*, p. 101 (IV, 446).

12 CPR A 534, B 562.

13 CPR A 534, B 562.

14 CPR A 533, B 561.

15 I Analogy: Principle of Permanence of Substance. III Analogy: Principle of Coexistence, in accordance with the Law of Reciprocity or Community.

16 CPR A 189.

17 CPR A 532, B 560 fin.

2

The Leading Question of Philosophy and Its Questionability.
Discussion of the Leading Question from Its Own Possibilities and Presuppositions

§ 6. Leading Question of Philosophy (τί τὸ ὄν) as the Question Concerning the Being of Beings

What does it mean to really ask this question? Nothing else but to allow everything *thought-worthy* in it to emerge, everything *worthy to be placed in question*. But that which is worthy of questioning encompasses everything *belonging to this question in its ownmost possibility*, everything implicated in its so-called *presuppositions*.

It is characteristic of any question that it does not, upon its initial awakening, already place in question everything belonging to its own presuppositions. And precisely the question concerning beings as such, this question which goes after the whole, necessarily begins by settling down comfortably in its first stage. But precisely in respect of *this* question, whose fundamental tendency is to question concerning the whole, which seeks what is primarily and ultimately worthy of questioning, it is not permissible to rest content with initial formulations.

To come to the point: what is supposed to be worthy of questioning in the traditional leading question of philosophy τί τὸ ὄν? What is worthy of questioning here is nothing less than that which is actually inquired into. The leading question 'what are beings?' must be brought to genuine questioning, so we must seek that which is asked in it, beings as such, ὄν ᾗ ὄν. But what is it that constitutes beings as beings? Can we call it anything else than just *being*? The question concerning beings as such is actually directed to being. It inquires into the *being* of beings, not into what beings are. What is worthy of questioning is precisely being.

Have we thereby exhausted what is worthy of questioning in the leading question? This is a genuine questioning only if it is concerned to discover that which *enables* the answer. Such enablement implies clarity about how the questioning proceeds, about what is sought therein. How then does this questioning of the being of beings proceed? What is sought in this questioning? Just that which determines the *essence of being*. It is a questioning which seeks determinations. It seeks to understand the origin of our understanding of the being of beings. Do we understand this, and if so *when*? We understand this at all times, without, however, knowing that we do so, without paying any attention to this fact. In what way do we already understand what 'being' means?

§ 7. Preconceptual Understanding of Being and Greek Philosophy's Basic Word for Being: οὐσία

a) The Character of Preconceptual Understanding of Being and the Forgottenness of Being

We need only recall what always happens in our Dasein. When we earlier asked if a treatment of the (special or particular) problem of freedom can be a genuine introduction to philosophy, we understood, still without taking the whole question into view, every word of this, including 'be'. We understood 'be' as related to the verb 'is'. If I say, and you in my audience understand, that the topic of the lecture course *is* human freedom, then we understand this 'is'. We understand something quite definite, and we can easily assure ourselves that what we mean by 'is' is not a stone or a triangle or a number, but simply 'is'. The same holds in respect of the forms 'was', 'has been', and 'will be'. We constantly hold ourselves and operate in such an understanding of what 'being' means, and not only, and not for the first time, when we employ these linguistic expressions. For example, if in listening to this lecture you silently think to yourselves that what I am saying is incorrect, you understand the 'is' and operate within this understanding. Or if, walking through the countryside and stopping for a moment, we look around and say to ourselves, aloud or silently, 'wonderful', we thereby understand that this surrounding countryside 'is' wonderful. It is wonderful just as it is and as it existingly reveals itself to us. It is not first by speaking and talking about beings, by explicit 'is' saying, that we operate in an understanding of 'is', but we already do this in all silent *comportment* to beings. Again, not only, and not initially, in contemplative enjoyment of beings, or in *theoretical* reflection upon them, but in all 'practical' judging and employment of beings. Not only in our comportment to the beings of our external environment do we understand that these beings 'are', and 'are' in such and such a way rather than in another, but we understand 'being' also in our comportment to ourselves and to others like ourselves. This being of beings of every kind is not first understood when we use words such as 'being', 'is', and 'was', but in all speaking whatsoever we understand beings in their so-and-so being, not-so-being, etc. Indeed, we can use the 'is' and 'was' and so forth because the being of beings is already self-evident to us prior to all speaking.

In understanding the being of beings, we always already understand being as *divided*. We can clarify this originary division in terms of 'is'. The earth 'is', i.e. as a planet it has 'actuality', it 'exists'. 'The earth is heavy', 'is covered by land and sea': in these latter cases being does not mean 'exists', but rather 'so-being'. 'The earth is a planet': being as *what-being*. 'It is the case that the earth moves around the sun': being as *being-true*. This is just an initial indication of the originary dividedness whereby we understand being as being-present, as what-being, as so-being, and as being-true.

At every moment we comport ourselves to the kind of beings which we as humans are, as well as to the kind of beings which we are not. We constantly hold ourselves in such an understanding of being. Our comportment is carried and governed by this *understanding of being*. Yet this fact does not occur to us as such. We do not attend to it at all, so that we must first be reminded of this self-evidency. We have forgotten it to such an extent that we have never actually thought about it. We begin our existence with this *forgottenness of our understanding of being*, and the more we open ourselves up to beings, the deeper becomes our forgetting of this one thing, that in all openness to beings we understand being. But this deep forgottenness is *no accident*. Above all, it is no disproof that we are governed by this understanding of the undifferentiated being of beings; on the contrary, it is evidence *for* this.

We said that the leading question of philosophy inquires into the *being* of beings. More precisely, what is sought is the origin of our understanding of being. This much is evident, that we do not understand being just now and again, but rather constantly in all our comportments. Everyone understands the 'is' and 'being', and everyone has forgotten that he thereby holds himself in an understanding of being. Not only does *everyone understand it while no one properly grasps it,* but everyone is greatly embarrassed if asked what he really means by 'being' and 'is'. Not only are we embarrassed for an answer, but we are quite unable to indicate from where an answer might be found.

If we ask what a table is, we could say that it is an object of use. Even if we are not in a position to give a correct definition of its essence, we nevertheless always already operate within an understanding of such things. Or if we are asked what a triangle is, at least we can say that it is a spatial figure. We already operate within knowledge and perception of space and spatiality. The region *from where* we define table and triangle – object of use, space – stands open for us so to speak, as that *to which* our understanding of such things is referred. The same applies in respect of every being, whatever it happens to be; every being that we know as such is already somehow understood in respect of its being. Not only do we understand and know the being, but also, albeit in an *implicit* way, we understand its *being.* So the question remains as to the origin of our understanding of being and the 'is'. Being must somehow be interpreted, for otherwise we could not understand it, and we do understand it when we say 'is', confidently distinguishing this 'is' from 'was'. We can indeed deceive ourselves in trying to ascertain whether, now and in a particular place, a particular object exists, or whether it rather *was* at a former time. But we cannot be deceived about the distinction between 'is' and 'was' as such.[1]

We all understand being and yet we do not grasp it, i.e. we are not able to explicitly define *what* we mean by it. We operate within a *preconceptual* understanding of being. We thereby refer to the puzzling fact that already, and precisely in our everyday existence, we understand the being of beings. We have, moreover, now become acquainted with some *characteristics* of this understanding of being: 1. the scope of being (all regions of beings, in some sense the totality of beings) wherein we hold ourselves; 2. penetration into every kind of human comportment; 3. unspokenness; 4. forgottenness; 5. undifferentiatedness; 6. preconceptuality; 7. freedom from deception; 8. originary dividedness.

When philosophizing as such breaks out and begins to develop itself through setting human questioning of beings over against itself, posing the question of what beings are as such, this means – however clumsy this questioning may appear – that not just the beings as such, but the *being* of beings, must somehow come to light.

This understanding of being which comes to expression in philosophy cannot be invented or thought up by philosophy itself. Rather, since *philosophizing is awakened as a primal activity of man*, arising thus from man's nature prior to any explicit philosophical thinking, and since an understanding of being is already implicit in the pre-philosophical existence of man (for otherwise he could not relate to beings at all) philosophy's understanding of being expresses what man is in his pre-philosophical existence. This awakening of the understanding of being, this self-discovery of the understanding of being, is the birth of philosophy from the Dasein in man. We cannot here follow this *birth of philosophy* as *the awakening of the understanding of being in Western history*, but must be content with a schematic indication.

b) The Ambiguity of οὐσία as Sign of the Richness and Urgency of the Unmastered Problems in the Awakening of the Understanding of Being

The awakening of the understanding of being means understanding beings as such *in respect of* their being. In this way being comes into the sight and view of an understanding which remains quite hidden from itself. Nevertheless, the hiddenness of this understanding of being is such that being must somehow or other be illuminated. Whenever and wherever beings are so experienced, the being of beings must stand in the – albeit hidden – *illumination of an understanding*. But wherever beings are experienced through *explicitly* and *deliberately* interrogating them as to what they are, in some sense the being of beings is discussed. Experience of beings as beings means that the understanding of being must somehow come to expression. Wherever philosophizing takes place, the understanding of being is somehow understood and grasped, i.e. seen in the light of . . . – of what?

The way in which ancient Greek philosophy – Western philosophy in its decisive beginnings – understands being must be discoverable from its *basic word* for being. We inquire into the ancient Greek word for being as such, i.e. not for that which is, although then as now the two meanings, both inside and outside of philosophy, run through one another. When we encounter the word 'being' in contemporary as well as in previous philosophical literature, this always means beings. But we are seeking the Greek terminological characterization for being, not that for beings.

The Greeks refer to that which is, beings, as τὰ ὄντα (πράγματα), or in the singular τὸ ὄν, the being. τὸ ὄν is the participle of the infinitive εἶναι. τὸ ὄν means every existing thing, irrespective of whether one knows anything about it. τὸ ὄν is like τὸ κακόν, the bad, everything bad there is, all present bad things. But by τὸ ὄν, and correspondingly by τὸ κακόν, we mean something else. We say, for example, that this thing we encounter is a κακόν, something bad, i.e. not only is it a present bad thing, but it belongs to what is bad in general: τὸ κακόν, that which is a bad thing, not all presently existing bad things taken as a whole, but *the bad* as such, whether present or not.

Likewise, τὸ ὄν does not mean all existing beings taken together, but the beings as existing [*das Seiend-seiende*], i.e. what a being is when it is, despite the fact that there is no necessity for it to be. Just as τὸ κακόν is the collective name for everything belonging to the realm of the bad, i.e. refers to this *realm* itself, so is τὸ ὄν the *collective name* for all present beings, for what falls within the realm of that which is, for what we mean by an existing thing.

The double meaning of such words is no accident but has a deep metaphysical reason. However obscure and trivial this distinction and its constant obfuscation may seem, it leads us to the abyss of a central problem. One can understand the inner greatness, e.g. of the Platonic dialogues, only if one follows the way in which the many intertwined and seemingly empty debates about words steer toward this abyss, or more precisely, how they hover over it, thus bearing the whole disquiet of the primary and ultimate philosophical problems.

Τὸ κακόν is a collective name and the name of a region. In the latter meaning it refers to the bad beings as such, to all beings insofar as they are determined by badness, by κακία. Likewise, τὸ ὄν is a collective name and a regional name; in the latter meaning it refers to the existing beings as such, to all beings insofar as they are determined by beingness [*Seiendheit*], by οὐσία. That by which a being is determined as such is the beingness of the being, οὐσία τοῦ ὄντος

The present (existing) bad	– the present being
The bad beings as such	– the beings as such
Badness (that which constitutes the bad beings)	– the beingness of beings (being)

Now just as in the case of τὸ κακόν the collective meaning and the regional meaning can change and be confused with one another, as the bad thing itself or as badness as such (being bad), so can the meaning of the word 'badness', wherein the essence of being bad is intended, also be used as a collective description, i.e. 'the badness in the world', the actually existing bad. The word 'being' is likewise employed in the meaning of present beings.

In everyday as well as in vulgar-philosophical discourse 'being' usually means beings. Accordingly, what the ancient Greek question τί τὸ ὄν actually seeks, but which just for this reason is not, despite its familiarity to us, clearly and properly known, receives the designation οὐσία. Initially, however, our task must be to hold on to this question τί τὸ ὄν and arrive at a preliminary answer, that is to say, we must first bring οὐσία into view. What thus emerges is a bewildering variety of possible meanings for οὐσία, so much so that Plato and Aristotle, in their original reflections on this problem, were unable to see their way forward. The light which was at that time breaking through was so bright that these great thinkers were blinded, so to speak, and could only register what was proximally presented to them. The initial great harvest first had to be brought in. Ever since that time, the history of philosophy has been threshing this harvest, and now it is only empty straw which is being threshed. So we must go out and bring the harvest in anew, i.e. we must come to know the field and what it is capable of yielding. We can only do this if the plough is sharp, if it has not become rusted and blunt through opinions and gossip. It is our fate to once again learn tilling and ploughing, to dig up the ground so that the dark black earth sees the light of the sun. We, who have for all too long unthinkingly taken the well trodden roads.

The word οὐσία means many things. Therefore the *ambiguity* of this basic word, as we find it in Plato and Aristotle, is not at all an accident, nor is it a sign of slackness in terminology, but rather *indicates the richness and unmastered urgency of the problems themselves*. Yet precisely if we hold fast to this variety of meanings for οὐσία, i.e. for that which was and still is intended by being, then we must be able to understand something unitary within this diversity, even without being capable of properly grasping it.

What does this ambiguous word οὐσία really mean? Are we capable of discovering a meaning which the Greeks themselves were unable to express? Were not the Greeks in the same situation as we ourselves? We understand 'being', 'is', 'was', 'will be', etc. very readily, such that there seems nothing more to understand or ask about. What is supposed to drive us on to further questioning? Just this, just the remarkable fact that we take what is designated by being, οὐσία, as 'this' and 'this' – as what?

The table *as* an object of use, the triangle *as* a spatial figure. Being as . . .? Being in the sense of . . .? Of what then? This is the question.

But perhaps someone could, in the final analysis, deter us from this question about the meaning of being, namely by pointing out that being cannot be viewed in the same way as a table or a triangle. These are particular things, i.e. beings, about whose being it is possible and necessary to ask. But *being* – in the end this is just the beings themselves as such; being is not itself a being. We thus have no right to interrogate it as if it were a being. This is a convincing argument. Appealing to the completely different character of being in comparison with beings it is insisted that questions properly pertaining to beings cannot be simply transferred to the *being* of beings.

What justification is there, however, for appealing to the completely different character of being in comparison with beings? This presupposes that we already know about the different and particular nature of being, i.e. that we know the latter's essence. Do we indeed know this? Or do we make this appeal on the basis of an obscure intimation that 'being' and 'is' and 'was' are not like the things of which we can say that they are or were. Can we know, can we want to know, something of the essence of being, if at the same time we bar the way to its interrogation? Clearly not. Therefore we must *ask* about what *being* means. And even if the question of what we understand by being is *linguistically* similar to the question concerning our understanding of *this being* – table – it does not follow that questioning and understanding has the same character in both cases. What emerges from all this is just that the question concerning being cloaks itself in, and must cloak itself in, the same outward form as the question concerning beings. The question concerning being is hidden behind a form which is alien to it, and will remain unrecognizable for whoever is used to asking only about beings. So we must follow the philosophical path, the path which is remote from ordinary understanding, or better, we must *try* to follow this path. At any event, the necessity of the question remains, namely this question concerning the meaning of the fundamental word of Greek philosophy, οὐσία. If this word is not just sound and fumes, but was able to challenge the genius of Plato, what does it mean?

Οὐσία τοῦ ὄντος means in translation: the beingness of beings [*Seiend-heit des Seienden*]. We say, on the other hand: the being of beings [*Sein des Seienden*]. 'Beingness' is a very unusual and *artificial* linguistic form that occurs only in the sphere of philosophical reflection. We cannot say this, however, of the corresponding Greek word. οὐσία is not an artificial expression which first occurs in philosophy, but belongs to the everyday language and speech of the Greeks. Philosophy took up the word from its pre-philosophical usage. If this could happen so easily, and with no artificiality, then we must conclude that the *pre-philosophical* language of the Greeks was already *philosophical*. This is actually the case. The history of the basic word of Greek philosophy is an exemplary demonstration of the fact that the *Greek language is philosophical*, i.e. not that Greek is loaded with philosophical terminology, but that it philosophizes in its basic structure and formation. The same applies to every genuine language, in different degrees to be sure. The extent to which this is so depends on the depth and power of the people who speak the language and exist within it. Only our German language has a deep and creative philosophical character to compare with the Greek.[2]

c) Everyday Speech and the Fundamental Meaning of οὐσία: Presence

If we wish to hearken to the fundamental meaning of this basic word οὐσία, we must pay attention to everyday speech. We soon see that in everyday linguistic usage there is no sharp distinction between beings and being. So also in Greek, οὐσία means beings. To be sure, not just any beings, but such as are, in a certain way, *exemplary in their being*, namely the beings that belong to one, one's possessions, house and home, the beings over which one has disposal. These beings stand at one's disposal because they are fixed and stable, because they are *constantly attainable and at hand* in the immediate or proximate environment. Why do the Greeks use the same word for beings as such that they use for house and home, possessions? Why is *precisely this kind of being* exemplary? Clearly, only because this being corresponds in an exemplary sense to that which, in everyday understanding of being, one implicitly understands by the *beingness* of a being (its being). And what does one understand by being? We shall be able to comprehend this if we succeed in determining what is *exemplary* about house and home.

What is this exemplary character? House and home, possessions, are constantly attainable. As constantly attainable they lie close at hand, presented on a plate as it were, *constantly presenting themselves*. They are what is closest and in this constant closeness they are present and at hand in a definite sense. Because they are present and at hand in an exemplary sense, we call possessions, house and home, etc. (what the Greeks call οὐσία) *estate* [*Anwesen*]. In fact, by οὐσία nothing else is meant but *constant presence* [*ständige Anwesenheit*], and just this is what is understood by beingness. By being we mean nothing else but constant presence, enduring constancy. What the Greeks address as beings proper is what fulfils this understanding of being as *being-always-present*.

We asked how it comes about that *these* particular beings – house and home – become exemplary for beings as such, i.e. for beingness? When we asked in this way, it first appeared as if we meant that the word οὐσία, with its indicated fundamental meaning, was simply there, such that the Greeks then asked which among the many beings best deserved this designation. The actual situation was the reverse: the word οὐσία in its linguistic connections with ὄν and ὄντα first arose in the experience of these beings. To be sure, this could only occur because what is meant by the word already existed: *constant presence*. For the most part, and especially where, as in the case of this fundamental word, it is a matter of something ultimate and essential, man has long had an implicit understanding of what he means, yet without the right word occurring to him. In this case house and home, possessions, etc. were the particular beings which exemplified beings as such, and this is something that could only occur because beingness – prior to the formation of the word οὐσία – was intended and understood as constant presence.

In summary, the everyday meaning of οὐσία refers to house and home, etc. But the Greeks only intend this because of their precursory understanding of constant presence. They understand constant presence in a pre-understanding, yet without this coming thematically to expression. This everyday usage of the word οὐσία, as the self-evident and implicit fundamental meaning, is overlooked in the philosophical usage of the word. *This fundamental meaning* then made the word possible as a technical term for that which is intended and sought and pre-understood in the *leading question* of philosophy.

d) The Self-concealed Understanding of Being (οὐσία) as Constant Presence. Οὐσία as What Is Sought and Pre-understood in the Leading Question of Philosophy

But can we base an interpretation of the concept of being in Greek philosophy on this simple explanation of the everyday meaning of οὐσία? Is it not a violent, artificial, and *external* approach if we try to extract the substantive problem of Greek philosophy from an isolated word-meaning, especially when the result – the meaning of being as constant presence – is nowhere explicitly enunciated in Greek philosophy? However, it is precisely the fact that Greek philosophy never *explicitly* states what it means by οὐσία that makes it necessary for us to inquire into this question. But what about the *violence, artificiality* and *externality* of our interpretation?

To be noted here is that we have not appealed to etymology for the disclosure of anything originary from the word stem – a process subject to great misuse and errors, but which if practiced in the right way and in the right context can also be fruitful. We have *not merely seized* on the word οὐσία and analysed its meaning, but we have entered into the *thing itself* named by this word in common usage. We have taken the word as *expressing an essential comportment* of man to the beings of his *constant and most proximate environment*. We have taken language as the primordial revelation of the beings in whose midst man exists – man, whose essence is to exist in language, in this openness. The Greeks experienced this essential character of man as no one else before or after them. Existing in language was grasped by the Greeks as the crucial moment of the essential definition of man. For they said: ἄνθρωπος ζῷον λόγον ἔχον, man is a living being possessed of language, i.e. which holds itself within the manifestation of beings in and through language.

Our interpretation does not amount to an external registration of a word meaning by reference to a dictionary. Above all, however, what we have said about οὐσία is not a final statement, but only prepares us for the philosophical interpretation of the word. Our interpretation does not proceed by assembling the meanings of the word from various passages of philosophical writing, but by exhibiting it as a basic word, so that we can bring to light the innermost problematic of Greek metaphysics, where οὐσία is understood from and in the leading question of philosophy. To be sure, such a topic could occupy an entire lecture course.

At this point we are content just with some indications within the contexture and limits of our own questioning. The *contexture* and *perspective* for the problem of freedom is the question of what beings are. How does this question involve a challenge? To *make a decision* on this problem we must *actually* pose the leading question, i.e. we must place in question precisely what is most worthy of questioning! We are inquiring into beings as such! And how must we inquire into them, in order that an answer should become possible? What does being mean? From where do we understand it? It is understood in the understanding of being, and indeed not only or for the first time in philosophy, but the other way round: philosophy arises from the awakening of an understanding of being. In such an awakening there occurs a speaking-out. Thus, in the awakening of philosophy, in this decisive event of antiquity, the understanding of being comes to speak out. Already in ordinary language the word for being is οὐσία, which means house and home, estate, etc. Our interpretation showed that *the pre-understanding of being contained in this everyday meaning of οὐσία comprehends the beingness of beings as constant presence.*

If being is understood as constant presence, *from where does such understanding receive its illuminating power? In which horizon does the understanding of being operate?* Before we expressly answer this crucial question we must show *that* and *how* precisely philosophy, insofar as philosophy is guided by the question τί τὸ ὄν, also understands being as constant presence, and is itself to be grasped from this understanding. Here we must content ourselves with some minimal references to Plato and Aristotle.

§ 8. Demonstration of the Hidden Fundamental Meaning of οὐσία (Constant Presence) in the Greek Interpretation of Movement, What-Being, and Being-Actual (Being-Present)

We have set out from the everyday meaning of the word οὐσία, or more precisely, we have set out from what is intended in this word's pre- and extra-philosophical usage: beings *qua* house and home, or in the broader philosophical sense, every present being as present. If, guided by the question of what beings are as such, we now attend to the beings we proximally encounter (the things around us, whether natural or artificial) and if we ask about what constitutes their beingness, this question appears clearly posed and ready for an answer. However, the entire history of philosophy shows that this elementary question, precisely because it is elementary, is of the very greatest difficulty, and is ever again insufficiently prepared, i.e. elaborated.

a) Being and Movement: οὐσία as παρουσία of the ὑπομένον

When we inquire into what constitutes the being of a present thing, e.g. a chair, then we immediately ask about how we conceive a chair, or whether we can conceive it at all. But if we disregard the groundless and senseless question of whether we grasp a psychical image of the chair or the actual chair, if we hold fast to this present thing before us, everything is not yet in readiness for asking about what constitutes the thing's presence. There is a lot of talk in philosophy about objects and their object- ivity, but without prior indication of what it means when e.g. someone has a chair present before him. We could say that things have now changed in this regard. We now see clearly that the chair standing there, in the room or in the garden, is not like a stone or a piece of wood from a broken branch, but that it (and similar things such as tables, cupboards, doors, steps) has a *purpose*. This purposiveness does not attach to such things in an external way but determines what and how they are. To be sure, it is important to characterize objects of use in this way. But this still does not provide an answer to the question of the kind of presence possessed by such things. It is only preparation for this, i.e. for actually asking this question, and indeed it is only *one* specifically oriented preparation. This characterization contributes to our understanding of what and how a chair is, but it is incomplete. Indeed, something quite crucial is missing.

But what else are we supposed to discover about the chair, or more accurately, about its way of being, when it just stands there? That it has four legs? It could if necessary stand on three. And even if it had just two legs, in which case it would be lying on its side, it would still be a present chair, albeit a broken one. In fact, there are chairs with just one leg. We can say whether it has a back-rest or not, is upholstered or not, is high or low, comfortable or uncomfortable. But we are asking about its way of being simply as there to use, however it may be constructed and irrespect- ive of whether it is standing or has fallen over. So it stands or lies. It does not, therefore, run about, thus it is not an animal or a human. But we are asking about what it is, not about what it is *not*. It stands, i.e. it rests. Now it is not a great piece of wisdom to establish this. And yet everywhere, and precisely where one cannot shout loudly enough that chairs and tables are things and not just representations in us, the much proclaimed 'being-in- itself' of such things has been stubbornly ignored. But what do we ourselves want with all this? What is obtained from this advice that the present chair rests? Just that the chair's 'resting', its 'standing', its 'having a stand', indicates the fact that it exists in movement. But we said that it rests and we placed particular emphasis on this. To be sure, but only something whose nature belongs in movement can rest. The number five does not and can never rest. This is not because it is constantly in movement, but because it cannot come into movement at all. Whatever rests is in movement, i.e. *movability* belongs to the being of that which rests. Thus one cannot, without going into the essence of movement and movability, problematize the being of the present chair which stands there. On the other hand, in problematizing the essence of movement, questioning comes into the proximity of the question of being. If we ask about the essence of movement, it is necessary to speak of being, even if not explicitly and thematically.

So it is with Aristotle, of whom we have already said that he grasped the problem of movement for the first time, albeit in such a way that he neither saw nor grasped its inner connection with the problem of being. But he understood that if being-in-movement is a determination of natural things and of beings as such, then the essence of movement is needful of discussion.

Aristotle carried out this discussion in his great lectures on 'physics'. This latter word is not to be taken as equivalent to the modern concept of physics, but not for the reason that Aristotle's physics is primitive and proceeds without mathematics. It is because Aristotle's physics is not natural science at all but rather philosophy, i.e. philosophical knowledge of the φύσει ὄντα, knowledge of present things as present. Aristotelian physics is not only not more primitive than modern physics, but it is the latter's necessary presupposition, both substantively and historically.

The thematic discussion of movement occurs in the third, fifth, and eighth book of the *Physics*. The first book has an introductory character. Aristotle exhibits the *inner necessity of the problem of movement* by showing how the primary and ultimate problematic of all previous philosophy presses toward this problem. In this connection he discusses the difficulties which face any new treatment of movement. Many things about movement (the essence of movement) are problematized. Aristotle inquires into the *origin* of movement in its intrinsic nature. He calls that which determines the inner possibility of something the ἀρχή, principle. The fundamental nature of movement is μεταβολή, change. This is change from . . . to . . . If, for example, this piece of chalk for some reason (γένεσις) becomes red, we can take this in two ways: as a change from white-coloured to red-coloured, or as a becoming-red of the chalk. In the latter case white does not become red, but the white piece of chalk becomes a red piece of chalk, not just a τόδε γίγεσθαι (τόδε) ἀλλὰ καὶ ἐκ τοῦδε . . .[3]; it does not happen that a red thing originates from the chalk. A third principle belongs to the inner possibility of the γένεσις ἔκ τινος εἴς τι: the ὑπομένον, i.e. what *stays the same* throughout the change. But this, the chalk, a singular thing, has a twofold εἶδος: first its being-chalk, which does not necessarily involve being-white, and secondly this being-white itself. These must be *different* if change is to be possible, namely change as a going-over to something different to and absent from the initial state, στέρησις. So γένεσις in the proper sense involves these three principles: 1. ὑπομένον, 2. εἶδος, 3. στέρησις. 2 and 3 refer to the ἐναντία. For καὶ δῆλόν ἐστιν ὅτι δεῖ ὑποκεῖσθαι τι τοῖς ἐναντίοις καὶ τἀναντία δύο εἶναι.[4] Thus three ἀρχαί: on the one hand ὑπομένον, on the other hand the indicated opposition, which itself consists of two principles. At least these three (two) ἀρχαί are necessary; no more are required. τρόπον δέ τινα ἄλλον οὐκ ἀναγκαῖον.[5] In another sense, however, the principles governing the possibility of μεταβολή need not be regarded as three. ἱκανὸν γὰρ ἔσται τὸ ἕτερον τῶν ἐναντίων ποιεῖν τῇ ἀπουσίᾳ καὶ παρουσίᾳ τὴν μεταβολήν,[6] as it suffices for the possibility of change that one thing displaces another, i.e. that change is brought about simply by ἀπουσία (absence) or παρουσία (presence).

This passage, considered in its total context, is of significance for us in several respects. Initially there are two linguistic forms of the familiar word οὐσία. These forms bring to expression two possible meanings of οὐσία: ab-sence [*Ab-wesenheit*] and pre-sence [*An-wesenheit*]. They clearly indicate that *the concept of* οὐσία *involves absence and presence*. At the same time, however, one can also say that if ἀπουσία-παρουσία means absence-presence, then οὐσία just means essencehood [*Wesenheit*], i.e. something which hovers over both without being either. So what we have maintained is not the case, i.e. οὐσία does not mean *presence* at all. The Greeks express presence by παρουσία. This formal linguistic objection appears irrefutable. In fact, it cannot be refuted at a linguistic level, nor by appealing to what is directly and expressly *intended* in everyday usage of the word, because our thesis that οὐσία means constant presence simply does not rest on such considerations.

What we intend by the asserted fundamental meaning will be discussed below. For the moment we hold to the meaning of οὐσία in its possible modifications as absence and presence.

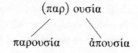

The παρουσία which is explicitly set off against ἀπουσία presupposes the primordial παρουσία. Just how this is possible remains problematic, not merely in the sense of a philological difficulty concerning the interpretation of Greek philosophical concepts, but as a fundamental substantive problem.

Before entering into this problem in more detail, we must note the implications of the quoted passage for our task of interpreting the fundamental word οὐσία. That the interpretation and description of μεταβολή is oriented to absence and presence – indeed that this was, in a certain sense, already the case with Plato, who speaks of change from nothing to being and *vice versa* – to clearly see and understand this is of the greatest importance. Change in colour, for example, is conceived as the *disappearance* of one colour and the *appearance* of another. In the case of processes, i.e. of what we call 'becoming' in the narrower sense – a white piece of chalk becoming a red piece of chalk – there is something which underlies this change: ὕπο, something *remains*: μένον. *The interpretation of the essence of movement proceeds through determinations of remaining and not-remaining, of remaining present and remaining absent.*

To be noted is that becoming and origination basically mean: obtaining being, coming into being, coming to so-and-so-being. It is evident that change involves *being*-other, and thus a connection between being and constancy. To be constant (to remain) means to endure in constant presence; beingness, οὐσία, is understood as constant presence.

Yet we have already seen that what we attributed to οὐσία is in fact only expressed in παρουσία: παρά means 'next to', 'being adjacent' in a series, being immediately present. To be sure, these are the moments of meaning which are immediately intended when Greeks understand οὐσία in the *usual* sense. So we are forced to the thesis that οὐσία always means – whether or not this is made explicit – παρουσία, and that only for this reason can ἀπουσία express deprivation, i.e. lack of presence. In absence it is not essence but presence which is lacking; thus 'essence-hood', οὐσία, at bottom means *presence*. The Greeks understood *beingness in the sense of constant presence.*

b) Being and What-Being. οὐσία as the παρουσία of the εἶδος

It would, admittedly, be a very great error were we to think that everything has now been clarified. We would completely close ourselves off from the correct interpretation of the Greek understanding of being were we to overlook the fact that the clarification of this particular kind of understanding – the understanding of something self-evident yet also ungrasped (constant presence, presence in general, οὐσία; more sharply: παρουσία) – involves constant struggle.

At first, the Greeks find this almost natural meaning of being, which we now formulate as presence, so very problematic that they cannot even discover what, at bottom, is problematic about it. For this reason their questions and answers move hither and thither in seeming disorder. On the one hand we discover the much proclaimed self-evidence of being; on the other hand we find, stubbornly juxtaposed to this, that the way in which the proper being of beings is to be grasped from presence remains incomprehensible.

I would therefore like to quote a very striking example from a Platonic dialogue, the *Euthydemus*. In doing this I must forgo describing the situation of the dialogue, the interlocking and overlaying of the two conversations, as well as the course, content, and intention of the work. The relevant passage can be fairly easily lifted out and treated on its own.

Socrates recounts to Crito a philosophical-sophistical conversation between Dionysodorus, Euthydemus, Cleinias, and Ctesippus. In the relevant passage,[7] Socrates tells of his own contribution to this conversation: 'And I asked Cleinias why he was laughing in this way over the most beautiful and serious things'. Dionysodorus now took Socrates at his word and asked him, according to Socrates' report: 'Have you, Socrates, ever seen a beautiful thing?' 'Indeed', said Socrates, 'many, and of many kinds, my dear Dionysodorus'. The latter: 'Were these (the many beautiful things) other than the beautiful itself or one with this?' Socrates: 'I was totally embarrassed by this question, found no way out (ὑπὸ ἀπορίας), and had to admit to myself that it served me right for being so uppish. Nevertheless, I replied to the question by saying that "the individual beautiful things are something different to the beautiful itself. However, in every one of them something of (like) beauty is present"'.

Here – in the crucial answer of Socrates – there occurs, and quite naturally so, the word that is important to us, i.e. πάρεστιν, παρεῖναι, παρουσία. For what question is under consideration here? It is the question concerning what beautiful things are. It is not the question of what distinguishes beautiful things from ugly things, but of how we are to understand the *being-beautiful* of these individual beautiful things.

Being-beautiful (beauty) pertains to every beautiful thing as beautiful. But how? If beautiful things are different from being-beautiful, then they are not themselves beautiful. Or if *the* being-beautiful of many things is the same as this (beauty), then how can there be many beautiful things? Socrates' answer, i.e. Plato's response and solution to this problem, asserts two things: 1. that beautiful things are distinct from beauty. 2. that nevertheless, *beauty* is present in each of them. This presence constitutes the *being*-beautiful of the individual things. Is the problem solved in this way? Not at all. It is only posed and made explicit, in that the 'being' of beautiful beings is spoken of, and indeed *in the sense of being as presence*. Despite everything, this 'presence' is utterly obscure, so that Socrates' answer is neither intelligible nor valid for the other participants in the conversation. This is shown by the way that Dionysodorus responds to Socrates. If the being-beautiful of a beautiful thing is supposed to consist in the presence of beauty, then the following results: if παραγένεται σοι . . ., 'if an ox comes to stand alongside you, and is present beside you, are you then an ox? And are you, Socrates, perchance Dionysodorus, because I, Dionysodorus, now stand beside you (πάπειμι)?' Socrates' thesis that being-beautiful, or more generally, that the so- and what-being of an individual being consists in its presence, leads to obvious nonsense. In this way Plato wants to show that the situation in respect of this παρουσία, i.e. of the beingness of a being, is anything but self-evident. And if it is not self-evident, then the problem must be posed and worked through.

From this, as from many other passages, we can conclude that precisely where the pure so-being and what-being of things – rather than, e.g. their origination and dissolution – is spoken of, this word παρουσία is employed. παρουσία is not necessarily oriented to ἀπουσία as a counter-concept, nor is it used only in such contexts. On the contrary, παρουσία stands simply for οὐσία, and expresses the meaning of οὐσία more clearly. This is shown by the fact that precisely where the οὐσία of the ὄν, e.g. the being-beautiful of existing beautiful things, becomes a problem, παρουσία crops up as a perfectly natural expression.

It would, however, be hasty and superficial to take our thesis that οὐσία, being, means constant presence, as the key which immediately opens all doors – as if, wherever we encounter expressions concerning being, it merely sufficed to insert the meaning 'constant presence'.

c) Being and Substance.
The Further Development of the Problem of Being as the Problem of Substance. Substantiality and Constant Presence

Nevertheless, we have obtained a crucial guideline for the interpretation of Greek philosophy, and indeed for the whole development of Western philosophy until Hegel. At any event, since antiquity the *traditional conception and development of the problem of being* has been governed by the fact that οὐσία is comprehended as *substance*, or better, as *substantiality*: substance as the proper beingness of a being. That this occurred, that the problem of being took the form of the problem of substance and led all further questioning in this direction, is no accident. The original impulses thereto can already be found in Plato and Aristotle. This cannot be demonstrated here, but we can at least provide some indications of how the rigidified problem of substance can be loosened up.

Substantia: *id quod substat*, that which stands under, ὑπόστασις. We have already encountered this ὑπο in the Aristotelian interpretation of movement. The first structural moment is the ὑπομένον, i.e. that which is preserved through all changes of properties and thus through the transformation of the thing, that which is fixed so to speak, κεῖσθαι. Thus the expression ὑποκείμενον very often stands for ὑπομένον. *The innermost content of the concept of substance has the character of an enduring remaining, i.e. of constant presence.*

d) Being and Actuality (Being-Present).
The Inner Structural Connection of οὐσία as παρουσία with ἐνέργεια and Actualitas

Summarizing what we have so far said concerning the Greek concept of being (οὐσία), three things emerge:

1. The interpretation of movement as a fundamental characteristic of beings is oriented to ἀπουσία and παρουσία, absence and presence.
2. The attempt to clarify the what-being of beings, e.g. beautiful beings as such, is oriented to παρουσία.
3. The traditional conception of οὐσία as substance likewise involves the primordial meaning of οὐσία *qua* παρουσία.

After all this, the fundamental meaning of οὐσία in the sense of παρουσία still remains obscure.

Our thesis that being means constant presence can itself be demonstrated from the problematic, especially since we do not maintain that the Greeks explicitly recognized this understanding of being and made it into a thematic problem. We are only saying that their questioning of beings proceeds within the horizon of this understanding of being.

But our thesis fails at a decisive point, namely if we focus on the concept of being predominant in ordinary employment of the word 'being': being as distinct from not-being. Being or not-being – that is the question. Being means being-present, *existentia*. For example, the earth is, God is, i.e. exists or is actual. Being in the sense of *actuality*. To be sure, we saw that this is *only one* of the meanings of being belonging to the originary structure of the concept of being in everyday understanding. It would, therefore, be a fundamental misunderstanding of the problem of being were we to pose it as exclusively or primarily the problem of actuality. Nevertheless, and precisely in regard to antiquity, we cannot pass over the question of whether and how the concept of actuality – existence in the traditional sense, as e.g. in Kant – involves the fundamental meaning of οὐσία as constant presence. We can immediately see that no progress can be made if we remain at the level of linguistic discussions.

To comprehend what is problematic in the word 'actuality', we must inquire into the philosophical term to which it corresponds. 'Actuality' [*Wirklichkeit*] is a translation of the Latin word *actualitas – ens in actu*, i.e. a being in so far as it is actually present, as distinct from an *ens ratione, ens in potentia*, i.e. a being insofar as it is merely possible. However, *actualitas* is itself the Latin translation of the Greek word ἐνέργεια. Our word 'energy', in the sense of *force*, has nothing to do with this. What ἐνέργεια means, as a philosophical expression for existence, actuality, being-present, is something totally different from 'force'. To conceive ἐνέργεια as force betrays an external and superficial understanding of the concept, in a similar manner as Dionysodorus' argumentation in respect of παρουσία. ἐνεργείᾳ ὄν means actual beings as distinct from δυνάμει ὄν, mere possible beings.

How then is this actuality of the actual to be comprehended? What does ἐνέργεια mean in its substantive meaning, not just according to the dictionary? Does this understanding of being support our more general claim that being means constant presence? What does ἐνέργεια have to do with constant presence? We certainly cannot discover this without entering into the ancient Greek problematic of being (Plato and Aristotle).

However, we have already seen how Aristotle develops the problem of being in terms of the problem of movement, where the latter means change, μεταβολή. Change involves the disappearance of something and the appearance of something else: ἀπουσία and παρουσία. Now it is very significant that Aristotle, precisely where he presses forward into the genuine depths of the essence of movement, avails himself of the concepts ἐνεργεία and δύναμις, and in such a way that, roughly speaking, ἐνέργεια is attributed to that which is proximally grasped through παρουσία.

$$\begin{array}{c} \mu\varepsilon\tau\alpha\beta o\lambda\grave{\eta} \\ \diagup \quad \diagdown \\ \begin{array}{c|c} \grave{\alpha}\pi ou\sigma\acute{\iota}\alpha & \pi\alpha\rho ou\sigma\acute{\iota}\alpha \\ \delta\acute{\upsilon}\nu\alpha\mu\iota\varsigma & \grave{\varepsilon}\nu\acute{\varepsilon}\rho\gamma\varepsilon\iota\alpha \end{array} \end{array}$$

These concepts of actuality and possibility, which following the long tradition of philosophy (including Kant) we so routinely employ today, these fundamental concepts of being arise for the first time in Aristotle's treatment of the problem of movement. To show what occurs there, and to what degree the connection between ἐνέργεια and παρουσία is there demonstrated, would lead us too far afield. I choose a shorter way of clarifying the fundamental meaning of ἐνέργεια, which simultaneously clarifies the connection between the philosophical/pre-philosophical meaning of actuality and the understanding of being as constant presence.

The word ἐνέργεια stems from ἔργον, work [Werk]. ἐν ἔργον, in work, means more precisely: self-holding (self-maintaining) in the activity of work. The workhood of work is the essence of work. The Greeks, and above all Aristotle, see the workhood of work not in terms of its origin, nor in terms of the person who sets the work into motion, but in the moment of being finished and ready.[8] To be sure, the Greeks also see the intention of the work, its directedness-to, but they do not regard this as the decisive and essential moment. The workhood of work consists in its *being finished*. And what does this mean? Being ready and finished is the same as producedness. And again, not necessarily in the sense of being produced rather than growing up by and of itself. Rather, the understanding is directed towards the inner content of producedness, to being brought to stand forth from here to there, and, as such, to be now *standing there*. So producedness means there-standingness [*Da-stehendheit*], and ἐνέργεια means a self-holding in producedness and there-standingness.

We can now easily see how the crucial moment shines through: the presence of the finished thing as such. It is from here that we must seek the way to a proper philosophical interpretation of that aspect of Aristotle's doctrine of being which has been so misinterpreted and deformed that attention has been diverted far away from the genuine problem. This is the doctrine of ὕλη and εἶδος, of matter and form. In the usual conception, and often with seemingly just reference to Aristotle's words, the actuality of a thing consists in the actualization of its form, εἶδος, in matter. The form of the chair, which the craftsman must previously imagine in his mind, εἶδος, ἰδέα, is actualized in matter, e.g. in wood. And then one wonders about how a 'spiritual' form can be located in something material. People think it particularly characteristic of Aristotle that he brought idea (form), located by Plato in a supersensible world, back to matter and the things themselves. This common interpretation of Aristotle's philosophy, which one can find in any decent textbook, does not recognize the childishness which it attributes to both Plato and Aristotle, and simply repeats everything that has been said since philosophy declined – to the level of compilers and schools – from the heights achieved by these two thinkers. To do the history of philosophy in this way would be analogous to deriving our interpretation of Kant from what a journalist wrote at the 1924 Kant jubilee.

However, what is the situation with respect to this actualization of form in matter (whereby the actuality of the thing is to be secured)? First, this *fails to clarify the essence of actuality* unless one previously indicates what *actualization* is supposed to mean. Further, it is not an interpretation of the Greek concept of actuality unless it has been shown that the Greeks understand actuality from the act of actualization, which is precisely not the case. Above all, however, these discussions concerning form and matter continue and proliferate without ever appropriating the standpoint, or even asking about it, within which εἶδος and ὕλη are supposed to illuminate the actuality of the real. It is not a matter of the embodiment of form in substance, nor of the *process* of production of beings, but of that which resides in the producedness of the produced thing. The question concerns the way in which *workhood* must be conceived if it is to announce the being of beings. The answer is that precisely the *look* [*Aussehen*] of the thing comes to expression in its producedness. οὐσία, *the being-present of a being as actually present, consists in the παρουσία of the εἶδος, i.e. in the presence of its look. Actuality means producedness, there-standingness as the presence of its look.*[9]

When *Kant* goes on to say that we do not know the thing-in-itself, i.e. that we do not have an absolute intuition of this but only see an appearance, he does not mean that we grasp a pseudo-actuality or something that is only half actual. If that which is present (the beings themselves) is conceived as appearance, this means nothing else but that the actuality of the actual consists in its character as appearance. To appear is to come into view, i.e. into the presence of a look, into the fully determining determinedness of the self-showing beings themselves. Kant has the same understanding of being as Greek philosophy. It was not his fault, it was not his doing, if the primordial connection between the concept of appearance and the radically conceived problem of being had to remain hidden. Instead, when we talk about Kant and others in the usual glib way, it is we who are at fault, it is we who belong to the debris rubbed off from the spirit of history.

In summary, we can say that the Aristotelian concept for the actuality of the actual, i.e. the concept of ἐνέργεια as well as the later concept of *actualitas* (actuality) determined by this, does not initially confirm our thesis of 'constant presence' as the fundamental meaning of being in Greek philosophy. However, if we do not play games with words, crudely attempting to derive actuality [*Wirklichkeit*] from working [*Wirken*], but rather immerse ourselves in the Greek conception and interpretation of ἔργον as such, then we immediately become aware of the inner structural connection between the philosophical concept ἐνέργεια and οὐσία as παρουσία. At the same time, we thereby obtain an insight into the basic concept of the Platonic doctrine of being: ἰδέα, εἶδος. To grasp the Platonic doctrine of being as the 'doctrine of ideas', if this concept is taken purely doxographically, is admittedly an error. For Plato, being means what-being, and the 'what' of something is given in its look. The latter is the way beings present [*präsentieren*] themselves and *are present* [*anwesend*]. In the look of a thing there resides its *presence* (being).

That work in its workhood and producedness as such – whether as product of craft or as genuine art work – plays an essential role in the formation of the Greek concept of being must be clarified in terms of the fundamental attitudes of Greek Dasein. What these attitudes show is the wrenching of things and forms from and in the fearfulness [*Furchtbarkeit*] of existence. They expose the lies about the cheerfulness of Greek Dasein. Especially noteworthy is that, from an early date and for a long time, the word τέχνη stood for knowledge as a whole, i.e. simply for the making manifest of beings. τέχνη neither means technique as *practical* activity nor is limited to craft knowledge, but it signifies all *producing* in the broadest sense, together with its guiding knowledge. It expresses the struggle around the *presence* of beings. We cannot enter now into a discussion of other fundamental words of Greek ontology and their broad implications. In discussing the concept of ἐνέργεια reference has already been made to Kant's concept of *appearance*. That beings as such have the character of appearance just means that the being of beings is understood as self-showing, as being-encountered, as presence. This interpretation of the Kantian concept of appearance, likewise our earlier interpretation of the Greek concept of being, goes beyond what is expressly stated by Kant and the Greeks; that is, our interpretation returns to that which stood within the horizon of their understanding of being. If we directly ask whether and how Kant himself explicitly interpreted and determined the actuality of actual beings, we can discover the following statement in the *Critique of Pure Reason*: 'That which is bound up with the material conditions of experience, that is, with sensation, is actual'.[10] Actuality means a connection with sensation. We must, however, likewise forgo discussing how a sufficiently concrete interpretation of this determination of the essence of *actuality* supports what we have just said concerning Kant's concept of appearance.[11]

§ 9. Being, Truth, Presence
The Greek Interpretation of Being as Being-True in the Horizon of Being as Constant Presence. The ὄν ὡς ἀληθές as κυριώτατον ὄν (Aristotle, Metaphysics Θ 10)

a) Where the Inquiry Stands.
The Previously Discussed Meanings of Being and the Exemplary Status of Being-True

Our proposed elaboration of the leading question of metaphysics through to the fundamental question proceeds from the thesis that being means constant presence. We attempted to validate this thesis by an interpretation of the Greek concept of being – οὐσία – in its principal meanings. Clearly, everything that follows depends upon the validity of this interpretation. If this interpretation of being as constant presence is not correct, there can be no basis for unfolding a connection between being and time, as demanded by the fundamental question.

Yet although Greek metaphysics as such, together with the subsequent tradition of Western metaphysics, is of great significance for our problem, its implications do not extend this far. For even if for some reason or other our interpretation of Greek ontology could not be carried through, what we have asserted as the fundamental orientation of the understanding of being could be exhibited from our own immediate comportment towards beings. So we unfold the leading question of metaphysics in the direction of the fundamental question (being and time) not because the Greeks already (albeit implicitly) understood being in terms of time, but simply because – as will be shown – we humans *must* understand being in terms of time. Wherever being becomes thematic, the light of time must come into view. Our thesis that οὐσία means constant presence, i.e. this interpretation of the history of metaphysics, can never itself ground the problem of being and time, but serves merely to illustrate the unfolding of the problem. Moreover, the relevant features of Greek ontology can only be discovered if we have already assured ourselves, in a philosophical manner, of the substantive connections.

However, the history of metaphysics provides us with more than just examples. Of course, we can never rely on the authority of Plato or Kant to ground a thesis or problem. But history offers us more than a picture of earlier and superseded stages of thought. Apart from the fact that progress does not exist in philosophy, so that every instance of genuine philosophy is on the same level as regards greatness and smallness, earlier philosophy has a constant (albeit hidden) influence on our contemporary existence. If we try to grasp the Greek concept of being, this is not a matter of acquiring external historical knowledge. We shall see that, in altered form, the Greek concept of being is still present in Hegel's metaphysics. We shall not enter into the inner connection between Hegelian metaphysics and Greek philosophy, especially since we have followed the Greek concept of being only in some aspects. We have limited ourselves to a purely systematic-substantive characterization of the understanding of being. We spoke of the original dividedness of being, which we further clarified in terms of the various meanings of 'is'.

Let us explain this once again by an example: 'the chalk is white'. The 'is white' expresses the white-being, thus the so-and-so-being of the chalk: it is so-and-so. This so-and-so does not *necessarily* pertain to it, for it could also be red or green. When we say 'the chalk is a material thing', we also refer to the being of the chalk, but in this case not to anything arbitrary, rather to what *must* belong to it for it to be what it is. This being is not an arbitrary so-and-so-being, but a necessary what-being. When we say 'the chalk is', perhaps in response to a claim that we have only imagined it, then being means being-present (actuality). Again, if we enunciate these sentences with a specific emphasis – 'the chalk *is* white', 'the chalk *is* a material thing', 'the chalk *is* present' – then by this emphasis we also intend a specific kind of being. We now want to say that it is true – the what-being of the chalk, the being-a-thing, the being-present. We now mean the *being-true*.

We have interpreted the Greek concepts of being corresponding to the first three of these meanings of being and have shown them to be grounded in 'constant presence'. In respect of being-true, however, we have thus far given no proof, remarking only that this would be too difficult and involved.

so-and-so-being	what-being	being-present	being-true
(now this – now that)	(possibility)	(actuality)	?
ἀπουσία – παρουσία	Plato:	ἐνέργεια	
	παρουσία	ἔργον	
		παρουσία	

Various investigations have shown me that understanding the first three meanings depends on clarifying the fourth. We can conclude this substantively from what we have just seen, namely being-true as that which is intended by emphasis. Even without emphasis, the meaning of being-true is included in all the others. Being-true is therefore an especially comprehensive meaning of being. Accordingly, I shall now briefly attempt an interpretation of being-true.

In what way does the asserted fundamental meaning of constant presence also apply to being-true? What connection can we see between being-true and being as such? To exhibit this connection is difficult, not only because we run up against the common opinion of being-true, but also because the Greek doctrine of being-true, especially Aristotle's doctrine thereof, has been interpreted in terms of this same common conception. It has thus come about that Aristotle's genuine problematic has been comprehensively misunderstood. In such cases the most convenient way out is to alter the text so that it can correspond to the common opinion and cause no embarrassment.

Our interpretation of being-true, which aims to show that this too relates to the indicated fundamental meaning, will proceed by reference to a particular Aristotelian text. We shall show *how the Greek concept of being-true is also understood in terms of constant presence*.

b) Four Meanings of Being in Aristotle.
The Exclusion of the ὄν ὡς ἀληθές in Metaphysics E 4

First a general preview of the substantive problem. We have learnt that the leading problem of ancient metaphysics, as formulated by Aristotle, is τί τὸ ὄν. What is inquired into is the ὄν ᾗ ὄν. Now Aristotle repeatedly emphasizes, especially wherever he is introducing a fundamental problem of metaphysics, that τὸ ὄν λέγεται πολλαχῶς, i.e. that 'being is said in many ways'. Now πολλαχῶς is itself ambiguous. On the one hand it signifies the diverse meanings of being, but it also refers to a diversity within one of these meanings, i.e. within the categories. The ὄν of the κατηγορίαι is itself multiple, such that one can again inquire into a πρώτως ὄν, i.e. a primary being.

Beings as such are addressed in various ways, or, more clearly, we understand being in various ways.[12] Aristotle identifies four ways, which do not immediately coincide with the fourfold structure of being given above. The four modes in which we understand that which is, ὄν, and accordingly also that which is not, μὴ ὄν, are as follows.

1. τὸ ὄν κατὰ τὰ σχήματα τῶν κατηγοριῶν (τῆς κατηγορίας) – ὄν καθ' αὑτό, beings as they show themselves in *the categories*. For example: 'this chalk is white', *this* chalk, this present thing *here*: category of the τόδε τι. Being white, i.e. to be of a certain *quality*: ποιόν. The chalk lies here on the lectern: ποῦ, *place*.

2. τὸ ὄν κατὰ συμβεβηκός, beings in respect of their *contingency*, their so-and-so-being, the being of beings which just happen to be such-and-such at a particular time, e.g. being-red, being-white.

3. τὸ ὄν κατὰ δύναμιν καὶ ἐνέργειαν, beings in respect of their *being-possible and being-actual*.

4. τὸ ὄν ὡς ἀληθὲς καὶ ψεῦδος, beings in respect of *being-true and being-false*.

The inquiry into the ὄν ᾗ ὄν must already be clear about the various meanings of the ὄν. Such clarity was originally lacking. Only slowly was this clarity attained, and even Aristotle is content just to factually distinguish these four meanings. No explanation is given as to why just these, and these alone, are distinguished, nor does Aristotle explain the principles for distinguishing them. At this point, what is important for us is that *being-true is explicitly identified as one of these four meanings*. Now must philosophy in the proper sense, i.e. the philosophy which inquires into what beings as such actually are, must this philosophy inquire into all four modes of being, or only into those beings and their being which manifest themselves precisely as proper beings [*das eigentliche Seiende*]? Clearly, philosophy is concerned only with the latter. For if the essence of being were clarified by reference to proper beings it should be possible to clarify the essence of non-proper beings [*das uneigentliche Seiende*].

This is the way Aristotle proceeds in *Metaphysics* E (VI), where he outlines the thematic field of philosophy in terms of the four indicated meanings of ὄν. In so doing, he excludes the ὄν κατὰ συμβεβηκός (the second meaning of being) and the ὄν ὡς ἀληθές (the fourth meaning of being) from the field of metaphysics. Only the first and the third meanings remain, which are treated later in the central books of the *Metaphysics*, i.e. Z, H, Θ, I (VII–X). Why does Aristotle exclude the second and fourth meanings? We have already indicated that these are senses of being wherein the being of proper beings, thus also proper being, does not manifest itself. Why not? The ὄν κατὰ συμβεβηκός is ἀόριστον, it is *not determinate* in its being but is sometimes such and sometimes so; it does not refer to anything constantly present, not πέρας and μορφή, εἶδος, but to something that occurs at one time only to disappear. Thus Aristotle says: φαίνεται γὰρ τὸ συμβεβηκὸς ἐγγύς τι τοῦ μὴ ὄντος.[13] It is not, therefore, beings proper which are here intended. And why is the ὄν ὡς ἀληθές excluded? To put the matter briefly: truth and falsity pertain to knowledge of beings, to propositions, to the λόγος (discourse) concerning beings. Aristotle calls this τῆς διανοίας τι πάθος,[14] a character not of the beings themselves but of their determination in thought. Being-true pertains to grasping beings in thought, not to beings themselves. To formulate the matter in traditional terms, the problem of being-true (truth and falsity) belongs in logic and epistemology, not in metaphysics. The exclusion of the second and the fourth meanings of being is thus quite in order and immediately convincing. Metaphysics, as knowledge of beings as such, is concerned only with the ὄν of the categories and with the ὄν κατὰ δύναμιν καὶ ἐνέργειαν. The ὄν of the categories – especially the first category, upon which all the others are founded – is treated by Aristotle in *Metaphysics* Z and H, while the ὄν κατὰ δύναμιν καὶ ἐνέργειαν, i.e. being in the sense of possibility and actuality, is treated in *Metaphysics* Θ. Furthermore,

LEADING QUESTION OF PHILOSOPHY

Book Θ presents ἐνεργεία (ἐντελέχεια) as *the* fundamental meaning of the actuality of that which is properly actual. The being proper is the ὄν ἐνεργεία. Those beings to which, according to our own interpretation, constant presence must be attributed, i.e. those beings properly deserving of the name, are ἡ οὐσία καὶ τὸ εἶδος ἐνέργεια ἐστιν.[15] So it is Book Θ of Aristotle's *Metaphysics* which discusses the being of proper beings.

c) Thematic Discussion of the ὄν ὡς ἀληθές as the κυριώτατον ὄν in Metaphysics Θ 10 and the Question of Whether This Chapter Belongs to Book Θ.
Connection Between the Textual Question and the Substantive Question of the Relation Between Being Qua Being-True and Being Qua Being-Actual (ἐνεργεία ὄν)

Book Θ concludes with Chapter 10, which itself begins as follows:

Ἐπεὶ δὲ τὸ ὂν λέγεται καὶ τὸ μὴ ὂν τὸ μὲν κατὰ τὰ σχήματα τῶν κατηγοριῶν, τὸ δὲ κατὰ δύναμιν ἢ ἐνέργειαν τούτων ἢ τἀναντία, τὸ δὲ κυριώτατα ὂν ἀληθὲς ἢ ψεῦδος, τοῦτο δ᾽ ἐπὶ τῶν πραγμάτων ἐστὶ τῷ συγκεῖσθαι ἢ διῃρῆσθαι, ὥστ᾽ ἀληθεύει μὲν ὁ τὸ διῃρημένον οἰόμενος διῃρῆσθαι καὶ τὸ συγκείμενον συγκεῖσθαι, ἔψευσται δὲ ὁ ἐναντίως ἔχων ἢ τὰ πράγματα, πότ᾽ ἔστιν ἢ οὐκ ἔστι τὸ ὡς ἀληθὲς λεγόμενον ἢ ψεῦδος; τοῦτο γὰρ σκεπτέον τί λέγομεν.[16]

The terms 'being' and 'not-being' are used not only with reference to the categories, and to the potentiality or actuality, or non-potentiality and non-actuality, of these, but also, in the strictest sense, to denote truth and falsity. This depends, in the case of the objects, upon their being united or divided; so that he who thinks that what is divided is divided, or that what is united is united, is right; while he whose thought is contrary to the real condition of the objects is in error. Then *when* do what we call truth and falsity exist or not exist?[17]

Thus τὸ δὲ κυριώτατα ὂν ἀληθὲς ἢ ψεῦδος. What is going on here? The explicit theme is the ὄν (ὡς) ἀληθές. At the close of the properly central book of the *Metaphysics*, Aristotle takes up a topic from logic, i.e. a topic which he himself, earlier in E4, had explicitly excluded from the domain of first philosophy. It is thus immediately clear that this chapter is out of place and does not belong where we discover it. This is externally indicated by the fact that it stands at the end of the book. Therefore, although its overall content is indisputably Aristotelian, someone must have added it later. There is no difficulty in assuming this to be the case, for Aristotle's *Metaphysics* is not a continuously composed work but a collection of self-contained treatises which belong together because of their affiliated content. Furthermore, that this chapter on being-true cannot belong to Θ, which concerns actuality as such, is quite clear from the fact that the ὄν ἀληθές, being as being-true, is introduced as even more proper than the ἐνεργείᾳ ὄν, which contradicts everything that precedes it and everything we know of Aristotle.[18]

We can see how the *textual question of the correct positioning of this final chapter of Book Θ also raises the substantive problem of the meaning of being-true itself, or more precisely, the question of the relation between being qua being-true and being qua being-actual*. Yet for the traditional, as also for the most recent interpretation and treatment of this Chapter 10, there is no problem here at all, because there can be none. For after all, every beginner in philosophy knows that the problem of truth belongs to logic and not to metaphysics, especially not to a treatise concerned with the fundamental problem of metaphysics. Such considerations lead *Schwegler*, to whom we owe a valuable Hegelian commentary on the *Metaphysics*, to say flatly: 'This chapter does not belong here'.[19] Werner *Jaeger*, the author of a very valuable study of the composition of the Aristotelian *Metaphysics*,[20] is convinced by Schwegler's view: 'So the chapter just stands there, devoid of all connections'.[21] Unlike Schwegler, however, Jaeger believes that Aristotle, despite this chapter's disconnectedness with the book as a whole, himself added it as an appendix.

α) The rejection of Θ 10's placement in Θ and the traditional interpretation of being-true as a problem of logic and epistemology (Schwegler, Jaeger, Ross). The erroneous interpretation of κυριώτατα resulting from this interpretation

If, like Jaeger, one adopts Schwegler's view that a chapter on logic could not substantively belong in the *Metaphysics*, then for the sake of consistency one should not attribute the addition of this chapter to Aristotle himself, especially considering the manner in which Aristotle's chapters and books are composed and constructed. Jaeger's opinion becomes all the more curious when, to justify the rejection of Chapter 10's placement in Θ, he goes even further than Schwegler. Jaeger sees the main 'external' hindrance to accepting Chapter 10 in the fact that the ὄν ἀληθές not only supposedly relates to the principal theme, but that this ὄν is taken as κυριώτατα, i.e. that beings as being-true are understood as the most proper beings. 'To me this is very improbable, and it will strike everyone else likewise.' 'If anyone were to support the placement of Θ10 on the ground that only here is the κυριώτατα ὄν attained, he would mis-understand the wording, and besides, he would be thinking in an un-Aristotelian way.'[22] Jaeger wants to say that whoever maintains that Aristotle in Θ10 conceives being-true as the most proper being does not understand what κυριώτατα means, moreover has a concept of being quite foreign to Aristotle.

I maintain, by contrast, that anyone who conceives Θ10 as belonging to Θ, and sees it as the genuine culmination of Θ and of Aristotle's *Meta-physics* as such, thinks not just in properly Aristotelian terms, but simply in Greek terms. The fact that Aristotle closes with Θ10, interpreting being-true as proper being, *indicates that Greek metaphysics' fundamental conception of being here comes to its first and ultimate radical expression.* Only someone who uncritically accepts long-standing traditional platitudes about Aristotle could regard this as un-Aristotelian.

Thus it is clear that the apparently external question concerning the placement of Chapter 10 in Book Θ can only be resolved by going into the problems treated in the chapter and book respectively. We must inquire into what fundamental meaning of being makes it *possible* as well as *necessary* to treat being-true in the context of being-actual, and indeed such that being-true constitutes the most proper meaning of being. Before answering this question, and thus positively establishing the inner necessary connection between Θ10 and Θ, the doubts concerning this connection must be briefly dealt with. We shall begin by discussing the argumentation directed against the κυριώτατα.

If one assumes from the start that Θ10, since it concerns the ὄν ἀληθές, relates to a *problem of logic* and as such does not belong to the overall theme of Θ, then one must deny the possibility that the ὄν ἀληθές could be referred to as the most proper being, κυριώτατα ὄν. This κυριώτατα must therefore be removed. There are two alternatives here: 1. striking it altogether out of the text, 2. reinterpreting it, so that it conforms to the presupposed content of the chapter. The second procedure is adopted by Schwegler and especially by Jaeger. The first procedure is to be found in the most recent treatment by Ross: *seclusi: an post* μὲν (a34) *transpo-nenda*?[23] There is not the slightest justification for such a violent interven-tion in the text, which is completely in order at this point. It is just that the κυριώτατα is anomalous vis-à-vis the presupposed content of the chapter. Schwegler's commentary simply bypasses the κυριώτατα. What this implies can be seen from his translation of the *Metaphysics*, where he trans-lates κυριώτατα by 'mainly': being is 'mainly' addressed as being-true.

Jaeger holds to the same conception of κυριώτατα: κυριώτατα ὄν 'is the most common meaning of being, the most frequent meaning of being in everyday usage'. 'And it is plain that this is the *esse* of the copula.'[24] What can we say about this view? There is no evidence for it in Aristotle. That the 'is' for the most part functions as the copula is correct, but it is not the case that the copula for the most part means 'is true', being-true. This is not because the copula only seldom has this meaning, but because it always does, whether explicitly or not. To say, with Jaeger, that the copula mostly means being-true is like saying that 2 plus 2 mostly comes to 4. But while being-true is always intended by the copula, 'being' is for the most part not understood in this way, but in the sense of what-being, so-being, being-present. There is no substantive basis for the thesis that 'is' mostly means being-true, and thus there is no basis for claiming that ἀληθὲς ὄν as κυριώτατον means being in its usual employment. Above all, however, κυριώτατον never refers, neither in this context nor anywhere else, to frequency of employment. It is for this reason that Schwegler and Jaeger omit any linguistic evidence for their arbitrary interpretations.

Κυρίως, κύριος: the master, the possessor, the owner of something. κύριος, κυρίως taken in its characteristic and proper meaning: when κυρίως pertains to a word, what is intended is not primarily frequency of use, but just the word itself in its proper meaning. This proper meaning is also the most frequently occurring meaning, while the transferred meaning, μεταφορά, is less frequent, foreign, unusual. κυρίως ὄν means what a being properly is. κυρίως is often employed by Aristotle to distinguish from κατὰ μεταφοράν, i.e. a word in its proper meaning as distinct from a word in its transferred meaning.

To be sure, κύριον, that which predominates or rules, is also employed by Aristotle in the meaning of 'the usual'; in accordance with the meaning of κύριος, master, τὸ κύριον thus means the main or primary linguistic usage. The less common or unusual employment of language is, accordingly, denoted by τὸ ξενικόν. In the *Rhetoric* Γ2 Aristotle says: ἔστω οὖν ἐκεῖνα τεθεωρημένα καὶ ὡρίσθω λέξεως ἀρετὴ σαφῆ εἶναι,[25] every discourse possesses excellence, ἀρετή, to the degree that its words make clear what is meant: σαφῆ μέν ποιεῖ τὰ κύρια.[26] However, if discourse is not to be vulgar, ταπεινή, it also requires ξενικά, unusual non-standard words. Metaphors and provincial expressions, etc. belong here. In respect of the employment of language, therefore, Aristotle uses κύριον in the sense of what is common or usual. But the primary and proper use of language is common because it is proper, not the other way around. The proper meaning is the reason for frequency in language use. Thus the primary and proper meaning of κύριον is properness. Metaphysics is in no way concerned with what is common or normal. The latter issue plays no substantive role within it at all.

We must therefore ask what κύριον means elsewhere within Aristotle's philosophical terminology. In Book 6 of the *Nichomachean Ethics* we read: Τρία δή ἐστιν ἐν τῇ ψυχῇ τὰ κύρια πράξεως καὶ ἀληθείας, αἴσθησις νοῦς ὄρεξις.[27] There are three things in the soul which together make up the κύρια, i.e. that which is proper in action and knowledge: perception, thought, and will. It would be completely nonsensical to translate κύρια here as 'usual'. Again in Book 9, Aristotle says, in connection with the problem of friendship and man's self-love: εἰ γάρ τις ἀεὶ σπουδάζοι τὰ δίκαια πράττειν αὐτὸς μάλιστα πάντων ἢ τὰ σώφρονα ἢ ὁποιαοῦν ἄλλα τῶν κατὰ τὰς ἀρετάς, καὶ ὅλως ἀεὶ τὸ καλὸν ἑαυτῷ περιποιοῖτο, οὐδεὶς ἐρεῖ τοῦτον φίλαυτον οὐδὲ ψέξει. If a man is always concerned to do the right and proper thing, in general striving to be noble, nobody will censure him as an egoist. And yet precisely such a man possesses proper self-love: μᾶλλον εἶναι φίλαυτος . . . καὶ χαρίζεται ἑαυτοῦ τῷ κυριωτάτῳ,[28] for he appropriates for himself what is most noble and best, is inwardly bound to what is most essential and proper in himself. Here too it would be senseless to translate κυριωτάτῳ as 'the usual'. And again in Book 1, Aristotle says that ethics is the ἐπιστήμη πολιτική, for this is the ἐπιστήμη κυριωτάτη,[29] i.e. the highest and most proper science which as such encompasses and guides all human action. Thus Aristotle speaks, in this same sense, of ἀκρότατον ἀγαθόν or κυριώτατον ἀγαθόν, i.e. the most proper good, the good simply and as such.

In a manner completely in line with this latter passage, Aristotle speaks in *Metaphysics* Θ10 of proper beings. However awkward, this must be left standing! To be sure, Jaeger is right to maintain that κύριον can mean the most common or usual. But we must insist that, substantively speaking, this does not apply to being-true, either in vulgar usage or in Aristotle. The κυριώτατα is not to be shaken: it stands firm, announcing Aristotle's intention not only to treat being-true within his metaphysics, but to interpret this as the most proper mode of being, and to close his treatise on proper being precisely in this way.

β) Demonstration of Chapter 10's proper placement in Book Θ.
The ambiguity in the Greek concept of truth: truth of things and truth
of sentences (propositional truth).
The thematic discussion of the being-true of (proper) beings
(ἐπὶ τῶν πραγμάτων), not of knowledge, in Chapter Θ10.

Aristotle's straightforward claim is that being-true constitutes the most
proper being of beings, i.e. that being-true as such announces the most
proper essence of being. This problem arises where he consistently and
explicitly treats of proper being (ἐνέργεια, ἐντελέχεια), in Book Θ. How
the assertion can be justified is shown in Θ10. In short, the chapter is
concerned to unfold the proof of the thesis that *being-true constitutes
the most proper being of proper beings*. The theme is the being-true of beings,
i.e. he asks about how beings in themselves must be, in order that they
may be true, and about the being-true itself which is thus made possible.
How does this relate to the proper being of beings?

It must first be shown that the being of beings also remains the theme
in Θ10, and that being-true is drawn into this guiding theme. So after
introducing the ἀληθὲς ὄν, i.e. that which is true, as that which most
properly is, Aristotle immediately says: τοῦτο, namely being-true, τοῦτο δ᾽
ἐπὶ τῶν πραγμάτων,[30] this being-true is applicable to the existing things
themselves. Being-true is the being-true of the πραγμάτων, the things,
thus is not a property of conceptual thought of things, is not truth as
pertaining to knowledge of beings, is not a property of propositions, of the
λόγος about beings, does not concern opinion of . . . as such; none of that,
but being-true pertains simply to the beings themselves. From the first
sentence of the chapter it is evident that the theme differs utterly from
what it has traditionally and uncritically been taken to be, i.e. that it does
not at all concern being-true as pertaining to conceptual thought and
assertion. As to the latter, we read in E 4: ἐπεὶ δὲ ἡ συμπλοκή ἐστιν καὶ ἡ
διαίρεσις ἐν διανοίᾳ ἀλλ᾽ οὐκ ἐν τοῖς πράγμασι, τὸ δ᾽ οὕτως ὂν ἕτερον ὂν
τῶν κυρίως,[31] namely the categories, . . . ἀφετέον. Analysis and synthesis
pertain to the thinking of beings, not to the actual beings which are
thought, thus they and all their properties, thus also being-true and
being-false, are left aside.

Σκεπτέον δὲ τοῦ ὄντος αὐτοῦ τὰ αἴτια,[32] the beings themselves must be
considered in relation to what makes them possible as beings. In Θ10,
however, as in Book Θ as a whole, it is not the being-true of thought but
only the beings themselves, ultimately their being-true and its possibility,

which is inquired into. And it is maintained that the being-true of beings constitutes the most proper being of beings. Thus not only is the problem situated completely within the domain of πρώτη φιλοσοφία, but it is itself the latter's most radical problem. Θ does not address problems of logic or epistemology at all, but rather the fundamental problem of metaphysics. Can any doubt remain as to whether this chapter belongs to Book Θ, i.e. to the book which brings the leading question of Greek metaphysics to its highest development? Must not the chapter necessarily belong there? The chapter is not at all unconnected to the rest of the book, and certainly Aristotle did not, despite its alleged unconnectedness, just add it on.

But how could the real theme of the chapter be so crudely and stubbornly overlooked? The commentators and those who cite them have, to be sure, also read the chapter and interpreted it. Certainly, but there is reading and reading. The question is whether we read in the right way, i.e. whether we are adequately prepared for seeing what is in front of us, whether we measure up to the problematic or not, whether we understand the problems of being and truth and their interconnection in a sufficiently primordial manner, whether we are thus able to move within the horizon of the philosophy of Aristotle and Plato. Or whether we rush at the philosophical tradition with worn-out philosophical concepts and their pseudo-problems, expecting that with such miserable qualifications we can decide which additions the text requires, and what Aristotle must have thought. This is what happens in the case of Schwegler. The problem of truth is known to belong to logic. Being is in any case self-evident and does not need to be placed in question. So if Aristotle includes, in the main book of his *Metaphysics*, a chapter which treats of truth from the very first sentence, this cannot properly belong here. Irrespective of its crudity or refinement, overall or in detail, nothing changes the fundamental untenability of such a procedure.

What therefore is the basic deficiency in the common interpretation of this chapter? It stems from the fact that the Greek understanding of the essence of truth is just as little interrogated as is the Greek understanding of being. This also applies to all subsequent philosophy. Indeed subsequent philosophy, for reasons we do not need to enter into now, has not even been able to take up and make fruitful what the Greek treatment of the problem of truth achieved. If this is the situation, then we certainly have no right to assume that in one chapter from one book, a chapter that asserts and discusses a connection between being and truth, everything will be carried through with perfect transparency. On the contrary, wherever the deepest problematic is attained, there remains, despite all acuity of questioning, the greatest obscurity.

What then do the Greeks understand, pre-philosophically and philosophically, by truth?[33] Ἀλήθεια, unhiddenness [*Unverborgenheit*]; not hidden, but brought out from hiddenness. So already and from the outset truth as unhiddenness does not pertain to the knowledge and conception of beings, but to beings themselves. Thus when Aristotle inquires into the unhiddenness of beings, into the truth of beings, this is, for the Greeks, the natural and proper way of inquiring into truth. From the very beginning, the problem of truth is not a problem concerning knowledge and conception. It only becomes this in a secondary sense, insofar as the knowledge which grasps beings in their unveiledness, unhiddenness, is also for its part 'true', i.e., in Greek terms, it is such as to appropriate, communicate, and preserve the unhiddenness of beings. The proposition is not what is primarily true in the sense of unhiddenness, but is the means by which we humans preserve and secure truth, i.e. the deconcealment of beings: ἀληθεύειν.

Ἀληθεύει cannot be said of beings themselves; rather, beings are ὄν ἀληθές in the primordial sense. However, that which ἀληθεύει (unveils), i.e. that which (the λόγος) can be called true in the derivative sense, is ἀληθής. ἀληθές means 1. beings as deconcealed, 2. grasping of the deconcealed as such, i.e. to be deconcealing. Thus ἀληθές and ἀλήθεια contain an ambiguity – and indeed a necessary one, an ambiguity to which we must hold fast if we want to get anywhere with the problem of truth.

What now is the situation in regard to the counter-concept of truth, i.e. untruth? Untruth is not just hiddenness, but distortion. A corresponding distinction can also be made between falsity and untruth. For untruth is not simply non-truth – the beautiful is also this – but exists where something is lacking in truth. Untruth exists where there is indeed unhiddenness, yet distortion predominates, i.e. where something is, but where this something presents itself as what it is not.

At the beginning of Chapter 10, Aristotle makes it perfectly clear that the issue is the being-true of beings: οὐ γὰρ διὰ τὸ ἡμᾶς οἴεσθαι ἀληθῶς σὲ λευκὸν εἶναι εἶ σὺ λευκός, ἀλλὰ διὰ τὸ σὲ εἶναι λευκὸν ἡμεῖς οἱ φάντες τοῦτο ἀληθεύομεν.[34] ἀληθεύειν is also grounded in the ἀληθὲς ὄν. But since the primordial Greek understanding of the essence of truth, along with the Greek understanding of being, is no longer taken seriously, this *ambiguity in the concept of truth* is overlooked. τὸ ἀληθὲς λεγόμενον, i.e. that which is true in the primordial sense, that which can be addressed as the deconcealed, is the beings themselves, the ὄν.

d) The Greek Understanding of Truth (ἀλήθεια) as Deconcealment
The Being Which Is True (ἀληθὲς ὄν) as the Most Proper Being
(κυριώτατον ὄν)
The Most Proper Being as the Simple and Constantly Present

Aristotle now poses the problem: πότ᾽ ἔστιν ἢ οὐκ ἔστι τὸ ἀληθὲς λεγόμενον ἢ ψεῦδος.[35] When does truth exist and when does it not, i.e. when are beings such that they can be true? How must the being of beings be, such that beings can be true, i.e. deconcealed? When can beings be properly true as such? Answer: when every possibility of the untruth of beings is in every respect excluded. When is that, and what does truth thereby mean? Answer: when truth belongs to being. How is that possible? Answer: when being-true constitutes what is most proper about being as such. But what is being? Answer: constant presence. Thus, when truth is nothing but the highest possible and most proper presence, then truth exists. This is a metaphysical question of the purest kind and has nothing to do with so-called epistemology. How can being-true belong to the being of beings? What is being-true itself, such that it can belong to the being of beings? Aristotle must ask these questions if he wants to show that being-true not only belongs to beings, but constitutes the most proper being of beings: ἀληθὲς ὄν as κυριώτατον ὄν. And clearly, only proper being-true, not just any arbitrary deconcealment of arbitrary beings, can constitute the most proper being of beings.

α) The correspondence between being and being-true (deconcealment).
Two fundamental types of being and their corresponding modes of being-true

What solution to this problem does Aristotle provide? After everything that has been said, we cannot expect this highest point of the Greek ontological problematic to show, in Aristotle's specific treatment, a different character to that of the Greek problematic in general. Here too the problem stands within the illumination provided by the natural or everyday understanding of being, but without this illumination itself being clarified. I shall sketch out the Aristotelian treatment of the problem only in its main features. A full interpretation would take us too far afield and would presuppose a thorough familiarity with the Aristotelian metaphysics.

Three things should be borne in mind in relation to this problem. First, that which properly exists is the ὄν ἐνεργείᾳ. ἐνέργεια is proper being in the sense of self-holding in constant presence. Secondly, truth is the deconcealment of beings, and only on the basis of and in relation to this deconcealment can truth apply, in a derivative sense, to that which determines and conceives beings: ἀληθεύειν, the φάναι or καταφάναι τὸ ἀληθές. Thirdly, it is precisely because the essence of truth is the deconcealment of beings that the various kinds of truth are determined by the various kinds of beings, i.e. in accordance with the being of these beings. If one grasps and holds fast to the essence of the Greek concept of truth, this correspondence between modes of deconcealment and kinds of beings is clear and obvious. By the same token, if this correspondence comes to clear expression with the Greeks, this reflects their fundamental conception of truth as the truth of beings (deconcealment). So Aristotle says, clearly and simply at the end of *Metaphysics* α 1: ἕκαστον ὡς ἔχει τοῦ εἶναι, οὕτω καὶ τῆς ἀληθείας,[36] as each thing is in respect of being, so it is in respect of truth (deconcealment). The mode of being of beings determines the mode of their possible deconcealment. The latter goes together with being. Proper being-true thus belongs to proper beings.

It is our claim that, in Θ10, Aristotle poses the problem of how the being of beings makes it possible for beings to be true, i.e. deconcealed. What is the proper being-true of beings? It should now be clear that the problem became unavoidable for Aristotle and the Greeks only after the leading question τί τὸ ὄν was awakened. This is obvious. We can also see why Aristotle unfolds this problem in the particular direction he does. For if his thesis is that the ἀληθὲς ὄν is the κυριώτατον ὄν, the most proper being, then he must set out from the question of the being of proper beings. The problem does not concern any arbitrary kind of truth of any arbitrary being, but the truth of proper beings, i.e. proper truth. *The connection between being and truth must come into view from consideration of the proper truth of proper beings*, i.e. it must be shown how *truth as such constitutes the proper being of beings*.

We have thus already sketched out the course of discussion in Θ10. The thematic treatment of the problem begins at 1051 b 9 and continues until 1052 a 4. The earlier sections introduce the problem. We have previously treated the most important matters: the thesis, the framework of questioning, the truth of things (πράγματα) as the ground of the possibility of assertoric truth. What is discussed after a 4 are implications. Given the profundity of the problem, Aristotle's construction of the thematic discussion as well as his brevity, acuity, and clarity, are utterly astonishing.

The deconcealment of beings is governed by their mode of being, τὸ δὲ ἀληθὲς ὡς τὸ εἶναι. When considering the overall classification of beings, we discovered a kind of being of which Aristotle remarks: ἐγγύς τι τοῦ μὴ ὄντος,[37] it is akin to non-being. This is, to be sure, still a being, but not a proper being, i.e. this ὄν κατὰ συμβεβηκός is such that it just happens to occur on a particular occasion. For example, the white-being of the chalk. Chalk does not need to be white. By contrast, the materiality of an existing piece of chalk does not just occur now and again, συμβεβηκός, but is a συγκείμενον, inseparable from the chalk, συν-κείμενον with the ὑποκείμενον. Chalk and materiality are here ἀδύνατον διαιρεθῆναι, impossible to separate. On the other hand, while all kinds of things may change an existing piece of chalk, deceitfulness, for example, can never belong to the chalk. It is impossible, in an unveiling determination of the chalk, to say 'the chalk deceives'. Aristotle says: ἀδύνατον συντεθῆναι. As already mentioned, there are some things that may or may not happen to the chalk. What then does being mean with respect to the materially existing chalk as such, i.e. the materiality of the chalk? It means to be together-with and in this togetherness to be one. By the same token, being-deceitful and being-chalk can never possess this togetherness.

Aristotle begins the thematic discussion by clarifying and defining these different modes of being: εἰ δὴ τὰ μὲν ἀεὶ σύγκειται καὶ ἀδύνατα διαιρεθῆναι, τὰ δ᾽ ἀεὶ διῄρηται καὶ ἀδύνατα συντεθῆναι, τὰ δ᾽ ἐνδέχεται τἀναντία τὸ μὲν γὰρ εἶναί ἐστι τὸ συγκεῖσθαι καὶ ἓν εἶναι, τὸ δὲ μὴ εἶναι τὸ μὴ συγκεῖσθαι ἀλλὰ πλείω εἶναι.[38] This is just the interpretation of the what-being and so-being of beings. In this interpretation we can discover tangible evidence for our general thesis on being. As the being of what-being (materiality of the chalk), being means togetherness, συγκεῖσθαι. But we recall that ὑποκείμενον means ὑπομένον. Thus συγκεῖσθαι means not just togetherness in the sense of co-givenness but constant co-presence. The chalk is what it is only through the constant co-presence of materiality. By contrast, chalk and deceitfulness form a constant non-togetherness, i.e. the chalk can never contain such a thing within itself and nothing of this sort can occur to it. The one must be constantly absent from the other.[39] Finally there is that which is not constantly present but sometimes present and sometimes absent, i.e. *the accidental*. If one does not, from the very outset, realize that being means constant presence, one cannot make even the first step towards understanding this decisive passage in Aristotle.

We now have *two basic kinds of being*: συγκεῖσθαι and συμβεβηκέναι. Here it is crucial to notice that each of these kinds of being has its own specific way of *not-being* or *absence*. Only after Aristotle has defined these kinds of being (what-being and so-being) does he proceed to the genuine problem, i.e. to the question of how the being-true and deconcealment (uncoveredness) corresponding to these different kinds of being is possible. He begins by interpreting the deconcealment of those beings which can be sometimes this, sometimes that, i.e. he begins with non-proper beings, with beings whose being is most remote from the essence of being as constant presence. When and how does the unveiling (truth) of non-constant or accidental beings occur? The deconcealment of the accidental does not always occur, and indeed precisely does not occur when the accidental is how it is. The essence of accidental beings is such that its truth is not always what it wants to be – truth. Truth becomes untruth. It is, therefore, not primarily our own doing if from time to time we err and think wrongly. How then can the deconcealment of the accidental be such that, according to its own essence, it is not always what it is, i.e. that deconcealment can itself turn into untruth, and that beings themselves can change independently of our conception of them? We see this chalk and say 'the chalk is white'. This is a true assertion because it takes up what this chalk is in its unhiddenness. We hold fast to this true assertion, we preserve this truth and go home with it. We can meet and talk about the object, describing it in our imagination. If, however, someone has in the meantime painted the chalk white, or if for some other reason the chalk has changed colour, then our true assertion, without any doing on our own part, has become untrue. Indeed, it becomes untrue precisely because we hold fast to our true assertion, merely through the beings themselves and their way of being as sometimes this, sometimes that. By the same token, the incorrect assertion 'the chalk is red' can become uncovering. Our assertion has become false, i.e. it no longer unveils but rather distorts. In our assertion, 'white' conceals what the chalk is revealed (deconcealed) to be, namely red. Not only do we cover this up, but because we claim to say something true about the chalk we present it as what it is not. We conceal and distort it in what it is and so we deceive ourselves and others. The λόγος becomes ψευδής – not only does it become incorrect, but it leads astray. We are led into error. So at any time the deconcealment of the accidental, by virtue of its own intrinsic nature, can change quite independently of us. The truth of accidental beings is non-constant, so that one and the same assertion, which itself grasps truth, can sometimes reveal and sometimes conceal. περὶ μὲν οὖν τὰ ἐνδεχόμενα ἡ αὐτὴ γίγνεται ψευδὴς καὶ ἀληθὴς δόξα καὶ ὁ λόγος ὁ αὐτός, καὶ ἐνδέχεται ὁτὲ μὲν ἀληθεύειν ὁτὲ δὲ ψεύδεσθαι.[40] The same being in its so-being, and quite apart from any change in human conception, can, according to its nature, be deconcealed at one time and distorted at another time. This change can be regarded as an occurrence, i.e. it just happens. Aristotle does not explain the ground of the possibility for this change. Since the essence of the truth of the accidental involves the constant possibility of untruth it is not itself proper truth.

What about the truth of the συγκείμενον, of what-being? The deconcealment of the what-being of beings is constant, whether we make use of it or not. Seen from the side of beings, as unveiled in their what-being, beings are not at one time uncovered and at another time covered up. Thus they are not exposed to the possibility of untruth. Yet the συγκείμενα are not absolutely and in every respect immune to the possibility of distortion. To be sure, the what-being of the chalk is never such that it could change through the determination 'deceitful' becoming applicable to it. Nevertheless, the chalk, determined in its what-being as this and this, is always found together with particular determinations such as materiality and extension, such that many other determinations are essentially excluded from it. Anything with the way of being of the συγκείμενον has an essential relation to what *cannot* belong to it. The possibility thus arises of attributing to it something which does *not* belong, i.e. the possibility of distortion. Thus περὶ δὲ τὰ ἀδύνατα ἄλλως ἔχειν οὐ γίγνεται ὁτὲ μὲν ἀληθὲς ὁτὲ ψεῦδος, ἀλλ᾽ ἀεὶ ταὐτὰ ἀληθῆ καὶ ψευδῆ.[41] So in respect of that with which it belongs together it is constantly deconcealed, and in respect of that with which it does not belong it is constantly distorted. Since it is not possible for this deconcealment to change over to distortion, a superior kind of truth belongs to the what-being of beings. This is because beings are constantly present as what they are revealed to be. Nevertheless, the deconcealment of what-being still involves a possible distortion, but this latter lies outside of truth, precisely because the distortion too is constant.

β) Truth, simplicity (unity) and constant presence.
The simple (ἀδιαίρετα, ἀσύνθετα, ἁπλᾶ) as the proper being and its
deconcealment as the highest mode of being-true

We can see, therefore, that the more proper the being of beings the purer
and more constant is their presence, i.e. the more does deconcealment
belong to beings as such and the more distortion is ruled out. Yet as long as
truth as such remains related to the possibility of untruth, it is not the
proper and highest truth. Only this latter can constitute the proper being
of beings. Is there then a kind of being-true which as such cannot be
related to untruth, which *absolutely* excludes the possibility of distortion?

In line with the foregoing development of the problem, this question
must be formulated as follows. Is there, in addition to the various modes
of being already discussed, a mode of being to which there belongs the
most proper being-true? The latter must be defined by the being of the
most proper beings. This is the next question to be addressed. Now it is of
crucial importance for the content and problem of Θ10 as a whole that,
precisely in respect of the question concerning the most proper being-
true, the methodology changes. Aristotle does not begin by inquiring into
the being of proper beings in order to then discuss their characteristic
being-true, but he immediately inquires into the being-true of proper
beings, in order to then determine their being – in other words and more
pointedly, in order to define this being-true itself as the most proper being
of the most proper beings, as that which is most proper about proper
beings.

At two points within his preparatory discussion Aristotle says:
ὥσπερ ... τὸ ἀληθὲς ... οὕτως ... τὸ εἶναι.[42] and τὸ δὲ εἶναι τὸ ὡς
ἀληθές.[43] What he had said earlier was ὥσπερ τὸ εἶναι, οὕτως τὸ ἀληθές;
now, by contrast, he does not proceed from the being of the συμβεβηκός
to the being of the συγκείμενον and then to the corresponding deconcealment, but he inquires first into deconcealment. And how does he
inquire? It is now clear that the question must be: what is the most proper
truth which absolutely excludes the possibility of distortion? When does
this occur?

The last kind of being considered was a συγκείμενον, e.g. the chalk and
its determination of materiality. Another example would be a diagonal
and its incommensurability with the side of a square. συγκείμενα are
ἀδύνατα διαιρεθῆναι, i.e. there is no possibility of separation in the
determination of the being in question. This is what Aristotle refers to as

ἀδιαίρετα.[44] Is there anything which resists separation of its moments to a still greater degree than such cases of constant and necessary co-belonging? Clearly there is, namely where there is no togetherness at all, no συν, i.e. in the case of the ἀσύνθετον. Briefly and positively, the ἀσύνθετα can be grasped as τὰ ἁπλᾶ, the simple. So the investigation proceeds as follows: συμβεβηκότα, συγκείμενα, ἀδύνατα διαιρεθῆναι, ἀδιαίρετα, ἀσύνθετα, ἁπλᾶ.

While not every ἀδιαίρετον is a ἁπλοῦν, the reverse applies: every ἁπλοῦν is a ἀδιαίρετον, indeed in the highest and proper sense, for in the case of the ἁπλοῦν not only is there no possibility of separation but nothing can be found which belongs together in the first place. When, therefore, the pure simple is deconcealed in what it is, nothing else is involved which could define it. It is never manifest as this or that but purely in itself as itself. The deconcealment of the simple can never be distorted by something not belonging to the simple. This deconcealment cannot change over to distortion, and not because what belongs together with it is constantly revealed but because the simple does not admit of togetherness at all. The deconcealment of the simple completely excludes the possibility of untruth. Such deconcealment not only never changes over into distortion but does not even have any relation to the latter. The only possible opposite to this kind of deconcealment is un-deconcealment [Unentborgenheit], which, however, can never, according to its own nature, be distortion or untruth. The deconcealment of the simple as such is therefore the highest possible mode of being-true, i.e. proper being-true. And what is this proper deconcealment? Deconcealment is the manifestness of something which can present itself as itself. The deconcealment of the simple is the presence of the simple in and of itself. This presence is absolutely unmediated, i.e. nothing can intervene. Further, this unmediated presence is prior to all other presence. It is the highest and most original kind of presence. However, this completely unmediated constant presence of itself, *this most constant and purest presence, is nothing else but the highest and most proper being*. If, accordingly, the ἁπλᾶ are the most proper beings, if this deconcealment is the highest and most proper, and if, furthermore, this proper being-true is nothing but absolutely constant presence, then the beings which are properly true are the most proper beings: the ἀληθὲς ὄν is the κυριώτατον ὄν. It remains to show more precisely: 1. that Aristotle takes the ἁπλᾶ as the most proper beings, 2. that the essence of the most proper truth is nothing but constant presence.

Let us recall the leading question of philosophy: τί τὸ ὄν, what is being? This question inquires into the inner possibility of beings as such, into their ἀρχή (principle) or αἰτίαι (ground). Now Aristotle says that μᾶλλον ἀρχὴ τὸ ἁπλούστερον,[45] that which is simpler, more primordial, is more of a principle. The closer we come to what is simple, the closer do we come to principles. The more primordially we know, i.e. the more primordial the deconcealment of the deconcealed, the more ἁπλούστεραι αἱ αἰτίαι καὶ ἀρχαί.[46] But the question concerning beings as such, precisely as knowledge of the ground of beings, is the most primordial knowledge, thus the simplest. And what is this which universally belongs to beings as such? It is being itself, αὐτό τὸ ὄν, the beings themselves considered purely in their being. Being does not just sometimes belong to beings and sometimes not, but belongs to them constantly and before everything else. Being as such, simplicity, unity, cannot be further analysed. Being is the simple itself, and as such it is the primary and ultimate ground of the possibility of every actual and conceivable being. That which is most simple is also that which is most proper in beings.

Now what does Aristotle say about proper beings, i.e. about the beings which have constant presence as their ground (principle, ἀρχή)? τὰς τῶν ἀεὶ ὄντων ἀρχὰς ἀναγκαῖον εἶναι ἀληθεστάτας.[47] The ἁπλᾶ are most concisely conceived in Θ10: ἔστιν ὅπερ εἶναί τι καὶ ἐνεργείᾳ.[48] These principles of proper beings, i.e. being itself as such, is what is most true and deconcealed before everything else. Our more radical conception of the problem means that, *if beings are to be discoverable and determinable at all, being must be constantly deconcealed.* Whether or not we actually conceive and interrogate being, it is always already unveiled. Being as such stands in deconcealment. What does it mean to say that the most simple is the most true and deconcealed? What, at bottom, does deconcealment mean? We thus come to the second thesis, i.e. the thesis that *the essence of proper truth is nothing but absolutely constant presence.*

γ) Deconcealment of the simple as pure and absolute self-presence

In the same chapter Aristotle says: τὰ τῇ φύσει φανερώτατα πάντων,[49] i.e. that which in its inner nature is most primordially manifest and thus most purely present, is the ἀρχαί. That the deconcealment of the simple is nothing other than an exemplary presence can be seen from what Aristotle identifies as the specific mode of accessibility belonging to the simple.

Let us first recall the deconcealment of beings in the proximal sense, i.e. the conceiving of an accidentally (contingently) existing thing as that which it reveals itself to be. In saying something about such a thing we make an assertion, e.g. we attribute whiteness to the chalk. We claim the white thing to be this or that. Our discourse, λόγος, is a καταφάναι; we attribute something to the chalk, καταφάναι τὸ ἀληθές. However, since the simple does not admit of analysis, it can only be addressed as itself and not as something else, i.e. it can only be *named*. Aristotle indicates as much in Θ10: there is no καταφάναι in respect of the simplex, but only φάναι. The simple is grasped in its deconcealment only through simple inspection, i.e. only if we do not allow anything else to intervene. Likewise when Aristotle characterizes the φάναι τὸ ἀληθές of the ἁπλοῦν: this is a θιγεῖν, a touching, a simple grasping, not a conceptualization, not a conceiving of the simple as something else. There can no longer be ζήτησις (inquiry) or διδάξις (explanation) in the usual sense, but in the case of the ἁπλᾶ a ἕτερος τρόπος (different approach) is necessary.[50] Such simple grasping is the only possible mode of access to that which presents itself purely as itself. *This deconcealment is just the pure presence of the simple in itself, absolute presence*, which according to its essence completely excludes everything not yet or no longer present.

If the simple in this way constitutes that which is most proper to beings, and if the deconcealment of the simple is nothing else but the purest presence, prior to everything else (as constant), then this highest truth of the simple is the most proper being of the most proper beings, i.e. the τὸ ὂν ἀληθές is the κυριώτατον ὄν.

What about the exclusion of the ὂν ἀληθές in Chapter E 4?[51] Only now can we see why the ἀληθὲς ὄν is ruled out. For the ἀληθὲς ὄν is there conceived as the ἀληθές of the διάνοια, as ἀληθεύειν. There is also a reference to the ἀλήθεια of the ἁπλᾶ, which, it is said, will be treated at a later point.[52] Yet also in the case of the ἁπλᾶ there is an ἀληθεύειν of νοῦς *qua* νόησις. Neither is this latter the proper theme. So either (perhaps owing to an editorial error) the exclusion is somehow wrong, or something else is intended with διάνοια. This ἀληθεύειν is not excluded because it pertains to a subjective condition but because it is a matter here of the kind of being-true and being-distorted which can change over to one another. This ἀληθεύειν is not at all bound to proper beings. On the other hand, every ἀλήθεια of the νόησις is simply what it is. The exclusion occurs because the mode of being of the ἀληθεύειν in question is not itself determined by beings. At bottom, the truth of διάνοια does not (even where, as ἀληθεύειν, it refers to beings) reveal anything completely autonomous in proper beings themselves: ἀληθεύειν οὐκ ἐν τοῖς πράγμασιν (ἐν διανοίᾳ). The ἀληθές, however, does indeed concern ἐπὶ τῶν πραγμάτων (περὶ τὰ ἁπλᾶ . . . οὐδ' ἐν διανοίᾳ).[53] But we already indicated that being-true is always co-intended with the copula. How is this connection between being and being-true possible? Only now do we discover the dimensions of the problem. The later deformation of the problem in terms of subject–object, act and being, etc. remains fundamentally inadequate.

e) The Question of the Being-True of Proper Beings as the Highest and Deepest Question of Aristotle's Interpretation of Being.
Θ10 as Keystone to Book Θ and to Aristotelian Metaphysics in General

Once this thematic content of Θ10 has been brought to light through an interpretation informed by the Greek understanding of being and truth, κυριώτατον as the character of ἀληθὲς ὄν will no longer be found disturbing. On the contrary, one would have to find it surprising if κυριώτατον did not appear where it does. At the same time it should be clear that the way Aristotle develops the problem of being-true has nothing to do with logic or epistemology. *The question concerning being-true unfolds as the fundamental problem of the proper being of beings themselves* and as such stands in the closest possible relation to what was treated in the foregoing chapters of Book Θ. Let me provide yet another indication of the unambiguously positive connection between Θ10 and Θ, in order to counter the possible view that, although Θ10 does indeed *relate* to Θ it does not actually *belong* to this book. The topic of Book Θ is δύναμις and ἐνέργεια, i.e. possibility and actuality as fundamental modes of being. It is shown that proper being is ἐνέργεια. Proper beings are those which exclude every possible change, every possibility of becoming-other. We are in the habit of saying that for something to be actual, it must first be possible. Thus possibility is primary and prior, before actuality. But Aristotle maintains the contrary position: πρότερον ἐνέργεια δυνάμεώς ἐστιν.[54] Actuality is prior and primary with respect to possibility. To be sure, this can only be maintained on the basis of the specifically Greek approach to the problem of being, including the fundamental conception of truth as deconcealment. This is not to be entered into now. We do say, however, that Θ10 discusses a fundamental aspect of the whole thematic question, i.e. the ever more comprehensive exclusion of the possibility of untruth from truth. *In Θ10 there is concentrated the most radical conception of the basic problem of* Θ. In a word: Θ10 is not a foreign appendix, but rather *the keystone of Book* Θ, which itself is the centre of the entire *Metaphysics*.

So from the textual question we have gained some insight into the fundamental Greek meaning of being-true as constant presence. As indicated at the outset, this conception of truth is not just Aristotelian, but simply Greek. We have become familiar with the leading question of πρώτη φιλοσοφία as the question of what beings are. This question inquires into the being of beings, into beings in respect of their constancy and presence, i.e. into the deconcealment of beings. Thus Aristotle can say: ὀρθῶς δ' ἔχει καὶ τὸ καλεῖσθαι τὴν φιλοσοφίαν ἐπιστήμην τῆς ἀληθείας.[55] It is quite proper to call philosophy knowledge of truth, i.e. philosophy is not the theory of truth considered as knowledge, but is knowledge of truth, i.e. knowledge of beings as such in their unhiddenness.

What has been clearly demonstrated is that the Greeks saw truth primarily as pertaining to beings themselves, i.e. that they took being-true as the proper being of proper beings. What this ultimately means the Greeks did not show, because they remained at the level of the leading question, i.e. they did not develop the question of being to the level of the fundamental question. Neither was this shown subsequently, for everything became covered up by pseudo-questions such that the problem was lost sight of altogether. The connections we have exhibited require a much deeper clarification – which must proceed from the problematic of being and time. It does not suffice to place intuitive truth [*Anschauungswahrheit*] prior to assertoric truth if the truth of intuition itself remains unclarified. Truth must be clarified in such a way that the necessary subordination of assertoric truth to primordial truth can also be comprehended.

We can now close this excursus and return to the main topic. To what extent we have obtained substantive insights from this reflection will emerge at the appropriate point later. At this stage what we need to keep firmly in mind is just the *natural and self-evident way in which the Greeks grasp being as constant presence,* and how, from the very beginning, *this understanding of being illuminates all steps of the inquiry.* The *source of this illumination,* however, the *light* of the same, is *time.*

§ 10. The Actuality of Spirit in Hegel as Absolute Presence

Another thing to remember is that this understanding of being as constant presence not only continued from antiquity right through to Kant, but that this interpretation of being comes to clear expression precisely where Western metaphysics attains its genuine fulfilment, i.e. where the basic approach of Greek philosophy, together with the essential motives of subsequent philosophical questioning, are brought to a full and unified presentation, with *Hegel*.

Hegel's *fundamental metaphysical thesis* can be seen in his statement: 'In my view, which can be justified only by the exposition of the system itself, everything turns on grasping and expressing the True, not only as Substance, but equally as Subject'.[56] What this means is that, although it is indeed the case that substantiality constitutes the being of beings, substantiality must itself, in order for the being of beings to be fully comprehended, be conceived as *subjectivity*. To be sure, subjectivity in the modern sense of the concept relates to that which has the character of the I [*das Ichliche*]. But for Hegel, subjectivity is not the I-ness [*Ichheit*] of the familiar empirical egos of individual finite persons, but rather the absolute subject, the pure self-grasping of the totality of beings which in and for itself grasps the whole multiplicity of beings as such, i.e. which can grasp all otherness of beings from itself as the mediation of its self-othering.[57] 'That the True is actual only as system, or that Substance is essentially Subject, is expressed in the representation of the Absolute as *Spirit* – the most sublime Notion'.[58] 'The spiritual alone is the actual.'[59] Hegel means the proper beings. Accordingly, the being of these beings – beings as spirit [*Geist*] – tells us how to understand being as such.

So how does Hegel conceive the being of beings *qua* spirit, or the *actuality* of this actual? 'The spirit . . . is eternal',[60] the way of being of the spirit is *eternity*. 'Eternity will not be, nor was it, but it *is*',[61] 'the eternal [is] . . . *absolute presence*' [*absolute Gegenwart*].[62] This is not the presence of the momentary now which immediately flows away, nor is it just lasting presence in the usual sense of what continues to endure, but it is a presence which stands by itself and through itself, in self-reflected duration, a presence of the highest constancy, which itself makes I-ness and self-abidingness possible.

From this brief discussion of Hegel we conclude two things: 1. Hegel, who raises the problematic of Western metaphysics into a new dimension by grasping substance more radically as subject, *also* understands being as 'constant presence'. 2. Precisely because this interpretation of the actuality of the actual is expressed as the overcoming of being *qua* substance, Hegel's metaphysics retains a conscious inner connection to the Greeks.

Summarizing our entire discussion of the fundamental meaning of οὐσία, being, we can see that even a fleeting look into the world of the great thinkers places us before *one* simple and forceful fact: the understanding of being, not just in the everyday existence of man and not just at the beginning of Greek metaphysics but in the whole history of Western philosophy, is oriented to being as presence and constancy. This understanding owes its clarity to the illumination provided by the spontaneous implicit understanding of presence and constancy. We have thus succeeded in answering the question as to how being is understood. The leading question of metaphysics – τί τὸ ὄν – inquires into the *being* of beings. It was a matter of really asking this question. We ourselves attempted to do this by posing two questions: 1. What does the question ask about? (being). 2. How is being understood? (constant presence).

The following series of questions arose: τὶ τὸ ὄν, what are beings? What are beings as such? What are beings in respect of their being? What is being? What is being understood *as*? We have, so to speak, *dug more and more into* the content of the leading question, and thereby *dug out* more primordial questions. This is what must occur if we are to really ask the leading question, if we are, furthermore, to experience the challenging character of philosophical questioning, if we are to understand what it means for philosophy to go-after-the-whole, and finally, if we are to grasp the problem of freedom precisely as the problem of metaphysics, and so be adequately prepared for its discussion.

Notes

1 What does it mean to possess something in its truth? How is this possible? Complete freedom from deception?
2 Cf. Meister Eckhart and Hegel.
3 Aristotle, *Physics* 190 a 6. ('We say not only "this becomes so-and-so", but also "from being this, comes to be so-and-so"', trans. Hardie and Gaye.)
4 *Physics* 191 a 4 f. ('It is clear that there must be a substratum for the contraries, and that the contraries must be two'; trans. Hardie and Gaye.)
5 *Physics* 191 a 5 f. ('Yet in another way of putting it this is not necessary'; trans. Hardie and Gaye.)

6 *Physics* 191 a 6 f. ('One of the contraries will serve to effect the change by its successive absence and presence'; trans. Hardie and Gaye.)

7 Plato, *Euthydemus* 300 e–301 a.

8 See Aristotle, *Metaphysics* Θ 8, 1050 a 21: τὸ γὰρ ἔργον τέλος, and Θ 1, 1045 b 34: ὄν . . . κατὰ τὸ ἔργον.

9 See below pp. 51 ff. on the ὄν ὡς ἀληθές and on *Meta*. Θ, 10 in particular.

10 CPR A 218, B 226.

11 On 'being is not a real predicate', see Heidegger's 1927 lectures, *The Basic Problems of Phenomenology* (trans. Albert Hofstadter, Bloomington: Indiana University Press, 1982), Part One, Chapter One.

12 *Metaphysics* Δ 7.

13 *Metaphysics* E 2, 1026 b 21: 'It seems that the accidental is something closely akin to the non-existent'; trans. Tredennick.

14 *Metaphysics* E 4, 1028 a 1.

15 *Metaphysics* Θ 8, 1050 b 2 : 'substance or form is actuality'; trans. Tredennick.

16 *Metaphysics* Θ 10, 1051 a 34–b 6.

17 The translation here is by Tredennick (modified, see next footnote).

18 The unmodified Tredennick translation puts 'in the strictest sense' in parentheses, with the note 'This appears to contradict VI. iv. 3. But it is just possible to interpret κυριώτατα (with Jaeger) as "in the commonest sense"'. The relevant lines of the Ross translation read: 'The terms "being" and "non-being" are employed firstly with reference to the categories, and secondly with reference to the potency or actuality of these . . . and thirdly in the sense of true and false' [Trans.].

19 A. Schwegler, *Aristoteles, Metaphysik*, 4 vols, 1846–47; unaltered reprint, Frankfurt am Main (Minerva) 1960. Vol. IV, p. 186.

20 W. Jaeger, *Studien zur Entwicklungsgeschichte der Metaphysik des Aristoteles*, Berlin 1912. See also W. Jaeger, *Aristoteles: Grundlegung einer Geschichte seiner Entwicklung*, Berlin 1923.

21 W. Jaeger, *Studien zur Entwicklungsgeschichte*, p. 53.

22 Jaeger, *Studien zur Entwicklungsgeschichte*, p. 52.

23 Aristotle, *Metaphysica* (Ross), Oxford 1924, Vol. II.

24 Jaeger, *Studien zur Entwicklungsgeschichte*, p. 52.

25 Aristotle, *Rhetoric* Γ 2, 1404 b 1 f.

26 *Rhetoric* Γ 2, 1404 b 6.

27 Aristotle, *Nichomachean Ethics* Z 2, 1139 a 17 f.

28 *Nichomachean Ethics* I 8, 1168 b 25–31.

29 *Nichomachean Ethics* A 1, 1094 a 25 ff.

30 *Metaphysics* Θ 10, 1051 b 2.

31 *Metaphysics* E 4, 1027 b 29 ff.

32 *Metaphysics* E 4, 1028 a 3.

33 Cf. Heidegger, *Being and Time*, translated by John Macquarrie and Edward Robinson, Basil Blackwell, Oxford, 1962, § 44.

34 *Metaphysics* Θ 10, 1051 b 6 ff: 'It is not because we think truly that you are pale, that you *are* pale, but because you are pale we who say this have the truth'; trans. Ross.

35 *Metaphysics* Θ 10, 1051 b 5 f.

36 *Metaphysics* α 1, 993 b 30 f.

37 *Metaphysics* E 2, 1026 b 21.

38 *Metaphysics* Θ 10, 1051 b 9 ff: 'If some things are always combined and cannot be separated, and others are always separated and cannot be combined, while others are capable either of combination or of separation, "being" is being combined and one, and "not-being" is being not combined but more than one'; trans. Ross.

39 Cf. Plato, *Euthydemus*. The beautiful things and the beautiful; παρουσία.

40 *Metaphysics* Θ 10, 1051 b 13 ff: 'As regards the class of things which admit of both contrary states, the same opinion or the same statement comes to be false and true, and it is possible at one time to be right and at another wrong'; trans. Tredennick.

41 *Metaphysics* Θ 10, 1051 b 15 f: 'As regards things which cannot be otherwise the same opinion is not sometimes true and sometimes false, but the same opinions are always true or always false'; trans. Tredennick.

42 *Metaphysics* Θ 10, 1051 b 22: 'Just as truth is not the same in these cases, so neither is being'; trans. Tredennick.

43 *Metaphysics* Θ 10, 1051 b 33: 'being in the sense of truth'; trans. Tredennick.

44 Aristotle, *On the Soul* Γ 6, 430 a 26 and b 6 ff.

45 *Metaphysics* K 1, 1059 b 35.

46 Cf. *Metaphysics* E 1, 1025 b ff.

47 *Metaphysics* α 1, 993 b 28 f: 'The first principles of things must necessarily be true above everything else'; trans. Tredennick.

48 *Metaphysics* Θ 10, 1051 b 30 f: 'With respect to all things which are essences and actualities . . .'; trans. Tredennick.

49 *Metaphysics* α 1, 993 b 11.

50 *Metaphysics* Z 17, 1041 b 9 f.

51 Cf. also *Metaphysics* K 8, 1065 b 21 ff.

52 *Metaphysics* E 4, 1027 b 27 ff.

53 Cf. *Metaphysics* E 4, 1027 b 25 ff.

54 *Metaphysics* Θ 8, 1049 b 5.

55 *Metaphysics* α 1, 993 b 19 f: 'Philosophy is rightly called a knowledge of truth'; trans. Tredennick.

56 G.W.F. Hegel, *Phenomenology of Spirit*, translated by A.V. Miller, Clarendon Press, Oxford, 1977, pp. 9–10.

57 Cf. *Phenomenology of Spirit*, p. 10.

58 *Phenomenology of Spirit*, p. 14.

59 *Phenomenology of Spirit*, p. 14.

60 Hegel, *Philosophy of Nature* (Part Two of Hegel's *Encyclopaedia of the Philosophical Sciences*), translated by A.V. Miller, Oxford, Clarendon Press, 1970, p. 35 (§ 258).

61 *Philosophy of Nature*, p. 36.

62 *Philosophy of Nature*, p. 36.

3
Working the Leading Question of Metaphysics Through to the Fundamental Question of Philosophy

We have not only identified the leading question of Western philosophy but we have teased out the more primordial questions contained therein. Has our questioning really come alive in this way? We have indeed answered these more primordial questions. The essence of an answer is to resolve the question to which it responds. Perhaps we have asked the leading question more primordially but in so doing precisely done away with it. Not only, just as was previously the case, have we not experienced the challenging character of the question, but even this possibility is now foreclosed if, namely, the challenge is supposed to reside in something other than mere questioning as questioning. At the outset, when we had only the rough leading question 'what are beings?' before us, at least we had some inkling of how such questioning could go to our roots. For we ourselves are beings and as such we are co-involved in this questioning. But now, after we have shown that the questioning of beings means understanding presence and constancy, we can no longer see what this understanding of being, this demonstration that being means constant presence, has to do with a challenge. To be sure, the leading question awakened a more primordial questioning. We thereby arrived at an answer, and indeed, as became plain, not just at an arbitrary private opinion but at an answer continually given by Western metaphysics, an answer which appears so self-evident that it does not even announce itself as an answer to a question. Being is understood in terms of 'constant presence'.

But how do we know that with this thoughtworthy question contained in the leading question, with this question about the understanding of being, we have exhausted our questioning? Should we be content with this unspoken answer? Is this answer – presence and constancy – the only answer which could bring us to ask more radically? Is it really so self-evident that being is understood as constant presence, and must we accept this self-evidence simply because the whole of Western metaphysics has uncritically held fast to it? Or may and must we ask what is happening when being is so unproblematically understood as constant presence?

§ 11. The Fundamental Question of Philosophy as the Question Concerning the Primordial Connection between Being and Time

If being stands in the illumination of constancy and presence, what light is the source of this illumination? Presence is a character of *time*. And 'constant'? Constancy means endurance, always enduring in every now. The now is likewise a determination of time. Constant presence therefore means the whole present, the now, that which is now, constantly in every now. Constant presence refers to concurrence in every now. Within the illumination which allows being to be understood as constant presence, the light which expends this illumination itself becomes visible. This light is *time* itself. Being, whether in ordinary understanding or in the explicit ontological problematics of philosophy, is *understood in the light of time*.

How does time come to perform this illumination? Why precisely time? Moreover, why time precisely in just one of its moments, the present, the now? *What is time itself, such that it can expend this light and illuminate being? How do being and time come into this primordial relation?* What is this relation? What does time mean? What does being mean? What, above all, does being *and* time mean? These questions, which once set loose storm over us, take us a long way from the self-evident. In saying *that* being is understood as constant presence we have not answered the leading question but have brought it before the abyss of its own questionability. And with the catchcry 'being and time' we have ventured the leap into this abyss, such that we now stand in utter darkness, lacking all support and bearings.

Being and Time – there is a book of this title. But this book-title as such is just as irrelevant as many others. What is crucial is likewise not the book itself but that the reader becomes aware of the fundamental occurrence of Western metaphysics, the metaphysics of our whole existence, an occurrence over which individual books have no power but before which everything else must submit. Being and time is not at all a novelty nor is it a so-called philosophical standpoint. Even less is it a particular philosophy whose revolutionary mood might appeal to contemporary youth. It is not a novelty, for already the ancients inquired into the essence of time, likewise Kant and Hegel and every philosopher. Indeed, just those great thinkers, Plato and Aristotle, who brought the leading question of philosophy to its first authentic awakening by reference to οὐσία, were also – especially Aristotle – the first to inquire into the essence of time. And yet to inquire into time, and also into being, does not mean understanding the problem of 'being and time'. Both being and time remained hidden in their innermost relation and so remained also in subsequent philosophy. The 'and' is the actual crux of the problem. The leading question – what are beings? – must itself be transformed into the fundamental question, i.e. into the question which inquires into the 'and' of being and time and thus into the ground *of both*. This fundamental question is: *what is the essence of time, such that it grounds being, and such that the question of being as the leading question of metaphysics can and must be unfolded within this horizon*?

Pressing forward from the leading question to the fundamental question, we discovered the *questionability* of the leading question. This was expressed through two questions. First, what is the *theme* of the question concerning beings? Answer: being. Secondly, *as what* is being understood? Answer: as constant presence. The answers to these questions propelled us forward into the problematic of being and time. Now we see that this problematic also rebounds upon the indicated questions and their answers. For it is only from the problematic of being and time that we can ask why being is understood, proximally and for the most part, from the specific temporal moment of the present (presence). And in respect of the first question we must still ask about the conditions of the possibility of the distinction between being and beings, which distinction itself allows the theme of the leading question to be more sharply determined. How does the problematic of being and time help to illuminate the essence of the distinction between being and beings, this distinction which, in our comportment to beings, allows us to always already understand being, i.e. to exist within the understanding of being?

So the fundamental question broadens out the whole questionability of the leading question. A whole world of interconnected and equally essential questions opens up, from whose perspective the leading question itself appears crude and inadequate, though not as superfluous. On the contrary, it is only now, from our insight into the understanding of being and into the connection between being and time, that the original leading question, which seemed to have come from nowhere in particular, receives its inner necessity. Only now does the question concerning beings obtain its full scope in the fundamental question of being and time, and thus also do all the questions contained therein receive their full questionability. Does the purported challenging character of the authentically posed leading question now become visible? For the latter is the *third* of the three questions from which we proceeded, in order to show that the problem of freedom is a genuinely philosophical question, i.e. a question which goes-after-the-whole while at the same time going-to-the-root. We asked three things.[1] First: in what way does positive freedom signify a fundamental broadening of our problem? Our answer referred to autonomy, absolute spontaneity. Secondly: what perspective does this broadening open up? Answer: absolute spontaneity, causality, beings, the leading question. Thirdly: does this perspective allow us to experience the philosophical going-after-the-whole as a going-to-our-roots? We now grasp the perspective of the leading question by working through the fundamental question (being and time). The schema for this perspective has come into view: being *and* time – time – constant presence – being – beings as such – positive freedom.

But we still cannot discover the challenging character of the questioning of the fundamental question. Perhaps we shall not experience this at all as long as we are merely looking, having forgotten that we can only experience it through genuine questioning. But secondly, in genuine questioning we can only experience the *possibility* of this challenge, a possibility, however, of a quite distinctive sort. Why, now that the whole questionworthiness of the leading question has been released into the fundamental question, do we not even see the possibility of such an experience? Because all we have shown is *that* the leading question leads to the fundamental question. We have simply let the matter stand there, as previously with the case of the leading question. To identify and know the fundamental question is not the same as asking it. On the contrary, the more we come to know, and the more primordial questions we come to know, the stronger becomes the *illusion* that this knowing is already questioning. The more primordial the question known, the more obligatory does questioning become.

So everything begins over again with the fundamental question. If we really want to question, we must be clear over what we wish to place in question and in what way. The abbreviated formula is: being and time. The question concerns the 'and', i.e. the and-relation between the two elements. If this is not an external relation which merely juxtaposes two things, if it is rather a primordial relation, then it must originate equiprimordially from the essence of being and the essence of time. Being and time are interwoven with one another. *The 'and' signifies a primordial co-belongingness of being and time from the ground of their essence.*

We inquire neither into being by itself nor into time by itself. Neither do we merely inquire into them simultaneously; rather into their *inner co-belonging* and what originates therefrom. We can only experience their co-belonging by examining their respective essences. Therefore we must ask first about the essence of being and then about the essence of time. But as we unfolded the leading question it emerged that the question of being itself leads to the question of time, for no one will dispute that constancy and presence are in some sense temporal. We have therefore already encountered the co-belonging of being and time. We can now see more clearly that in inquiring into the essence of being we are compelled to inquire into the essence of time.

What are we inquiring into when we inquire into *time*? Time – we generally refer to this together with something else, i.e. together with space, as its sister so to speak. But time and space are not the same. So if we inquire into being and time, and if being is the broadest determination which encompasses everything that is, then this broadest determination is related to something which just exists alongside it, i.e. space. Why do we not with equal legitimacy speak of being and space, especially when we recall the everyday concept of being and the way it goes over into philosophy? Presence, the present: the being of the present is here determined not only by the now, but also by the 'here' as producedness [*Her-gestelltheit*], as there-standingness [*Da-stehendheit*]. The latter contain spatial determinations, which even seem to be the ones which are emphasized, e.g. by Dionysodorus in the *Euthydemus* dialogue. So focusing the problem of being upon the relation between being and time amounts to narrowing the primordial scope of the problem. Time does not have the same universality as being. Upon closer inspection, this is just an assertion, albeit an initially obvious one. It stems from the usual conception of time, which comes to expression in the usual juxtaposition of space and time.

§ 12. Man as the Site of the Fundamental Question.
Understanding of Being as the Ground of the Possibility of the Essence of Man

Like space, number, and movement, time counts as something which just occurs, and which as such is susceptible of philosophical examination and reflection. But hitherto, because the question of being has not been posed in a radical way, the primordial problem of time has never been treated. As can easily be shown, it is the ordinary conception of time which has determined the direction of its questioning, including the answers given as to its essence. So although the investigations of time by Aristotle, Augustine, Kant, and Hegel are of undoubted importance, they are subject to the fundamental deficiency that they proceed without an explicit orientation to the problem of being.

It remains true, however, that the traditional treatments of time provide us with important clues. If we disregard details and ask what is constantly said of time, it is this: time is not to be found somewhere or other like a thing among things, but in ourselves. Thus *Aristotle* says: ἀδύνατον εἶναι χρόνον ψυχῆς μὴ οὔσης.[2] 'Time could not be if the soul were not'. Likewise, *Augustine* says in his *Confessions*: *In te, anime meus, tempora metior . . . Affectionem, quam res praetereuntes in te faciunt et, cum illas praeterierint, manet, ipsam metior praesentem, non ea quae praeterierunt, ut fieret; ipsam metior, cum tempora metior.*[3] 'In you, my spirit, do I measure the times . . . When I measure time it is the present impression that I measure, and not the thing itself which makes the impression as it passes and moves into the past'. *Kant* conceives time as the form of our inner perception, i.e. as a mode of comportment of the human subject.

Soul, spirit, the *human* subject, are the loci of time. If we inquire into the essence of time we must inquire into the essence *of the human being. The fundamental question concerning being and time forces us into the question concerning the human being.* More generally, the question of beings, when we really unfold it into the fundamental question, leads to the question of man.

But we reached this point before, prior to our actual unfolding of the leading question. For it is clear that the question of man is included in the general question of what beings are as such. We already saw that this question *does not exhibit any challenging character*, for we are inquiring just as much into plants and animals and every kind of being, i.e. we are *dis*-regarding man as such in questioning beings in the whole. So ascertaining that the leading question *also* concerns man does not mean all that much, even if we now establish this from the connection between being and time. Still, are we at the same point as earlier in our considerations? Or is *the question of man as necessitated by our development of the leading question into the fundamental question of being and time a different question* of man to that contained in the leading question? This is indeed the case, i.e. not only is it different, but fundamentally so. When the problematic of being and time forces us to the question of man, we inquire into man not just as a being within the multiplicity of beings, but into man *insofar as time – the ground of the most radicalized ontological problem – belongs to man.*

The questioning of man and 'the question concerning man' are by no means the same. If we take man as one being among others, we inquire into man *within the framework of the leading question.* If we inquire into man in terms of our question of being and time, and of the essence of time, *we do not ask within the horizon of the leading question but from the ground of the fundamental question.* Nowadays, all kinds of anthropological studies are undertaken, e.g. in psychology, pedagogy, medicine, theology. Already this is no longer a fashion, but a plague. Even where man is treated in philosophical anthropology, it remains unclear in what way man is interrogated and in what way this interrogation is philosophical. Indeed, we must say that all philosophical anthropology stands outside the question of man, which can only emerge from the ground of the fundamental question of metaphysics. *This questioning of man from the ground of the fundamental question is what alone makes possible all philosophical questioning of man.* On the other hand, inquiring into man within the framework of the leading question is just an incidental inquiring into man. The questioning of man from the ground of the fundamental question is not only a different kind of questioning in regard to the order of problems, but also in regard to its content and basic problematic.

One difference is of particular importance to us here. The question of man, as posed within the framework of the leading question, is an also-questioning of man – its asks about, *among other things*, man. Man too must be questioned along with all other beings. On the other hand, the questioning of man which proceeds from the ground of the fundamental question does not serve just to complete the answer to the leading question, but is unavoidable in developing the ground of the leading question for the fundamental question. *The properly posed question of being, thus the question concerning being and time, concerning the essence of time, necessarily leads to the question of man.* Does this, perhaps, signify a challenge to man, a challenge that cannot be sidestepped but must be endured if we wish to genuinely ask the leading question rather than just to occupy ourselves with questioning? If we genuinely ask the leading question, are we, *remaining within* this question, i.e. asking it as the *fundamental question, compelled to inquire into the essence of time and thus into the essence of man*? Time and man? Certainly! Yet time and man: these are not the same; man is not just 'time', but has many other 'properties'. So while this questioning of man is indeed unavoidable, it is very one-sided: man is interrogated only in his relation to time. Above all, however, it is not the problem of time itself, but only the problem of the 'experience of time' that has to do with man. The question concerning the experience of time is a psychological-anthropological question, but this is not the question of the essence of time as such.

But all this forgets that we are not inquiring into time in any old way, nor are we inquiring into the experience of time, but we are inquiring into time *because*, and *in so far as*, being is understood from time, in the light of time. The *particular way* we are inquiring into time is already prescribed *by the question of being*, i.e. by what we already know about this question, quite apart from its connection with time.

What then do we already know about being? Just those things already indicated in our introductory discussion of the understanding of being, i.e. 1. its scope; 2. its penetration; 3. its unspokenness; 4. its forgottenness; 5. its undifferentiatedness; 6. its preconceptuality; 7. its freedom from deception; 8. its originary dividedness. To be sure, this is a great deal, and in the end it is also essential. But if we look more closely we can see that these things pertain to the *understanding* of being rather than to being as such. At best, only the fifth and eighth apply to being itself, i.e. being is undifferentiated and yet divided. We can now see that we *mixed together characteristics of being and characteristics of the understanding of being.* Did this occur because it was just a preliminary orientation, or does it have another reason? Is the *understanding* of *being* connected particularly *closely* with what it understands, i.e. precisely *being*? Is this connection quite different to what holds when we understand and know various beings? Clearly, if being and beings are not the same, there must be a difference. But is the relation between being and the understanding of being so straightforward that what holds for being also holds for the understanding of being, i.e. such that being is identical with its own deconcealment? So that the question of being as such can only be posed by inquiring into the understanding of being (deconcealing)? So that we must grasp the fundamental question as meaning: *the understanding of being and time*? These questions can only be answered through further substantive discussion of the problem of being.

Even if we leave open the inner connection between being and the understanding of being, one thing is certain, namely that we have access to the problem of being only through the understanding of being.[4] However, the understanding of being is, in general and provisional terms, a *comportment* of man. *In inquiring into being* we are not asking in an *arbitrary way after arbitrary properties of man* but we are inquiring into something *specific* in man, his *understanding of being*. The latter is not an arbitrary characteristic of man which he possesses along with many other properties, but it pervades all his comportments to beings, including his comportment to himself. Not only does the understanding of being pervade all comportments to beings, in the sense that it is present every-where, but it is the *condition of the possibility of any comportment to any beings whatsoever*. If man did not possess an understanding of being, *he could not comport toward himself as a being*: he could not say 'I' and 'you', he could not be 'he' himself, could not be a person. *Man would be impossible in his essence. Accordingly, the understanding of being is the ground of the possibility of the essence of man.*

When we inquire into being and the understanding of being, then not only are we compelled *in general* to inquire into man, but this becomes *unavoidable*. The question concerning the ground of the essence of man has thereby already become inevitable. In the root and rooting of our being human as such the leading question presses forward from its ownmost fundamental content.

If then the question of time is inseparable from the question concerning being and the understanding of being, if the *question of time* is even the *ground of the problem of the question of being*, we cannot inquire into time, and its belongingness to man, in just any arbitrary way. Rather, and from the very beginning, we must *inquire into time* in such a way that we can see it as the *ground of the possibility of the understanding of being*, i.e. *as the ground of the possibility of the ground of the essence of man*. But then time is not something that occurs only in man, which is the way Kant ultimately understands the matter. The question of the essence of being (the understanding of being), and the question of the essence of time, are both questions concerning man, or more precisely, they are questions con-cerning the ground of his essence. This is especially so when we inquire into the co-belongingness of being and time, i.e. into the 'and'. Not only does this kind of questioning, as required by the inner content of the leading question of philosophy, inquire into man in a way quite foreign to man's everyday self-reflection, but also it is a *questioning of man which goes beyond* anything that man's everyday self-questioning can bring into view. In short, our questioning of man is a questioning out beyond man as he ordinarily appears to be.

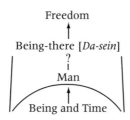

We are inquiring into the possibility of the understanding of being, i.e. into the possibility of the understanding of being in its entire scope, of the understanding which allows man to comport himself toward beings in the whole. With the fundamental question, we inquire into the totality of beings, and this questioning *is itself simultaneously directed to the ground of the possibility of being human*. It takes man into question in the ground of his essence, i.e. it harbours within itself the possibility of a challenge to man, a challenge which does not come from outside but rises up from the ground of his essence.

We can now see more clearly: 1. that the questioning of the leading question itself leads to the questioning of man; 2. that this is a questioning of man in the ground of his essence, i.e. in his roots; 3. that this questioning of the leading question is a questioning of beings in the whole and not specifically a questioning of man, which genuinely arises only through *radicalization of the leading question*. The leading question does not initially and directly pertain to man, but if its questioning is radical it rebounds on man and overpowers him in his ground. The questioning of beings in the whole, as a going-after-the-whole, is also a going-to-the-roots.

But this questioning of man is directed to man's essential ground. It thus inquires into man in general, disregarding particular human beings. Although we can see how the question of being and time connects with the question of man, we cannot see how we ourselves are specifically placed in question. We can only say that, insofar as it is we who pose these questions, we must be implicated in some way. In the end, however, this is so in respect of every human questioning, including the questioning which proceeds within the framework of the leading question, and for the purely formal reason that every universal implicates its particulars. Thus, however much we radicalize the leading question to the fundamental question, if the latter is the general problem of being and time we can treat it quite objectively and irrespective of whether it concerns man, such that the individual will *not* come into question. The problem of being and time is so general that it does not as such pertain to the individual. Nor does the fundamental question involve any serious challenge. It is only a challenge in general, i.e. it concerns nobody in particular.

Our discussions concerning the challenging character of the question of being have not been concerned with the possible practical-moral application of philosophical propositions by individual human beings, but only with whether and how the question itself, i.e. in the questioning demanded therein, involves a challenge. But the leading question cannot be substantively unfolded in any more primordial way than into the problem of being and time. In any case I see no further possibility. If anywhere at all, it is here that the challenge must announce itself.

§ 13. The Challenging Character of the Question of Being (Fundamental Question) and the Problem of Freedom. The Comprehensive Scope of Being (Going-after-the-Whole) and the Challenging Individualization (Going-to-the-Roots) of Time as the Horizon of the Understanding of Being

Being and time: with the problem of being in mind, we are inquiring into time, i.e. about whether and how it enables the fundamental condition of the possibility of human existence – the understanding of being. Being is the broadest horizon of all actual and thinkable beings. The condition of this breadth is supposed to be time. So time is supposedly the broadest breadth, in which the understanding of being encompasses all beings. But what and where is time? Where does time belong? *To whom* does it belong?

Everybody has his time. We have our time with one another. Do we all possess it in some loose way – our time, my time – such that we can cast it off at will? Or do we each of us possess our own proper portion of time? Do we each of us partake of time, or is it much more that we ourselves are possessed by time? And this not just in the indefinite sense that we cannot take leave of time, that we cannot escape its fetters, but such that time as in each case *our* time individualizes each one of us to his own self? Time is always time, where 'it is time', where there is 'still time' or 'no more time'. So long as we do not see that time fulfils its essence as temporal only by in each case *individualizing the human being to himself, temporality as the essence of time* will remain hidden.

But if temporality is at bottom individualization, then the *question of being and time* as such, in accordance with its own content, *necessarily leads to the individualization residing in time itself.* So while time as the horizon of being possesses the broadest breadth, it concentrates this breadth in the question concerning man's individualization. Not man as one of many present cases, but man in his individualization, i.e. in each case the individual as individual. Does not this most primordial content of the fundamental question, as unfolded from the leading question of philosophy, involve the possibility of a challenge, a challenge constant and unfailing in its target? This challenge is all the more threatening for appearing, as it did at first and for a long time subsequently, to have only general significance, i.e. as pertaining to everyone yet to nobody in particular. We can now see that *in the essence of time itself there lies individualization,* but not as the particularization of a universal, for time is never primordially universal. Time is always in each case my time, my and your and our time, not in the external sense of private bourgeois existence, but from the ground of the essence of existence, which is in each case individualized to itself. This individualization is the condition of the possibility for the division in the distinction between person and community.

Precisely when we obtain the greatest *breadth* for the problem of being and time as unfolded from the leading question to the fundamental question of philosophy, precisely when we really obtain this and do not merely talk about it, does the problem, in its basic content, come to focus on each individual as such. *The comprehensive scope of being is one and the same with the challenging individualization of time.* In the ground of their essential unity, being and time are such that, when they are placed in question, this questioning is itself *comprehensive and challenging.* Going-after-the-whole is a going-to-the-roots of every individual. Again, not subsequently and by way of a useful application; rather, the *content of the question* of philosophy – τί τὸ ὄν – demands a questioning whose ever more radical broadening implies an ever more certain focus on the *individual as individual, placing that individual in question.* The third of our three preliminary questions has thus been answered.[5] We asked: 1. Does the concept of positive freedom involve a fundamental broadening of the problematic? 2. What perspective does it open up? 3. Does this questioning have the character of a challenge? The inner connection of these three questions now reveals that *the question concerning the essence of human freedom is built into the leading question of philosophy. The latter has unfolded itself into the fundamental question (being and time). In its very content, this fundamental question shows that philosophizing involves the possibility of a challenge.*

The necessary preparations for treating our main theme have thus been finally completed. We now know the context of our theme, i.e. that it is built into the leading and fundamental questions of metaphysics. We can see that the question concerning the essence of human freedom, when properly posed, is a going-after-the-whole, which simultaneously, and according to its inner content, is also a going-to-our-roots. The theme and its manner of treatment in this lecture course are such that an introduction to philosophy can now be attempted. Yet the theme is particular, i.e. precisely freedom, not e.g. truth or art.

freedom
being-there
/ man \
↑
being and time
time
constant presence
being
τί τὸ ὄν
beings as such
beings
movement
causality
absolute spontaneity
autonomy
positive freedom
negative freedom
human freedom

§ 14. Switching the Perspective of the Question: the Leading Question of Metaphysics as Grounded in the Question of the Essence of Freedom

Our theme is human freedom in its essence. It is a matter, then, of really inquiring into this. Where and how do we find the object? To be sure, after our previous considerations we are no longer unfamiliar with it: negative freedom as freedom from . . ., positive freedom as freedom for . . . If we bear the above schema in mind, we can already see the whole domain of the problem of freedom in all its dimensions. But our unfolding of the horizon for the problem of freedom relied on Kant's interpretation of the problem. How do we know that this particular interpretation, however significant it may be, is philosophically central? How do we know that freedom must be conceived primarily in the context of causality? We have seen that this is *one* way of inquiring into freedom. But we are not entitled to assume that this is the *only and necessary way* of unfolding the problem.

If this is the situation, our whole orientation becomes dubious. At any rate we must put a qualification on our previous considerations. If, as with Kant, the problem of freedom is brought into connection with causality, then and only then does this lead into the further perspective which we ourselves have opened up. If freedom were to be defined differently from the outset, the perspective would also be different. Indeed, not only must we admit the possibility of various perspectives on freedom, we must above all be clear about where we situate freedom prior to the application of any further perspectives. This too has until now been left unspecified, for the fact that we take up different definitions does not explicitly indicate either the region where freedom belongs or how it is situated in this region. If our investigation of the essence of human freedom is to keep a steady course, we must assure ourselves of the field into which we must always be looking when inquiring into freedom, and when working toward the illumination of its essence.

This field seems so clearly defined that we can dispense with any lengthy discussion. The theme is human freedom, thus freedom in respect of man. Yet the nature of man is so enigmatic that this only indicates how totally indefinite and directionless our inquiry is. If it were only a matter of determining and discovering some insignificant property of man, we could hope to achieve this by running through all man's possibilities. In *the knowing of essence*, however, it is *crucial* that we have insight into essence *prior* to every concrete clarification and determination, and that this insight remains operative for *all subsequent investigation*. From the outset, therefore, our introduction must guide essential insight to the place 'where' we are to seek out freedom and which defines our standpoint. This *crucial leading of essential insight* must, initially, involve a violent redirection of our gaze. The correctness and necessity of this redirection can be established only from the content of essence. At the outset, the direction of our essential inquiry into the essence of human freedom can only be communicated in the form of a thesis. What is this?

In fixing the direction of our inquiry into essence, we must possess the diversity and breadth of a horizon. In respect of freedom, we have obtained something of the sort through our previous discussions. It now turns out that the course of these earlier discussions was by no means arbitrary. Let us recall our provisional schema of perspectives for the problem of freedom. With this in mind, we can establish, concerning the fundamental direction of our essential questioning, that *the essence of freedom only comes into view if we seek it as the ground of the possibility of Dasein*, as something *prior even to being and time*. With respect to the schema, we must effect a *complete repositioning of freedom*, so that what now emerges is that *the problem of freedom is not built into the leading and fundamental problems of philosophy, but, on the contrary, the leading question of metaphysics is grounded in the question concerning the essence of freedom*.

But if our essential questioning must take *this* direction, if the fundamental problem of philosophy must be viewed from this perspective, then it is irrelevant whether Kant was correct to interpret freedom within the framework of causality. Even if he was not correct in this, still, according to the new thesis, causality, movement, and being as such, are grounded in freedom. *Freedom is not some particular thing* among and alongside other things, but is *superordinate and governing in relation to the whole*. But if we are seeking out freedom as the ground of the possibility of existence, then *freedom must itself, in its essence, be more primordial than man*. Man is only an *administrator* of freedom, i.e. he can only let-be the freedom which is accorded to him, in such a way that, through man, the whole contingency of freedom becomes visible.

Human freedom now no longer means freedom as a property of man, but *man as a possibility of freedom*. Human freedom is the freedom that breaks through in man and takes him up unto itself, thus making man possible. If freedom is the ground of the possibility of existence, the root of being and time, and thus the ground of the possibility of understanding being in its whole breadth and fullness, then man, as *grounded* in his existence upon and *in* this freedom, is the site where beings in the whole become revealed, i.e. he is that particular being *through which* beings as such *announce themselves*. At the beginning of these lectures, we viewed man as one being among others, as a small, fragile, powerless and transitory being, occupying a tiny corner within the totality of beings. Seen now from the ground of his essence in freedom, something awesome [*ungeheuerlich*] and remarkable becomes clear, namely that man exists as the being in whom the being of beings, thus beings in the whole, are revealed. Man is that being in whose ownmost being and essential ground there *occurs the understanding of being*. Man is awesome in a way that a god can never be, for a god must be utterly other. This awesome being, that we really know and are, can only be as the most finite of all beings, as the convergence of opposing elements within the sphere of beings, and thus as the *occasion and possibility of the separation* of beings in their *diversity*. At the same time, it is here that the *central problem* of the *possibility of truth as deconcealment* resides.

If we view man in this way – and this is the view forced upon us by the fundamental content of the leading question of philosophy – if, in short, we view man metaphysically, then, provided that we understand ourselves, we no longer move along the path of egoistic reflection upon our I. We now stand in our own essence, where all psychology breaks down. It would be unfruitful to engage in further discussions or to put forward further hypotheses concerning this metaphysical experience of man. What this is, and how it sets itself to work as philosophy, is experienceable and knowable only in concrete questioning. Just one thing is clear. Man, as grounded in the freedom of his existence, has the possibility of penetrating into this his own ground, such that he *loses* himself in the truly inner metaphysical greatness of his essence and thus precisely *wins* himself in his existential uniqueness. For a long time, the greatness of finitude has been downgraded through a false and deceptive infinity, such that we are no longer able to reconcile finitude and greatness. Man is not the image of a god conceived in the sense of the absolutely bourgeois, but this latter god is the ungenuine creation of man.

Still, for the concrete unfolding and development of the problem of freedom, the question now arises as to how we can arrive at where our essential questioning leads us. What does it mean to say that freedom is the ground of the possibility of man's existence? Freedom is only revealed as this ground when our way of questioning, and the conciseness of our conceptual clarification, succeed in letting it be the ground. We therefore ask: what does the existence of man mean? What does the ground of existence mean? How do we encounter freedom here? This is one way to familiarize ourselves philosophically with the metaphysical problem of freedom.

However, I have chosen another way, which leads to the same goal, a way which forces us into constant dialogue with the philosophers, in particular with Kant. We remember that Kant was the first to see the problem of freedom in its most radical philosophical consequences. If we do not unfold the problem of freedom in a monologically free reflection, but rather in controversy and dialogue, this is not in order to provide historical knowledge of earlier opinions, but in order to understand that problems such as ours have their genuine vitality only in such historical controversy, in a history whose occurrences lie outside the course of given events.

In entering into controversy with Kant, we again bring the problem of freedom into the perspective of the problem of causality. The necessity of controversy is all the more pressing if we ourselves grasp freedom as the ground of the possibility of existence. The connection between cause and ground is uncertain.

We place the following considerations under the quite general heading of *causality and freedom*. I forgo developing the complicated programme of questions which lie hidden under this heading. My concern is that you travel a certain distance along the genuine road of 'research', albeit with the risk that, from time to time, you will lose your view of the whole. However, I shall briefly indicate, admittedly in what seem to be arbitrary formulas, the problematic which I see hidden in the general heading.

First of all, the relation between causality and freedom raises the question of whether freedom is a problem of causality, or causality a problem of freedom. If the latter, if freedom becomes the ground of the problem, how must freedom be conceived? Can it be conceived such that we can see from its essence how freedom can be both negative and positive? Can it be shown how freedom, in its essence, is on the one hand freedom from . . ., on the other hand freedom for . . .? Where is the primordial unity of this dual structure to be found? Is this a more primordial or only a superficial view? All these questions reflect upon the fundamental problem of philosophy, upon being and the understanding of being.

Notes

1   Cf. above p. 19.
2   Aristotle, *Physics* Δ 14, 223 a 26.
3   Augustine, *Confessions*, translated by R.S. Pine-Coffin, Penguin, Harmondsworth, 1961, Book XI, p. 276 (translation slightly modified).
4   Cf. above, pp. 69 ff. on ἁπλᾶ and ἀληθές.
5   Cf. above, pp. 19 and 81.

PART TWO

CAUSALITY AND FREEDOM

TRANSCENDENTAL AND PRACTICAL
FREEDOM IN KANT

1

Causality and Freedom as Cosmological Problem.
The First Way to Freedom in the Kantian System: the Question of the Possibility of Experience as the Question of the Possibility of Genuine Metaphysics

Is freedom a problem of causality, or is causality a problem of freedom? We must at once ask more fully whether this either-or is relevant at all, i.e. even if the problem of causality turns out to be the problem of freedom, is freedom itself adequately conceived in this way? Does the essence of freedom ultimately amount to its status as ground of the problem of causality? If so, is it sufficient to conceive causality in the foregoing fashion? It is not! Must we not conceive freedom more radically and not merely as a kind of causality *precisely if* it is the ground of the problem of causality? Where can we find directives for a return to the more primordial essence?

Kant must have had compelling reasons for bringing freedom into such an intimate relationship with causality. Moreover, from our own thesis we can see that this connection between causality and freedom originates from the inner content of the problem and not from a mere standpoint. The content of the fundamental question led us to freedom as the ground of the possibility of Dasein, which is where the understanding of being occurs. Freedom reveals itself as ground. But cause (*causa*) is itself a kind of ground.

§ 15. Preliminary Remark on the Problem of Causality in the Sciences

a) Causality as Expression of the Questionworthiness of Animate and Inanimate Nature in the Sciences

If we take up the problem of freedom in connection with causality, it is incumbent upon us to give some definite indication of what we mean by causality and of the problems it poses. I shall attempt a concrete orientation to causality by reference to the Kantian treatment of the problem, where various historical motives, which are not important for us here, intersect (Leibniz, Hume). Before we look more closely at Kant's conception of causality some indication of the scope of the problem is required, and in a twofold aspect. The research and inquiry we call science has two main streams, relating to nature on the one hand, and to history on the other.

Nature	History (man and works of man)
Processes	Occurrences
Cause and Effect	Cause and Effect
Causality	Causality
?	?

Today, in these two main streams of scientific research, causality has become problematic in quite distinctive ways. If we look from outside at the diversity of investigations, which are no longer capable of being surveyed by the individual researcher in his discipline, if we observe the organization of the sciences in societies, institutes, and congresses, if we see the pace with which one result is overtaken by another and translated into so-called *praxis*, it appears that the only thing we still need to know is the extent and means of this gigantic business. Indeed, we still need to know just this, in order to combat the inner ruin. For everything, once brought within the process of a self-perpetuating technique, only maintains itself when the inner necessity and simple force of genuine motives have died out.

Despite this almost technical progress of scientific research, and despite this flourishing scientific industry, the sciences of nature and history are more fundamentally questionable today than ever before. The misrelation between routinely produced results on the one hand, and the uncertainty and obscurity of fundamental concepts on the other hand, has never been so great. Again, it has never been so clear, for those who can see at any rate, how the spirit can become confused, powerless, and rootless, yet at the same time hold the world in bated breath with an avalanche of results. I do not know how many really grasp this situation and can read the signs.

Let me comment on something seemingly external. At the end of April, the German Historical Conference took place in Halle. There was a discussion about whether history is a science or an art. But nobody really possessed the necessary means for this discussion. The methods for grasping this enigmatic problem, and for correctly situating it, were lacking. Only one thing became clear, namely that historians today do not know what history is, indeed do not even know what is required to arrive at this knowledge. It is obvious that one does not even know *why* it occurs that people borrow an opinion from a philosophy professor whom they meet by chance, or who happens to be a colleague.

What is the reason for this catastrophic situation, the seriousness of which is not diminished by the fact that all these helpless types calmly continue their detailed work the very next day? The reason is not that we are unable to define the essence of historical science, but that the historical occurrence as such, despite the multiplicity of events, does not announce itself with unifying force, so that its essential character remains misinterpreted and concealed by worn-out theories of historical science. The historical occurrence as such cannot announce itself if it does not encounter an experience that brings it to clarity, an experience that can illuminate the historicality of history. It must hereby be decided whether history is only a sequence of causally connected facts and influences, or whether the causality of the historical occurrence must be grasped in a completely different way.

The problem of causality is not a recondite question somehow conjured up in philosophy. It concerns the innermost necessity of our relationship to the historical as such and thus to the science of history (philology in the broader sense). The same applies to the other direction of scientific inquiry, the science of nature, whether it be about the lifeless (physics and chemistry) or about living nature (biology). It is said that the new physical theories – the electrical theory of matter, the theory of relativity and the quantum theory – have undermined the hitherto binding law of causality. The traditional conception of the process-character of material processes has become problematic. There is no possibility of a new positive definition of nature such that the new inquiries and new knowledge can obtain a genuine grounding. The same applies in respect of the essence of organism, i.e. the essence of life, the fundamental conception of the way of being of those beings which, we say, live and die.

To repeat, causality is not a remote free-floating concept but *expresses the innermost questionability of the constitution of animate and inanimate nature.* But man himself, standing in the midst of nature and bound to the occurrence of its history, totters and searches in this questionability and distress. At the same time, philosophy is familiar with the perspective implied by the concretely understood problem of causality in history and nature. But precisely this universal confusion, which makes everything shaky and fragile, is the proper time of philosophy. It would be naïve even for a moment to wish it otherwise, but it would be just as shortsighted to think of 'saving' this time through a system of philosophy. On the contrary, it is a matter of maintaining the genuinely experienced and experienceable distress. It is a matter of ensuring that this looming questionability, the precursor of great things, is not circumvented through cheap answers and superstitions.

It is unnecessary, therefore, to provide you with further assurances that the theme of this introduction to philosophy grows out from, and at the same time reflects back on, the great directions of research into nature and history, directions in which you yourselves stand through membership of various faculties of the university. Philosophizing is here no side activity serving private needs or edification but stands at the centre of the work which you have set down – or have claimed to set down – for yourself.

With these comments on the sciences of nature and history we did not want to confirm e.g. various errors and deficiencies in the sciences, nor a failure of philosophy, nor anything that could justify mutual accusations. Rather, all these are forebodings and signs of the real shocks and displacements suffered by our whole existence, in the face of which the individual can only try not to miss the new voices, difficult to hear as they are. It would be wrong to think that any individual could tear all this down by himself. This would only result in the disaster of all reform, which changes overnight into unendurable tyranny. But it is just as important to beware of accepting anything and everything without distinction, i.e. of becoming the victim of empty public opinion. What we are seeking is not the mediocre but the centre, the steadfast silence before the inner complexity and relationality of the essential, which can never be captured in formulas and can never be saved by just knocking down its opposite.

b) Causality in Modern Physics.
Probability (Statistics) and Causality

What then is *causality*? To begin with we wish to hear what *Kant* says concerning causality, and this for several reasons. First because he brings causality and freedom into a special relationship, then because he conceives causality primarily as the causality of nature, which leads to fundamental difficulties for the causality of history. Further, because in contemporary philosophical discussion concerning the problem of causality in psychology it is said that the Kantian conception is inadequate. Finally, because the Kantian problem of causality leads into a contexture with which we are already familiar, i.e. that of the connection between being and time. For in the *Kantian conception of causality* it is the *relation to time* that is immediately striking, even though the problem is not followed through to its ultimate implications. So we must first concretely exhibit the Kantian approach to the problem of causality.

A comment is necessary on the terribly confused discussions concerning the problem of causality in modern physics and their meaning for philosophy. The confusion has resulted from a talking-past-one-another, which itself is due to the fact that the real question has been seen in neither physics nor philosophy. The physicists say that the law of causality can now be seen not to be an *a priori* principle of thought, and that, accordingly, this law can only be assessed through experience and physicalistic thought. 'Contemporary physicists no longer doubt that whether causality is complete can only be decided through experience, i.e. they no longer doubt that causality is not an *a priori* necessity of thought.'[1] This latter remark naturally alludes to the Kantian conception of causality, whereby the first thing to be said is that Kant nowhere claims the law of causality as an *a priori* necessity of thought. What Kant does say is that the fundamental principle of causality as natural law can never be grounded in experience but is the condition of the possibility of experience of nature as such. The philosophers, on the other hand, adopt a superior attitude vis-à-vis the claims of physics: whatever physicists might say about the law of causality they do not, so the philosophers declare, possess the requisite means for grasping the problem of causality. Neither of these two positions is acceptable. The philosophical appeal to the *a priori* is just

105

as dubious as the physicalistic fixation on experience is confused. In the end both claims are correct, and yet neither possesses sufficient clarity and radicalism to see the crucial problem.

In what sense has the law of causality become dubious for modern physics? 'Classical dynamics is governed by the unconditional principle that knowledge of a state of affairs (the position and speed of material particles) at any one moment forever determines the course of a closed system; this is how physics understands the law of causality.'[2] It is claimed, however, that although a determining causality applies at the macroscopic level of natural processes, this is not so at the microscopic level, i.e. at the level of those atomic structures which are today regarded as the elementary physicalistic processes, corresponding to astrophysical processes (the movements of the planets).

Atomic physics has demonstrated that physical magnitudes are not uniformly distributed in nature. Motion does not occur continuously but there are leaps and gaps. Movements are not subject to unambiguous determination. Their lawfulness is not dynamical and continuously causal, but is determinable only at a mid-point, with statistical probability.

The law governing elementary natural processes is different, and if one calls this law the principle of causality, physics points to the necessity of redefining causality. So what does this mean? 'For the physicist, defining causality means nothing else than indicating how its existence or non-existence can be experimentally ascertained.'[3] It is thus already clear that with the advance of our observations, of our knowledge and experimental methods, the definition of causality must also change.

Here it becomes quite clear that defining causality means giving the possible ways in which its *presence* can be established. But what causality is must already be clear prior to ascertaining its presence or non-presence. Or must this also first be ascertained, and if so how? This is the question physics forgets to ask, but which is decided by philosophy all too quickly. It is true that, in order to ascertain causality in this or that instance, one must already know what one understands by causality, and one must possess this knowledge prior to all experiential ascertaining. But what this *a priori* is, how it is possible, and why it is necessary – this is not decided, and is certainly not decidable by appeal to Kant.

Although we should mistrust physics' claims to authority, it is not permissible to dismiss the content of its contemporary problems as so-called empirical material, for these might point towards new definitions of the essence of nature as such. On the other hand, we must also mistrust the overhasty protestations of philosophy, while not forgetting that its task, for which it alone has the means, is to problematize the inner possibility of physics and its object, provided, of course, that philosophy is itself guided by the true vitality of its most authentic problematic.

§ 16. First Attempt at Characterizing the Kantian Conception of Causality and Its Fundamental Contexture: Causality and Temporal Succession

Before asking about whether the causal law is logically necessary, and whether this kind of questioning concerning its validity has any sense at all, we must get some idea of what causality means as such. For this question we must in turn obtain the proper *basis for discussion*, namely the *fundamental contexture* in which causality belongs. We shall proceed from Kant. This can only provide us with clues, the correctness and primordiality of which are always subject to renewed assessment.

Kant treats of causality in the 'Second Analogy'. In Kant's terminology, the Analogies are a specific set of principles relating to 'the existence of appearances', i.e. the being-present of beings, 'nature' as accessible to us. Natural processes, i.e. relations between present appearances in time, stand under definite rules of determinability, rules which are not derived from accidental or frequently occurring relations of experience, but which determine in advance what belongs to the possibility of a natural process as such, i.e. a natural process experienceable by us. Thus the 'general *principle*' of the Analogies of Experience is given in the first edition as follows: 'All appearances are, as regards their existence, subject *a priori* to rules determining their relation to one another in one time'.[4] One of these rules provides the Second Analogy.[5] Kant has *different titles* for, and *different conceptions* of, this principle in the first (A) and second (B) editions. In A: 'principle of production',[6] in B: 'principle of succession in time, in accordance with the law of causality'.[7] In A, his conception of the principle is: 'Everything that happens, that is, begins to be, presupposes something upon which it follows *according to a rule*'.[8] In B: 'All alterations take place in conformity with the law of the connection of cause and effect'.[9]

The law of causality yields a *fundamental principle of temporal succession*. Causality is itself related to *temporal succession*. How does causality come into a relationship with temporal succession? What does temporal succession mean? A cause is always the cause of an effect. That which is brought about we also call the *outcome*. An outcome is something that follows from something else. So to bring about, to effect, means to let-follow. As the effecting of the effect, the cause lets something follow-on, and thus is itself prior. The cause–effect relation thus involves priority and outcome: the following-on of one thing from another, succession, which Kant conceives as temporal succession. We therefore see the *connection between causality and temporal succession*. This connection must be firmly borne in mind if we are to understand Kant's elucidation of the essence of causality.

Causality means temporal succession. But what does temporal succession mean? Literally, it means that one time follows-on from another time. For example, Kant says that 'different times are not simultaneous but successive'.[10] Time 'constantly flows'. Its 'constancy' is just this flowing. On the other hand Kant emphasizes: 'If we ascribe succession to time itself, we must think yet another time, in which the sequence would be possible'.[11] That would lead to an infinite regress, and is therefore impossible – presupposing, as Kant does without argument, that this 'another time' has the same character. If, therefore, there is no succession in time as such, neither does time flow. 'The existence of what is transitory passes away in time, but not time itself . . . [which is] non-transitory and abiding'.[12] 'Time itself does not alter, but only something which is in time'.[13] So temporal succession does not mean a sequence of times belonging to time itself, but the succession of that which is in time.

But Kant further says: 'Simultaneity and succession are the only relations in time'.[14] Can it be that simultaneity and succession are not relations of that which is in time, but belong in time itself? Does temporal succession belong to time itself? Does time itself contain a *succession of times* (nows)? There is an opposition here: time itself is constant, i.e. it does not pass away or alter, but rather abides – and yet it remains a *succession*.

Kant calls temporal succession *a mode* of time, and indeed *one* mode among others. 'The three modes of time are duration, succession, and simultaneity.'[15] *What is a mode of time* and how do these modes relate to one another? Are they at the same level or does one have priority? What kind of modalization of time is involved here? Why just these *three* modes? The three modes of time are seemingly different to the three parts of time generally recognized, i.e. present, past, and future. What kind of temporal characteristics are these latter, and how do they relate to the so-called modes of time (to which temporal succession belongs, and in relation to which causality is conceived)?

Our first attempt at characterizing the Kantian conception of causality has already brought us to the centre of major questions and difficulties. We must now observe more closely how Kant deals with these problems, and thus what we should more precisely understand by 'temporal succession' and 'principle of temporal succession'. For this we must try to grasp the *entire problem of the Analogies of Experience* in its genuine core, so that we can comprehend the contexture of the principle of causality, at the same time bringing to light the more primordial dimension of the relationship between causality and freedom.

§ 17. General Characterization of the Analogies of Experience

If we enter into a consideration of the Analogies of Experience, we do so with all necessary reserve. Clearly, a problem from the central part of the *Critique of Pure Reason*, addressing the most central problematic of philosophy, requires more extensive preparation than we have been able to undertake. A general overview is not at all sufficient; we wish, rather, to deal concretely with the text, albeit not by means of a thematically continuous interpretation.

a) The Analogies of Experience as Rules of Universal Temporal Determination of the Being-Present of That Which Is Present in the Context of the Inner Enablement of Experience

Temporal succession, to which the principle of causality is oriented, is *one mode of time*. The first mode is permanence, the third simultaneity. The three Analogies of Experience correspond to these three modes. The First Analogy is oriented to duration: the principle of the permanence of substance: 'All appearances contain the permanent (substance) as the object itself, and the transitory as its mere determination, that is, as a way in which the object exists.'[16] 'In all changes of appearances substance is permanent; its quantum in nature is neither increased nor diminished.'[17] The Third Analogy is oriented to the third mode of time, simultaneity: the principle of simultaneity according to the laws of reciprocal effect or community. 'All substances, insofar as they co-exist, stand in thorough-going community, that is, in mutual interaction.'[18] 'All substances, insofar as they can be perceived to co-exist in space, are in thoroughgoing reciprocity.'[19]

What is basically stated in these Analogies? The principles refer to rules. What is regulated by these rules? They are rules of universal temporal determination. What does 'universal temporal determination' mean here? Why are the Analogies necessary as rules of universal temporal determination? By addressing this latter question, i.e. by inquiring into *the underlying necessity of the Analogies*, we wish to obtain an initial view of their essence. This will enable us to proceed to the specific content of the Second Analogy.

The necessity of the Analogies is grounded in the *essence of experience*. Experience is the way present beings become accessible to man. The essence of this mode of accessibility is defined in terms of the inner possibility of experience. Kant says: 'Experience is possible only through the representation of a necessary connection of perceptions.'[20] Note that Kant does not simply say that the possibility (essence) of experience consists in the necessary connection of perceptions. Rather, the possibility of experience consists solely in the *representation* of the necessary connection of perceptions, i.e. of the necessary connectedness of what is given in perception.

What kind of necessary connections are these? Why do they constitute the prime condition of the inner possibility of experience? If the possibility of experience depends on the representation of necessary connections, then precisely the essence of *this* experience must exhibit a multiplicity which is connected or needful of connectedness.

How does Kant discover such a thing in experience? 'Experience is an *empirical* knowledge, that is, a knowledge which determines an object through perceptions.'[21] This means that the beings (objects) themselves are only knowable insofar as they somehow show and give themselves. In respect of what thus shows itself, in respect of the determination of the object in its objectivity, knowledge is primarily receptive, a letting-stand-over-against. This receiving – apprehension – occurs through perceptions as determined by sensory sensations. These perceptions are occurrences in man. Taken as such, it is evident that they follow-on from one another. No perception has priority over another, but they differ simply through their position in the sequence. In this sense 'perceptions come together only in accidental order'.[22] The 'succession in our apprehension [is] always one and the same'.[23]

We can express this somewhat more freely, yet at the same time more definitely. Perceptions come into a sequential relationship with one another, and are thus after, before, or simultaneous with one another, as mental occurrences. For example I now see the chalk, feel the heat, hear the sound outside, look at the lectern. This is not just a sequence or simultaneity of *perceiving* as comporting in the broader sense, but it is also a corresponding coming-into-connection (assembly) of the various things perceived in perception: chalk, heat, sound, lectern. Where is all this assembled? In the perceivedness *of a* perception, in the *unitary perceiving 'consciousness'*. If we take what is perceived as such in its perceivedness, then this reveals itself as having come together in and through the sequence of perceptions. The chalk and the heat and the noise and the lectern, simply as the beings they are, initially have nothing whatever to do with each other. They do not, considered merely in their respective whatness, possess a determinate and necessary relationship to one another. In other words: if experience of beings is understood merely in terms of the apprehensions belonging to it, then these beings can only be conceived as having come together. Why is this not the end of the matter? Clearly, because factical experience is *never just* an assembly of various elements, and further, because in experience we are *not at all* cognitively oriented to perceptions as mental occurrences in temporal succession. So to what *are* we oriented? To the beings themselves as announced in perception, i.e. to what appears in all its diversity (and indeed in respect of its being-present), to the connections between these present things. Experience always already places us before a unity of present beings. Experience is not knowledge *of* perceptions, but 'knowledge of objects through perceptions'.[24] It represents 'the relation in the existence of the manifold, not as it comes to be constructed in the time [of being perceived] but as it exists objectively in time'.[25]

What is experienced in experience is more than a mere assembly of perceptions. Rather, what is experienced is the unity of present beings in their being-present: in short, *nature*. 'By nature (in the empirical sense) we understand the connection of appearances as regards their existence.'[26] If experience is always the experience of nature, appearances must always already represent the unity of what is present. What is the origin of this particular representation? Since perceptions give only an assembly, this unity and connection cannot be provided by them. Further, since Kant claims that knowledge (experience) is constituted by perception and thought (sensibility and understanding), this unity can only originate from thought, or from a determinate unitary connection between perception and thought. But it is clear that thinking alone cannot define the unity of the presence of that which is present. How then is this unity supposed to be possible?

The presence of something present is always a presence in time. The *unity of nature* is therefore primarily determined as the *unity and connection of that which is present in time*. But precisely this determinate position in time, and the temporal relation between present beings, cannot be construed independently of thought. Nor can we directly perceive the temporal determination of something present in the context of the unitary temporal relations of nature. That would require reading off the temporal position of everything present from absolute time, which itself would presuppose that we could perceive time itself absolutely and as a whole. This, however, is impossible. In his discussion of the Analogies, Kant repeatedly emphasizes that 'absolute time is not an object of perception',[27] that 'time itself cannot be'.[28] 'Now time cannot by itself be perceived.'[29] 'Time cannot be perceived in itself, and what precedes and what follows cannot, therefore, by relation to it, be empirically determined in the object.'[30]

What is the ultimate reason for this? Kant did not and could not expressly provide the reason, for he lacked a metaphysics of Dasein.[31] 'There is *only one time* in which all different times must be located, not as coexistent but as in succession to one another.'[32] Temporal determination, and thus the unity of the presence of the present, i.e. nature, is neither perceivable nor *a priori* construable, but can only be ascertained through the empirical measurement of time, where both thought and perception play a role. This requires ascertaining in advance those temporal determinations which express the temporal relations of what is present. Empirical temporal relations are only determinable from the pure temporal relations which constitute the possibility of nature as such, whatever the factical course of nature happens to be. Now Kant calls the Analogies of Experience, i.e. the principles to which causality (Second Analogy) also belongs, *transcendental determinations of time*. They contain the rules of the necessary temporal determination of everything present, 'without which even empirical determination of time would be impossible'.[33] Through these rules we can 'anticipate experience',[34] i.e. it is not the factical course of experience in its factical constellations that we can anticipate, but rather what is prior to every factical occurrence insofar as it is natural. These rules of transcendental determination of time – which are not rules of pure thought – delineate the comprehensive unity of the natural totality, giving the form of all possible concrete connections between perceivable things. These connections no longer pertain to the course of mental occurrences, but to that which appears in perception insofar as this is already presented under pure temporal determinations. This anticipation is the representing spoken of by Kant in the general principle of the Analogies. Universal temporal determination anticipates by disposing over the possible modes of being-in-time of whatever is factically given in perception.

b) The Three Modes of Time (Permanence, Succession and Simultaneity) as Modes of the Intra-Temporality of That Which Is Present

Now we can better understand why these three Analogies, as rules governing the prior temporal determination of that which is present, are oriented *to the modes of time*. Being-present and the unity thereof means precisely presence (being-present) in time, i.e. unity and determinability of the contexture of those temporal relations which something present (as something 'in time') can and must possess. Accordingly, modes of time signify not so much an alteration of time as such but are ways in which present appearances 'are in time'. In brief, modes of time are not basic features of time as such (present, past, future) but are *modes of the intra-temporality of that which is present*. The *first mode* – permanence – expresses the relationship of appearances 'to time itself, as a magnitude',[35] i.e. it measures the *duration* in time of that which is present. The *second mode* – succession – expresses the relationship between present things in time as a sequence (of nows); seen under this sequential aspect, every present thing *follows on from* something else present. The *third mode* – simultaneity – expresses the relationship of that which is present to time as a *summation of everything present*.[36]

So time is viewed here in three ways: as magnitude, as sequence, and as summation. The extent to which time can and must be so viewed is a question we must pass over for the moment. One can compare the chapter 'The Schematism of the Pure Concepts of Understanding', where it turns out that the categories, the table of categories, the table of judgements, or in general *logic*, are also at work in this characterization of time as 'series', 'content', 'ordering', 'summation'.[37] Why then does Kant, where he treats the relations to time of beings which exist in time, speak simply of temporal relations? Because, for Kant, time is nothing else but that wherein the manifold content of inner and outer perception is ordered. Time is seen exclusively in its relationship to that which is within time. Thus temporal relations are *modifications* of the relation of time to that which is within time. The strength of Kant's problematic, but also its limits, reside in this conception of time.[38]

c) The Distinction between Dynamical and Mathematical Principles

To complete our general characterization of the Analogies of Experience, we must mention yet another – not immediately comprehensible – description which Kant gives of these principles. He calls them *dynamical* as distinct from *mathematical* principles. Kant also uses this distinction to divide the categories. The distinction pertains not so much to the character of the principles as such but more to their application, to the way they make possible that to which they are applied (perceivability, determinability in presence). 'Now all categories are divided into two classes: the *mathematical*, which deal with the unity of synthesis in the conception of objects, and the *dynamical*, which concern the synthetic unity in the conception of the existence of objects.'[39]

The *mathematical* principles and categories relate to the perceptual-substantive aspect of appearances, i.e., in the terminology of Kant and earlier metaphysics, *the real*.[40] Here the real does not mean, as it does in today's corrupted usage, the actual, but that which belongs to the *res*, the substantive constituting content. The mathematical principles give the substance of things, the *essentia*. In Kant's problematic, the mathematical principles are those ontological principles which define the *essentia* of a being.

Since ancient times, however, *essentia* has been distinguished from *existentia* (being-present, or in Kantian terminology, existence). Now where appearances are determined simply in respect of their presence (*existentia*), i.e. not in respect of their substantive content, Kant calls the determining principles *dynamical*. If the Analogies of Experience belong to the dynamical principles, this allows us to see their location within the context of traditional metaphysics. I should mention here that Kant, following Leibniz, developed the ontological problem of presence in connection with that of what-being, and in any case without posing the fundamental question concerning the origin of this distinction (between what-being and that-being) or placing his own problem within the dimension of the radically conceived problem of being. I mention this because in our discussion of the problem of freedom we shall come across precisely this question concerning the origin of what- and that-being, i.e. possibility and actuality. From a metaphysical point of view, the problem of freedom has its centre *here*, and *not* in the problem of *causality*.

Freedom is to be discussed within the context of causality. What is the essence of causality? How does Kant determine the essence of causality? What is the problematic within which this definition of essence occurs? Running ahead a little we can say that it is the question concerning the possibility of experience. Experience is the only way in which man has knowledge of beings. The question of the possibility of finite knowledge is thus the question concerning the essence of the finitude of existence. The problem of causality, and thus also the problem of freedom, stand within this context. Ultimately, this is the primary and ultimate context, the only primordial and genuine context, of the problem of freedom. To be sure, this does not mean that the problem of freedom must be oriented to the problem of causality. Causality is not what most primordially pertains to the finitude of existence. The latter is not by any means primarily to be conceived from experience, from knowledge, from the theoretical, or even from the practical. *So where is the deepest essence of man's finitude to be sought?* Just in the understanding of being, in the occurrence of being. These are questions which arise when we inquire into the proper dimension of the problem of human freedom. More concretely then, and with a view to working through the problem: how must the highest essence of the finitude of existence be interrogated, and in which direction must it be unfolded, in order that a concrete guideline for the problem of freedom can emerge?

d) The Analogies of Experience as Rules of the Basic Relations of the Possible Being-in-Time of That Which Is Present

Solving the preliminary question concerning the Kantian definition of the *essence of causality* means interpreting his doctrine of the *Analogies of Experience*. Our general characterization of the latter has been concluded, ultimately by treating them as *dynamical principles* and in terms of the distinction between the mathematical and dynamical (*essentia-existentia*). In Kantian terminology, the 'Analogies' circumscribe the problem of the being-present of that which is present. What we must now discuss is the connection between this latter problem and the problems of causality and freedom.

In the Analogies, Kant formulates rules which are always pre-represented in every human experience, rules which hold up, for every possible experience, the fundamental relations of the possible being-in-time of that which is present, i.e. which allow the encountered being to be understood *in the contexture of its being-present.* These rules embody that *aspect of the understanding of being* which pertains to the being-present of that which is present (nature). As the most general laws of nature, they set forth what nature is as such. They are laws which natural science can never discover, precisely because they must always be presupposed and pre-understood in all scientific questioning concerning *specific* natural laws. As the Second Analogy, the principle of causality is therefore a rule of transcendental determination of time. The problem of causality thus pertains to the being-present of that which is present, and to the objective determinability of the latter. To see this clearly is of the greatest significance for understanding the contexture into which the problem of freedom is forced when Kant brings it together with causality, and when he makes a basic distinction between the causality of freedom and natural causality. It is still precisely *causality* – causality as oriented to the contexture of the *being-present of that which is present.*

We must now attempt, departing from the guideline provided by our general discussion of the Analogies, to unfold the concrete problem of the Second Analogy. However, in order that the latter's specific characteristics may come to light, we shall begin by treating the First Analogy. This procedure is really unavoidable, for the First Analogy, in a certain sense, provides the foundation for the others.

§ 18. Discussion of the Mode of Proof of the Analogies of Experience and Their Foundation from the Example of the First Analogy. The Fundamental Meaning of the First Analogy

a) The First Analogy: Permanence and Time

A: 'All appearances contain the permanent (substance) as the object itself, and the transitory as its mere determination, that is, as a way in which the object exists.'[41]

The First Analogy is called the 'principle of permanence', i.e. it expresses the necessity, grounded in the essence of experience, 'of the ever-abiding existence, in the appearances, of the subject proper'.[42]

To begin with, we restrict ourselves to the treatment in the first edition (A). Kant is concerned not only with the explicit presentation of this principle, but equally with its correct demonstration. Indeed, Kant finds that 'in all ages, not only philosophers, but even the common understanding, have recognized this permanence as a substratum of all changes of appearances'.[43] It is just that the philosopher expresses himself rather more definitely, and says 'throughout all changes in the world substance remains, and only the accidents change'.[44] 'I nowhere find even the attempt at a proof of this obviously synthetic proposition. Indeed it is very seldom placed where it truly belongs, at the head of those laws of nature which are pure and completely *a priori*.'[45] To be sure, one grounds all experience in this principle, 'for in empirical knowledge the need of it is *felt*'.[46] One rests content with this, without pressing forward to an understanding, i.e. to a clarification of the inner possibility and necessity of this principle.

The First Analogy is to be demonstrated. What is there in it to demonstrate? First, 'that in all appearances there is something permanent, and that the transitory is nothing but determination of its existence'.[47] Secondly, that what is permanent is the object itself, the genuine being given in appearance. Something permanent is given in each and every appearance. It is not this or that occurrence of permanence, but the necessity of the permanent in all experience, which has to be demonstrated. This can only be done by showing what belongs to the very possibility (essence) of experience in general.

How does the proof proceed? Let us recall the two aspects of experience: the manifold of perception as the mere assembly of diverse elements, still needful of connection; 2. the connection, which must not be accidental but rather binding and necessary, i.e. in accordance with the binding character of what proceeds from the beings themselves and their specific being-present. The First Analogy (thus also the other two) formulates one of the necessary modes of connection (modes of unity) of everything experienceable. The First Analogy in particular is concerned above all to demonstrate the necessity of permanence in the permanent, as grounding all change and modification, thus the whole multiplicity of relations between that which is present. Thus the demonstration of this necessity of permanence must likewise set out from the merely assembled manifold of apprehension. The proofs of all three Analogies begin precisely here, with the primary succession of apprehension.

What do we find when we restrict ourselves to the sequence of perceptions? In this case we simply have constant change. From this alone we could never discover whether just one unitary object, or rather a succession of these, is given in the stream of perceptions. Such a decision concerning succession and simultaneity (i.e. temporal relations) is only possible if, from the very beginning, experience is grounded in something permanent and abiding, something in respect of which the indicated relations are modes. More precisely, the essence of succession and simultaneity as relations of being-in-time already implies the necessary grounding in something permanent, for these temporal relations can only 'be' if time itself constantly endures and abides. Time expresses permanence as such. Only where there is permanence can there also be duration as the measure of being-present in time. The succession of apprehension already refers to something permanent, i.e. something which turns out to be the primal form of permanence: time. Time is the substratum of everything we encounter in experience, it is the *pure intuition* which is always already spread out before our view. Change and simultaneity are comparable and determinable only in terms of time – presupposing that time itself is perceivable. But this is not so. Consequently, the possibility of experience presupposes a substratum in the real to which all temporal determination must be referred. This is the necessary condition of the possibility of all unity in the connection of perceptions – substance. 'This permanence is simply the mode in which we represent to ourselves the existence of things in the [field of] experience.'[48] Permanence is the presupposed horizon for our definition and representation of whatever we encounter as present.

b) The Questionworthy Foundation of the Analogies: the Unclarified Association of Time and 'I Think' (Understanding) in an Uncritical Approach to the Essence of Man as Finite Subject

In the end, just as with other proofs in Kant, you will not find the demonstrations of the Analogies immediately clear in either in their content or their rigour; indeed they will remain incomprehensible. This is not only for the external reason that you lack a complete knowledge of Kant's theories and discussions, but has internal grounds about which a brief remark is necessary, especially since Kant himself lays much stress upon his proofs, while those who link themselves with Kant emphasize the rigour of his proof procedures. However precisely one formulates the

Kantian proofs, they do not gain in rigour unless one has already understood their necessity. Any proof possesses validity only if it is necessary
as a whole, and if this necessity is made comprehensible, which comprehensibility does not have to rest upon theoretical proof. Now it may be
that the presuppositions required by Kant for the validity of his proofs
are untenable, because they stem from an *inadequate* examination and
essential determination of the situation upon which and *for* which the
whole problematic is grounded. If this were the case, if the necessity of the
Kantian proofs were ungrounded, then not only could their much praised
stringency not be maintained, but even their possibility would be doubt-
ful. *This in fact is the situation* in respect of the Kantian proofs, and not
only the proofs of the principles, but also those of the transcendental
deduction. Already in purely stylistic terms, and in Kant's presentation,
there is a peculiar affinity between the proofs of the principles and the
proofs of the transcendental deduction. Neither the principles nor
the transcendental deduction are necessary in the *form* Kant takes them,
and upon whose ground he must take them. This, however, is not to deny
that they harbour a problem.

Why is this so? Briefly stated, it is because Kant did not problematize in
a sufficiently primordial manner the finitude of man, i.e. the problem
from which, and for which, he develops the *Critique of Pure Reason*. To
show this is the task of a Kant interpretation, which, however, does not
have the pseudo-philological aim of presenting the 'correct' Kant – there
is nothing of the sort. *All philosophical interpretation is destruction*, controversy, and radicalization, which is not equivalent to scepticism. Or else it
is nothing at all, mere chatter that repeats more laboriously what was said
in simpler and better fashion by the author himself. This does not mean
that one can declare Kant's proofs correct and leave them to themselves.
On the contrary, it means that we must make these proofs genuinely
transparent, so that we can see the foundation upon which they rest, a
foundation uncritically presupposed by Kant.

In our case it is the conception of time on the one hand, and the conception of understanding on the other hand. More fundamentally, it is
the conception of the relationship between time and the 'I think' (understanding). Still more precisely, it is the uncritical and unclarified
juxtaposition of both in an uncritical approach to the essence of man as
finite subject. That this inner structural connection between time and the
I as 'I think' (understanding), thus also the fundamental relationship
between them as the essence of the relationship between subject and

object, remains unclarified, in short that transcendence is not sufficiently determined to really become a problem – this is the basic reason for the substantive difficulty of understanding e.g. Kant's proofs of the Analogies.

c) The Analogies of Experience and the Transcendental Deduction of the Pure Concepts of the Understanding. The Logical Structure of the Analogies of Experience and the Question of Their Character as Analogies

We wish to repeat once again the main steps in the proof of the fundamental principles, such that the foundations can emerge, and so we can understand why these principles are called 'analogies'.

1. All appearances, i.e. present beings themselves as accessible to man, exist in time and stand in the contextual unity of their being-present, thus in the unity of temporal determination. The basic way of defining something as something is by the determination of a subject through a predicate. Time itself is what is primordially permanent, such that the primordial unity of the being-present of that which is present is grounded in permanence. The permanent is the substratum of all appearances.

2. But time cannot be perceived absolutely, i.e. in and for itself. As that wherein everything present is placed, and as determining the specific locations of things, time is not directly perceivable. But as the permanent, time binds to itself all determination of the unity of beings-in-time.

3. So there must be a rule according to which something permanent is contained in everything which appears as subject, and such that the subject appears as substance. This rule is the principle of the permanence of substance. Its necessity is demonstrated from the essence of appearance, from the unity of time and the 'I think'.

We can now see why these kinds of principle are called analogies. According to Kant, there are analogies in mathematics as well as in philosophy.[49] An analogy is a correspondence of something with something, more precisely, the correspondence of one relation with another. In mathematics, analogies are correspondences between two quantitative relations, their proportion. If three values are given, the fourth can be mathematically determined. Analogies in mathematics amount to constitutive determination. In *philosophy* it is not a matter of quantitative, but of *qualitative* relations (Wolff). What is determinable here is only the way something must be if it is to be at all experienceable in its existence.

An example of the First Analogy is the correspondence between two relations: predicate to subject and accident to substance. The relationship between predicate and subject corresponds to the relationship between accident (as something encountered in time) and substance. The latter must exist as determinable and underlying – in temporal terms, as the permanent. The Analogy does not assert the being-present of substances, but provides the *a priori* rule for seeking the permanent in all appearances.

The Analogies are *ontological principles* concerning the *being-present of that which is present* (*existentia*). These ontological statements do not imply the being-present of the corresponding ontical, but rather the finite necessity, belonging to experience, of the determinate encounterability of that which is ontologically intended in the principle, here the permanent. 'Now, in respect to the objects of experience, everything without which the experience of these objects would not itself be possible is necessary.'[50] The necessity belonging to experience is conditioned, grounded in the *contingency* of experience: *if* finite man exists. This involves a new determination of the essence of the ontological.

On the other hand, previous metaphysics proceeded as follows: 1. ontological statements were proven by rational-logical means, not from the essence of experience. 2. These ontological principles led directly to ontical conclusions. In another sense, all four groups of principles corresponding to the four classes of categories are analogies, since they correspond to the four logical forms of possible representational connections. The four aspects in terms of which the various forms of judgement (categories) and the principles, are constructed in correspondence, stem from the traditional division of judgements (forms of judgement) in formal logic: quantity, quality, reality, modality.

As a category, permanence (substance) is a relation, and as Kant says,[51] not so much because it contains a relation, but because it is a condition of all relations: inherence and subsistence, *substantia et accidens*, causality and dependence (cause and effect), community (reciprocity of acting and suffering).[52] The guideline is the table of judgements, i.e. the 'relations of thought in judgements'. They are 'a) of the predicate to the subject, b) of the ground to its consequence, c) of the divided knowledge and of the members of the division, taken together, to each other'.[53]

d) The Fundamental Meaning of the First Analogy. Permanence (Substantiality) and Causality

We can already see from this how permanence emerges also as the condition of the possibility of the causal relation, and indeed emerges as *relation*. This is quite clear from the way Kant concludes his discussion of the First Analogy. He considers the concept of *alteration*, which only now can be conceived in the proper manner. 'Alteration is a way of existing which follows upon another way of existing of the same object.'[54] A sequence of different states one after another, one ending and another beginning, is a *change*. Alteration, on the other hand, is a sequence of states 'of one and the same object'. So only something which *endures* can be altered, or as Kant says, 'only the permanent (substance) is altered'.[55] An alteration, therefore, is only perceivable if, beforehand, something permanent is experienced. For it is only upon the basis of, and in relation to, something permanent, that a transition from one state to another can be perceived; otherwise there would be nothing but total displacement of one thing by another. Transition, however, itself involves a succession, and likewise *completed* transitions and alterations involve the simultaneity of that which has been completed. Succession and simultaneity are the basic relations of possible pure determination of time. It is thus evident that the permanent within appearances, i.e. substance, is 'the substratum of all determinations of time'.[56] 'Permanence is thus a necessary condition under which alone appearances are determinable as things or objects in a possible experience.'[57]

The *fundamental meaning of the First Analogy* has thus been exhibited, while an indication has also been given as to how the cause–effect relation treated in the Second Analogy, as a relation of temporal succession, is grounded in the First Analogy. In discussing the Second Analogy we must always keep the First Analogy in mind, i.e. we must understand how the problem of causality is connected with the problem of substantiality in the broader sense of permanence. We have in this way gained an orientation concerning the mode of proof of the Analogies and their fundamental character.

Now in respect of the *connection between permanence and causality*, the following question arises. If freedom is itself a kind of causality, in what kind of permanence is it grounded? The permanence of the acting person. Can this permanence be conceived as the temporal endurance of that which is present (nature)? If not, is it enough simply to say that the acting person (i.e. reason) is not in time? Or does the personality of the person, the being-human of the human, possess its own temporality and its own 'permanence', which determines the historicality of human existence (the essence of history in the proper sense) in a manner fundamentally different to the determination of the process-character of present nature? Further, is the temporal character of what is free in its essence such that causality is primarily decisive for its existence? If not, it would be necessary to completely remove the problem of freedom from the domain of causality, and to positively define a new more primordial domain of problems.

Permanence has in every case an inner connection to time. That permanence belongs to everything experienceable is actually demanded by the essence of experience, for everything experientially accessible is determined in advance as inner-temporal. The encounter with the permanent is constantly verified within experience itself, a fact not without significance for the formation and orientation of the understanding of being. We recall that proper beings are those which are constantly accessible, constantly present. Things of this kind, but also the constantly associated experience of one's ownmost *self-being, self-hood and self-constancy*, press the idea of permanency, and thus also the idea of substance, into the realm of our most proximate *everyday comportment to beings*.

§ 19. The Second Analogy.
Occurrence, Temporal Succession and Causality

a) Event (Occurrence) and Temporal Succession.
Analysis of the Essence of Event and of the Possibility of Its Perception

A: 'Everything that happens, that is, begins to be, presupposes something upon which it follows according to a rule.'[58]

B: 'All alterations take place in conformity with the law of the connection of cause and effect.'[59]

From the A version it is clear that the problem is about relating an encountered event back to something determining. In B, Kant takes up the concept discussed at the end of the proof of the First Analogy. Indeed, the link between the Second and First Analogies is still closer in B, for prior to the actual proof Kant formulates the 'preceding principle' in a way which allows its relation to the Second Analogy to more clearly emerge.[60] For the Second Analogy deals with occurrences as such, i.e. succession, which succession announces itself proximally as *change* – beginning and ending. Since the First Analogy requires the prior representation of something *permanent* in all change, the principle can be formulated as follows: 'All change (succession) of appearances is merely alteration'.[61] Succession is just this, and *not* an absolute origination and passing away of substance, i.e. a rising up from nothing and disappearance into nothing. In more ontological terms, the relation of the First Analogy to the Second is already determined in the First Analogy from the essential determination of the 'genuine object' of experience (nature), and so also is the essence of possible *movement* provisionally determined: succession is *only* alteration. The transitions are successions and sequences of beings and non-beings such that these do not just change, but succeed one another from the ground of something permanent, constituting the event we perceive in experience. We are referred to something which is always already present prior to all conception. It is here that the finitude of experience announces itself.

If we now ask how experience of occurrences as such (i.e. processes) is possible, this question no longer concerns just the possibility of the being-present of that which is present as the genuine object of experience, but the fundamental character of being-present as a contexture [*als eines Zusammenhangs*]. So how is experience of processes possible? Only through a rule of pure temporal determination, which can be expressed as the 'principle of succession in time, in accordance with the law of causality'.[62] Accordingly, if it is shown that *causality alone makes possible experience of processes*, then it is proven that *causality belongs to the enablement of experience as such*, i.e. to its essential content. In this way the *essence of causality* is itself brought to light, which is precisely what we are here concerned to do.

It is a matter, therefore, not just of acquainting ourselves with the principle of causality, but of grounding this in its essence, which means determining its essence. As with the First Analogy, the law as such is familiar and constantly applied, but not truly grounded, not known in its essence. The discussion of this principle by the English empiricist David Hume became an important impetus for Kant's own philosophizing.

Again we ask: how is experience of occurrences as such, of objective processes, possible? We must first look more precisely at *what* is experienced. Experience involves the perception of 'events'. What is an 'event'? An event occurs when 'something actually happens'.[63] What actually happens 'begins to be'. This beginning to be (to be present) is not an origination from nothing, but rather, according to the First Analogy, mere 'alteration'.[64] This means, however, that there is some underlying *permanent* thing which merely changes *states*, such that any given state follows on from *a prior state*. What begins to be, 'formerly' was not. However, this not-having-been is not absolute, but in relation to what is already present it is the earlier, not something empty, but that from which the presently existing arose. Nothing ever arises from an *empty time*, always from a *fulfilled* time, i.e. in relation to something already present. We shall shortly encounter this problem of empty time again.

Thus *perceiving an event* means not just perceiving something as it occurs, but knowing in advance that this follows on from something earlier. This relation can be very indefinite and multifaceted, but since it belongs to the essence of an event as such, it is always co-perceived in perceiving an event. However, an event is not just something that actually happens. In each case it happens *at a particular time*. Accordingly, the full perception of an event involves not only the presupposition of something preceding it, but the presupposition of something retrospectively encountered in the present event. Perception of the given thus involves taking-in-advance according to a definite rule. *The given* always somehow announces itself as *following on* from something. What follows on can only show itself as such if the perception of the directly encountered object already looks back upon what went before, upon that which can be followed on *from*. What we encounter in perception is thus only experienceable as an event if it is already represented according to a rule referring back to something that conditions it, i.e. to something from which the event necessarily follows. The given announces itself as having arisen in fulfilled time, i.e. as following on, and what follows on is the conditioned. So our analysis of the essence of an event and its perception has brought forth what belongs to its inner possibility.

b) Excursus: on Essential Analysis and Analytic

When we speak of analysis here, this has nothing to do with a superficial concept of description, as if the event were described simply as a thing would be described. Analysis belongs here to *analytic* as understood by Kant, i.e. basically as *inquiry into origin, into the inner possibilities of what belongs to the essential content of experience*. This involves seeing the connections by means of a specific method of investigation and research, a method possessing its own specific lawfulness. *By demonstrating inner possibility, analytic is the grounding of essence, essential determination*, not just reading off the being-present of essential properties.

Among other things, the *analytic of the essence of event* and its possible manifestness in an experience has shown the necessity of a rule, which rule is nothing but the Second Analogy. For Kant, however, the proof of this proceeds differently, for his misunderstanding of transcendence leads him to see the primary given in the succession of apprehensions within a present subject. We must proceed therefore according to Kant's conception of the matter. To be noted is that setting the task of the analytic does not itself accomplish anything, for the main task is to determine just *what* is to be subjected to the analytic. When and how is this completely set forth? According to what we have indicated above, not in Kant.

We wish to briefly enter into this question, but without spinning out empty considerations over method. Knowledge of the matters themselves must precede everything else. On the other hand, reflection on how we gain access to these matters, on how we remove them from unhiddenness, is not irrelevant. Such reflection serves to reassure us in our method and must always be undertaken where we are truly on the way. In our introduction we occasionally halted to clarify our path, thus to increase the possibility of substantive understanding. If we now reflect anew on our path and method, this happens at a particular point, i.e. precisely where we arrive at the fundamental metaphysical context of Kant's problem of freedom: causality and its essence.

Our questioning is constantly directed to the *essence* of human freedom; thus already in the first lecture we briefly alluded to the characteristics of essential knowledge, the clarification of essence. We indicated three levels: 1. determination of what-being, 2. determination of the inner possibility of what-being, 3. determination of the ground of the inner possibility of what-being. The connections between these levels were not further discussed, nor will we go into them now. It should be remembered, however, that the first level provides a key to the next two levels, while the third level reflects back on the first two. The levels do not represent a fixed and final sequence of steps, but always a movement back and forth, a gradual transformation which does not permit any finality.

There is prevalent today a peculiar misrecognition of the nature of essential knowledge. According to this, philosophical knowledge of essences is final and ultimate, while scientific knowledge is only preliminary. But the real situation is the reverse. Scientific knowledge is always final, for it necessarily operates in a domain, not defined by itself, that condemns it to finality. Science itself can never get beyond this finality, except insofar as new borders are set for it by a new definition of the essential constitution of its domain. Science and science alone must according to its ownmost intention be oriented to finality. *Philosophy*, on the other hand, is constant *transformation* – not principally because of changes in its so-called results, but because philosophy itself, in its questioning and knowing, is a transforming. To see this one must free oneself from erroneous opinions which, today more than ever, have become entrenched. Indeed, there is a danger of essential knowledge being reduced to a technique of teaching and learning, to the research programme of a school, i.e. such that essential knowledge is reduced to an affair of scientific inquiry.

The misinterpretation of the knowledge of essence is partly due to its characterization as essential analysis and essential description. Analysis means resolution, dissection. But analysis of essence is not like resolving the meaning of a word into its elements. Nor is it the dissection of a concept into moments brought together in accidental fashion without reference to their context and necessity. As we understand it, analysis is defined from the task of an *analytic of essence*, some principal features of which were already recognized by Kant and followed in his works. Analytic is not resolution and splitting up into pieces, but the *loosening up of the contexture of the cognitive structure*, i.e. *return to its unity as the origin of structuration*.

This already means that analysis of essence is not description in the usual sense. It is not like enumerating the properties and moments of something present. For example, defining the essence of 'event' is not such a 'description' but rather a questioning back into the inner possibility of event, a return to the ground of the co-belonging of what belongs together. Since analysis of essence concerns contexts of possibility and enablement, *mere* description is out of the question. If we still employ the fatal word 'description' in regard to essential analysis, this is because, for vulgar understanding, description is the determining comportment that holds itself wholly to what presents itself. Stressing the 'descriptive' character of essential analysis simply expresses the necessity of holding to what essence gives as essence. But the question is: how does essence and essential contexture [*Wesenszusammenhang*] exhibit itself? We can say, negatively, that it does not do so in the manner of something present. Our analysis of the essence of 'event', departing from what we encounter in temporal succession, inquired into the essence of appearance. It is not at all possible to clarify the essence of event without already having this primordial contexture in view; we cannot take one step forward without bearing in mind the essence of appearance, finite knowledge, finitude and transcendence. What we thus have in view is nothing present like a bare scaffolding into which we build something. The illumination of essence requires transformation, suspension, release from the one-sided fixing of the valid and knowable. As the preliminary leap into the totality of existence, it is the fundamental deed of the creative activity of philosophy, proceeding from the earnestness of thrownness [*Grundakt der schöpferischen Handlung der Philosophie aus dem Ernst der Geworfenheit*].

What can we conclude for our questioning? Preparation and orientation differ in every case of description. The context of our question requires a going-after-the-whole as a going-to-our-roots, for the essence of 'event' does not lead us back just to some arbitrary place, but to freedom as the interrogative ground of the possibility of event. This kind of analytic is directed at the manner of *thinking the whole*. The primary and ultimate decisions of philosophical controversy are made in this domain. And it is precisely here that there reigns the greatest and simplest unanimity, which, however, to those who merely learn philosophy and undertake it like a business, seems like a confused mass of opinions, standpoints and doctrines.

c) Causality as Temporal Relation.
Causality in the Sense of Causation Is Running Ahead in Time as Determining Letting-Follow

What we are conscious of in perception and experience is at first just a multiplicity of apprehensions succeeding one another. There is indeed a succession here, a before and after, but this succession is itself 'altogether arbitrary'.[65] In perceiving an event, on the other hand, we experience something as actually occurring, something which follows on from something else. What follows on is not determined by our perception but itself determines perception. From the standpoint of Kant, the question now arises as to how the subjective succession of occurrences becomes objective, i.e. in what way it obtains a 'relation to an object'.[66] What gives to an initially arbitrary and reversible succession the unity of a binding and irreversible succession? How is the experience of the binding character of objective succession, the experience of succession in the perceiving of events, possible? In considering this question we must always bear in mind that it pertains not to (indeterminate) perceptions as such but specifically to the perception of events, *present* occurrences.

Kant sets off this kind of perception from others by considering two cases: the perception of a house situated directly in front of me, and the perception of a ship sailing past me down the river.[67] In both cases, what is initially given is a succession of apprehensions. But there is an essential difference. In perceiving the house, my perceptions can proceed from the roof to the basement or vice versa, likewise from left to right or vice versa. 'In the series of these perceptions there was thus no definite order specifying at what point I must begin in order to connect the manifold empirically.'[68] Why is the succession of apprehensions arbitrary *in this case*? Because the appearances themselves, i.e. the properties and determinations of the house, do not involve any succession. Since there is no succession in the object itself, no particular succession of apprehensions is necessary. The being-present of the house, in the unity of its properties, does not involve a succession. It does not have the character of an event.

Kant's intention here is obviously just to highlight the difference between the revealing of a present house and the revealing of a present event. It is true that the succession of apprehensions is not bound to an objective succession of appearances, for the house is not an event. In the case of the house nothing 'happens' – it just 'stands' or 'rests'. On the other hand, the succession of apprehensions still has a binding character. For if my apprehension of the house begins at the roof, I do not take this as the beginning or foundation of the house. In the construction of the house, the roof comes last, and in the completed house it remains at the top. In other words, the succession of apprehensions is arbitrary only against the background of the binding character of the ordered constellation of elements making up the present house.

What is the situation in the case of the ship sailing down the river? One might initially think that here the succession of apprehensions has the same character as in the case of the house. For I can also begin my apprehension of the ship at the stern or bow or masthead or bulwarks. To be sure, but in that case I am limiting myself just to the perception of the ship and its present properties, which is by no means the experience Kant has in mind. Rather, what Kant intends is perception of the ship sailing down the river, i.e. of the ship in its movement, of 'an appearance, which contains an occurrence'.[69] What is perceived is the occurrence in its being-present. The question is now whether the succession of apprehensions is also arbitrary in this case. How do I perceive this occurrence? Clearly, by following the ship through the individual points of its movement downstream. How we fix these points and distinguish them from one another is here a matter of secondary importance.

In experiencing the ship moving downstream, we perceive the ship at a point more downstream than where we perceived it a moment earlier. 'It is impossible that in the apprehension of this appearance the ship should first be perceived lower down in the stream and afterwards higher up. The order in which the perceptions succeed one another in apprehension is in this instance determined, and to this order apprehension is bound down.'[70] In the perception of events, the succession of apprehensions is not arbitrary but fixed. By what is it fixed then? One will say: by the objective temporal succession of the processes themselves. To be sure, apprehensions occur in temporal order, but by virtue of what is this order binding? Time is admittedly subjective, and like the apprehensions themselves belongs to the subject. Yet time in itself is absolute.

The proof thus begins in a way which corresponds to the First Analogy. Absolute time 'is not an object of perception',[71] i.e. time as such – insofar as the totality of positions of intra-temporal beings is determined in it – can never be immediately given. The temporal positions of appearances, thus the successions of processes, 'cannot be derived from the relation of appearances to absolute time'.[72] Although time is given, the totality of intra-temporal beings in their total temporal determination is not given. But if the temporal succession of apprehensions is to have a necessity, time itself, wherein every being encountered in experience is located, must indicate how the perception of something objective – the binding character of the succession of apprehensions – is possible. Can time itself do this? Does it involve a lawfulness in respect of succession? It does indeed, for I can arrive at a later time only by way of an earlier time. While I can think of something which comes later without attending to its character as later-than, I cannot conceive it precisely *as later* except by reference to what preceded it. The earlier time necessarily determines the subsequent time. The subsequent time *cannot be* without the earlier time. But does the reverse apply? *Time is an irreversible succession, i.e. it has a definite direction.* So if an intra-temporal occurrence is to be determined in experience, this determination must hold to the direction of succession. Each and every determination of a specific factual connection is governed by this law. Thus what Kant says with his principle of causality amounts to this: every appearance having the character of a temporal event, i.e. which begins to be at a particular time, presupposes something that runs ahead of it in time and determines it as that which follows on.[73] Succession as *procession of a process* is experienceable only as always already related to what went before as determining. Thus the rule: in whatever occurs we encounter the condition from which it follows necessarily. This 'principle of the causal relation in the sequence of appearances' is the ground of the possibility of experiencing the succession of appearances in their context as present.[74] It is thus clear that the causal law as Kant develops it here is not just something we apply to encountered events (in their successions) in order that we may orient ourselves. Instead, *the preliminary transcendental representation of this law is already the condition of the possibility of us at all encountering events as such*. Even when we encounter events within which we are unable to orient ourselves, i.e. events whose connection is indeterminate, we must still understand what we encounter in terms of causality.

Neither does the proof of the Second Analogy clearly exhibit the analogical character of the principle of causality, a circumstance reflecting the inner difficulty of the Kantian position. However, we can conclude from the whole context that, as with the First Analogy, a correspondence between two relations is involved. What is decisive in this case is likewise a relation, conceived by Kant as a fundamental relation, which belongs to the nature of understanding and is expressed as the logical relation of ground and consequence. Just as a consequence necessarily implies a ground, so what occurs later in temporal succession is a causal consequence of what occurs earlier. However, *the principle of causality cannot be logically derived from the logical principle of ground*. Instead, its necessity is grounded in the fact that it is a *necessary element of the whole that makes experience as such possible*. This experience is neither just logical determination of objects, nor just the apprehension of representations as subjective occurrences in time, but is a specific unity of temporally guided perception and thought which determines what is perceived.

So what is causality? It is a relation which does not just occur in time, but which *is determined in its relational character as a temporal relation*, as a mode of being-in-time. 'Succession' is a relation which represents in advance, and as such makes possible the experience of intra-temporal occurrences, i.e. succession is pre-represented *in* and *for* all experiential representation (perception and thought). This relation is temporal in the sense that *causality (as causation) means: running ahead in time as determining letting follow on* such that what runs ahead is itself an event that refers back to something earlier that determines it. As such a relation, causality necessarily involves the temporal character as this going before. Whatever follows on depends on something which *was*. Nothing ever follows on from something which absolutely was *not*. An occurrence is not 'an original act'.[75] However, we saw that this determination of essence is reached through *a determination of the inner possibility (essence) of experience as the finite human knowledge of that which is present in the contexture of its being-present.*

§ 20. Two Kinds of Causality: Natural Causality and the Causality of Freedom. The General Ontological Horizon of the Problem of Freedom in the Definition of Freedom as a Kind of Causality. The Connection between Causality in General and Being-Present as a Mode of Being

The definition of the essence of experience as finite knowledge gives the provisional definition of the essence of possible objects of experience. For example, in the context of the Third Analogy Kant says: 'In respect to the objects of experience, everything without which the experience of these objects would not itself be possible is necessary'.[76] Now that which, according to its essence, gets encountered in experience as present (in the contexture of its being-present) is what Kant calls *nature*. The clarification of the essence of causality from its necessary role in experience thus concerns the causality of nature. To nature there belongs a definite causation as essentially determined from the unity of the contexture of the being-present of that which is present. 'Natural necessity is the condition . . . according to which efficient causes are determined'.[77] Kant distinguishes 'natural causality' from 'causality through freedom'.[78] 'Freedom as a property of certain causes of appearances',[79] 'freedom as a kind of causality',[80] 'causality as freedom'.[81]

The expression 'causality out of freedom' indicates that freedom is oriented to causality. But the question at once arises as to what causality means in this context. Clearly, causality cannot here mean natural causality out of freedom, for as Kant says, these two kinds of causality are 'mutually incompatible concepts'.[82] So with the concept 'causality out of freedom', Kant can only mean causality in a general sense, which requires specification as either natural causality or the causality of freedom. Kant calls freedom 'a supersensible object of the category of causality', which 'practical reason . . . provides reality to'.[83]

a) The Orientation of Causality in General to the Causality of Nature. Toward the Problematic of Freedom as a Kind of Causality

What does causality mean generally, such that it pertains sometimes to nature and sometimes to freedom? How is the universal essence of causality to be defined? Obviously, in a way that gives both natural causality and the causality of freedom their respective proper entitlements. Either there is no more general and higher category of causality than these two, or if there is, the concept of causality is *fundamentally ambiguous*: mere category of nature on the one hand, and schematized category, schema, on the other hand. The following problems then arise. How can pure concepts of the understanding have a categorial function for a (supersensible) being? What is the unschematic presentation and fulfilment here, or why is this not necessary here? Did Kant anywhere carry through this definition of the universal essence of causality? If not, does he in the end employ a *universal* concept of causality derived primarily from natural necessity? If so, with what justification? If justification is lacking, why does he proceed in this way? What influence has Kant's approach to the problem of causality and the categories exerted on the problem of freedom as such? These questions follow on from one another. This questionability pertains not only to Kant's treatment of the problem, but leads to a *question of fundamental significance*. This alone is crucial for our substantive unfolding of the problem of freedom.

If the definition of causality in general is oriented to the causality of nature, where nature means the being-present of that which is present (whether physical, psychical, or whatever else), then the way of being of causation becomes characterized as *being-present*. If the causality of freedom is defined in terms of this universal causation, then freedom (as *being*-free) itself takes on the fundamental chararacteristic of being-present. But freedom is the fundamental condition of the possibility of the acting person, in the sense of ethical action. Thus the existence of man, precisely through the characterization of freedom as causality (albeit as one kind thereof) is *conceived basically as being-present*. This turns freedom into its complete opposite.

Now one could say that Kant, by his emphasis on the *difference* between natural causality and the causality of freedom, obviously wants to stress the *specific character* of the ethical person as opposed to the thing of nature. This is indeed the case. But this intention does not in any way solve the problem. In fact, it does not even engage with the problem, which concerns the fact that the way of being of man cannot be primarily defined as being-present. The way of being of man remains at least undetermined and underdetermined, which in this context, where something fundamental is at stake, is a grave deficiency not to be remedied by subsequent external supplementation. The reason Kant does not arrive at the required determination is that, despite everything, he treats the ontological problem at the level of the problem of present beings. This in turn is because he does not recognize and develop the universal problem of being. So Kant, already in his treatment of freedom as causality, lacks the metaphysical ground for the problem of freedom.

b) First Examination of Causality's Orientation to the Mode of Being of Being-Present-in-Succession as the Distinctive Temporal Mode of Causality and Illustrated by the Simultaneity of Cause and Effect

We must first clarify Kant's standpoint in such a way that we can see the *fundamental metaphysical problem underlying his interpretation of freedom as a kind of causality*. We have seen that Kant is inclined to treat natural causality as causality itself, thus to define the causality of freedom from the ground of natural causality. In other words, he does not treat the causality of freedom primordially and in its own terms. 'I soon see that, since I cannot think without a category, I must first seek out the category in reason's idea of freedom. This is the category of causality.'[84] The 'concept of causality always contains a relation to a law which determines the existence of the many in their relation to one another'.[85]

Kant's orientation of causation to being-present, which he equates with actuality and existence as such, means that *he sees freedom and being-free within the horizon of being-present*. Since he *fails to pose the question concerning the particular way of being of beings which are free*, he does not unfold the metaphysical problem of freedom in a primordial manner. If this is so, and if it is also true that Kant takes freedom as primary and ultimate in philosophy ('The concept of freedom, insofar as its reality is proved by an apodictic law of practical reason, is the *keystone* of the whole architecture of the system of pure reason and even of speculative reason'[86]), then he must have reasons for letting the question of the essence of human free-dom finish with the positing of freedom as the self-legislation of practical reason.

So that we may see what is crucial here, namely the *connection between natural causality (interpreted as causality itself) and being-present as a mode of being*, we wish to consider briefly something Kant adds to his discussions of his proof of the Second Analogy. This will provide an opportunity for more explicitly defining a number of basic concepts important for what follows.

Kant begins with an objection to his own definition of causality as the determining letting-follow-on by something temporally prior. According to this definition, which takes the causal principle as a principle of temporal succession, the cause is prior and the effect is subsequent. It turns out, however, that 'the principle of the causal relation among appearances' is not limited to the serial succession of appearances, but also pertains to their simultaneity, i.e. cause and effect can be simultaneous.[87] Thus temporal succession cannot be the unique and infallible empirical criterion for a cause–effect relation. Since Kant holds exclusively to the concept of causality as temporal succession, how does he resolve this difficulty?

First an example of the simultaneity of cause and effect. 'A room is warm while the outer air is cool. I look around for the cause, and find a heated stove. Now the stove, as cause, is simultaneous with its effect, the heat of the room. Here there is no serial succession in time between cause and effect. They are simultaneous, and yet the law is valid.'[88] Kant com-ments that in fact 'the great majority' of natural causes are simultaneous with their effects, and that the before–after relation only indicates that 'the cause cannot achieve its complete effect in one moment'.[89] An effect must always be simultaneous with the causation of its cause. If the caus-ation of the cause were to cease to be immediately prior to the effect, there could be no effect at all. Only insofar as causes continue to exist in their causation can there be any effects. The two are necessarily simultaneous.

Nevertheless, this necessary simultaneity does not contravene the essential role of temporal succession in the causal relation. On the contrary, it is only by bringing this simultaneity to light that we can understand what is properly intended by temporal succession. The latter necessarily intersects with the duration of the presence of cause and effect. However small the span of time between cause and effect – it might be vanishingly small, i.e. they might be simultaneous – the relationship between the one as cause and the other as effect continues to hold. For this relationship, which is at all times determinable, refers to the connection between the one as prior and the other as subsequent, more precisely to the *irreversibility of their serial order*. In this context, therefore, succession does not mean just one thing after another in order of their appearance and disappearance, but a unidirectional irreversible succession. What is crucial to 'succession' as a mode of time is not the duration and speed of a sequence of events, but the *uniquely directed order in the presence* of the one and the other. In this sense, therefore, the cause, even when simultaneous with the effect, is incontrovertibly prior, and cannot become subsequent to the effect.[90] Succession pertains to the direction of a sequence, not to its character as process. But the direction of a sequence does not exclude the simultaneous presence of cause and effect. Kant does not mean that the cause must disappear when the effect occurs. In the sense distinctive to causality, succession as a mode of time is quite compatible with simultaneity of cause and effect.

This more precise determination of the character of succession as order and sequential direction allows us to see the connection between cause and effect more clearly. The connection pertains to present things in their so-being, other-being, and not-being. Occurrences can now be defined not as isolated events but as related back to what precedes them as causes. By the same token, causation is a relation specifically directed to that which it lets follow on.

c) Second Examination of Causality's Orientation to the Mode of Being of Being-Present in Terms of the Concept of Action.
Action as the Succession-Concept in the Connection between Cause and Effect

This *conception of causality* leads to a concept of importance for the problem of occurrences in general, and of occurrences pertaining to free beings in particular: the concept of *action*. We often make use of the Greek word for this, i.e. πρᾶξις (πράττειν, to carry something out), whereby we mean 'the practical' in two senses. First the 'practical man' who possesses abilities of a certain kind and knows how to apply them at the right moment. Secondly praxis and action in the specific sense of *ethical action*, i.e. moral-practical comportment. Kant includes this latter meaning in his concept of the practical. 'By the practical, I mean everything that is possible through freedom.'[91] 'Plato found the chief instances of his ideas in the field of the practical, that is, in what rests upon freedom.'[92]

So action is related essentially to freedom. But this is not quite the case for Kant, i.e. praxis and action do not altogether coincide. For Kant, 'action' is much more the expression for *effecting in general*. Action by no means primarily pertains to ethical comportment and moral/unmoral activity, nor just to rational activity, nor just to mental activity. It refers also to the occurrences of animate and especially inanimate nature. This has been frequently overlooked in the interpretation of Kant, so that action is taken merely in the ethical sense. This is not just a point about Kant's use of language but has implications of a fundamental nature. If action has the general meaning of effecting (bringing about), and pertains primarily to natural occurrences, then the concept of free moral action, or as Kant likes to say, of 'voluntary' action, is ontologically oriented, precisely *as* action, to being in the sense of being-present. In other words, it is oriented to just that kind of being which does not apply to an ethically acting being, the human being. This means that the existence of man – irrespective of whether a clear distinction is made between the factually existing moral person and the things of nature – remains subject to a fundamentally erroneous ontological definition, or at least to a fateful indefiniteness. For Kant, action means the same as effecting, as in the Latin *agere – effectus*. It is a broader concept than doing – *facere* – which is a particular kind of action, a particular kind of effecting and *effectus*: the work – *opus*.[93]

Every doing is an action, but not every action is a doing. 'Doing' in the sense of constructing, making, finishing, is itself distinguished from 'act' in the sense of ethical action, 'deed'. *For Kant, there is action also where no work is produced* – in *nature*. Accordingly, Kant employs the expression and concept of 'natural action'.[94] In the *Prolegomena* he speaks of the constant action of matter,[95] further claiming that every natural cause 'must have begun to act'.[96] In the Second Analogy of the *Critique of Pure Reason* the concept of action is more precisely defined: 'Action signifies the relation of the subject of causality to its effect'.[97] Action is not simply a happening, but is a process that itself contains an event, which event belongs to the occurrence.[98] However, 'subject' here does not mean 'I', 'self' or 'person', but rather that which is already present as underlying, as the cause. 'Subject' has just as broad a meaning here as 'action'. Since every event is conditioned and thus involves an effected occurrence, every event contains an action. Thus 'action' and 'force', as Kant says in the Foreword to the *Prolegomena*, are 'concepts of succession . . . of the connection of cause and effect'.[99]

The implications of a correct understanding of the Kantian concept of action for the problem of freedom are now plain to see. For when Kant refers to a 'free act' as an 'originary action',[100] this forces it within the horizon of the *general* concept of cause and effect as determined primarily through natural causality. The action of matter is not an original effecting. The action of the ethical person is an original effecting, i.e. it does not arise from some other origin but is itself an 'origin'. The *general concept of causality thus enters into the definition of freedom*. Thus we grasp ever more clearly the *general ontological horizon in which Kant situates the problem of freedom, just insofar as freedom is a kind of causality*.

This discussion of the concept of action provides us with a further and final characterization of the ontological horizon of the Kantian problem of freedom. In our transition from the First to the Second Analogy, we saw how Kant explicated the essence of possible movement *as alteration* on the basis of *permanence*. At the end of Kant's discussion of the Second Analogy, he defines the essence of alteration more precisely, by showing that the possibility of alteration is grounded in the *continuity* of the causality of action. This new moment was co-intended all along, but not emphasized as such. The law of the continuity of all alteration is grounded in the essence of time (intra-temporality), i.e. in the fact that time does not consist of (ever so small) parts. Every transition from one state to another, which states might exist in two instants, still happens in a time between the instants and thus belongs to the *entire time of alteration*. For this reason every cause of an alteration testifies to its causation during the whole time of the alteration. In other words, the action of matter is continuous. There is no such thing as a sudden occurrence which breaks out from prior nothingness. Here too time is the guideline for the definition of continuity, and indeed as the time of nature, as the time of the co-belonging of that which is present.

An adequate account of Kant's conception of the essence of causality has now been given. It gives the *ontological determinations of the contexture of the being-present of that which occurs as present*. The character of natural occurrences as movement is alteration, i.e. the occurrences occur on the basis of the permanent and in the mode of continuous action. The concepts of action and continuity are read off primarily from the being-present of corporeal things. One can consult Kant's own remark on the priority of this domain of beings in his intuitive presentation of the categories. Where he discusses causality in general, the *mode of being* he presupposes is that of *nature*. At the same time he continues to emphasize that freedom is a kind of causality. We have already verified this conception of Kant. What is thus far missing?

§ 21. The Systematic Site of Freedom according to Kant

a) The Systematic Site as Substantive Contexture Defining the Direction and Scope of Questioning

What has thus far not been shown is *where* Kant situates freedom, i.e. which substantive contextures of problems and motives lead Kant to the problem of freedom, and in what way this occurs. We obviously require a criterion here, for only thus can we assess how causality (the location of which in Kant's problem we have identified) relates to freedom. But this is not the only and not the properly crucial reason for our need to clarify *the site of the problem of freedom in Kant's system*. The really fundamental reason is that we ourselves *clarified the problem of freedom by situating it within the perspective of the fundamental problems of metaphysics*. We must now ask how our own locating of the problem of freedom relates to that of Kant. We do not pose this question with a view to historical comparison. Rather, from our differences with Kant, which always at the same time signify agreement of a sort, we wish to clarify the specificity of our own problematic. This will allow us to show how the positive side of the Kantian problem can be appropriated, albeit with modifications.

When we speak here of the site of freedom in Kant's system, this should not be taken in an external and rigid sense, as if the system were a fixed structure with compartments for each and every problem and concept. To be sure, Kant had a strong tendency to architectonic, guided in fact by traditional conceptual schemata. But while this greatly facilitated his inquiry and presentation it also led to many substantive issues and phenomena becoming hidden or distorted. *The systematic site of a problem is that substantive contexture which is dictated by the direction and scope of questioning*. This is simply the entire substantive contexture in the philosophical problematic, which, in accordance with how it is in each case seen and approached, defines the direction and scope of a problem. Possessing a system in the external sense, or trying to classify and arrange purportedly frozen knowledge, is very different from philosophizing in a 'systematic' way. By the same token, philosophy does not become substantively rooted in the force of its problems when one merely – in the manner of Kierkegaard's critique of Hegel – denounces the idea of system.

We saw that the Kantian problem of causality is to be located primarily within the problem of the possibility of experience, i.e. within the problem of finite human knowledge of present beings themselves. So where does Kant situate freedom, i.e. from what substantive contexture does the problem of freedom emerge? Does the domain of this problem have a necessary connection with the possibility of experience? Is it the same or completely different?

To understand and engage with the Kantian problem of freedom, it is of crucial importance to see two things. First, that Kant is led to the problem of freedom from two utterly different contextures of problems. Secondly, that owing to the universal ground from which Kant defines the problematic of philosophy as such, these two ways to freedom are equally necessary for him. These two problems belong together within the totality of metaphysical problems. It is now a matter of exhibiting them. We do not do this just to obtain a broader knowledge of the Kantian philosophy, but in order to lay out the perspective of philo-sophical questioning in a richer and more primordial manner. Of course, in this area especially, we must dispense with any complete thematic interpretation and proceed instead according to rough guidelines. However, the inner deficiencies of the following presentation have still another cause, which we cannot at the present time remove. Today, the problem of metaphysics is a long way from achieving the transparency and primordiality required to engage with the Kantian problematic in a positive and critical manner. For this is never a matter of a so-called cor-rect interpretation of Kant. Kant's two ways to freedom converge in the problem of metaphysics as such. But it is precisely this connection which remains problematic for Kant himself, so much so that he no longer sees this problem, and still less does he possess the means for awakening it. The reason for this is that also in the case of Kant the traditional leading question of metaphysics – what are beings? – is not developed into the fundamental question: what is being? The latter is also the question concerning the primordial possibility and necessity of the manifestness of being.

b) Kant's Two Ways to Freedom and the Traditional Problematic of Metaphysics. The Site of the Question of Freedom in the Problem of the Possibility of Experience as the Question Concerning the Possibility of Genuine Metaphysics

We find in Kant a radical redefinition of the essence of ontology, a redefinition without which (for example) Hegel's ontology would not have been possible. And yet this redefinition is on the whole a renewal of the Greek approach to the question of being. From the perspective of this fundamental question of philosophy, therefore, it is quite wrong to set Kant over against the Greeks (especially Aristotle) in the manner of nineteenth-century Neo-Kantianism. What the Neo-Kantians saw in Kant was a particular theory of knowledge, to which they opposed a purportedly different theory. This opposition was then enthusiastically taken up by Neo-Scholasticism, such that also from this side access to Greek thought became obstructed.

Kant's *two ways* to the problem of freedom are as follows. The first proceeds by way of the context within which the problem of causality was discussed: the *possibility of experience as finite knowledge of beings*. What led Kant to this question? Nothing less than the *question of the possibility of traditional metaphysics*. As traditionally understood, metaphysics means knowledge of supersensible beings, i.e. knowledge of those beings which lie out beyond that which is experientially accessible. Traditional metaphysics, to which Kant remains oriented in his *Critique*, defines these supersensible beings under the three headings 'soul', 'world', 'God'. Soul understood in respect of what especially concerns man, i.e. its simplicity, indestructibility and immortality. World as the totality of present nature, and God as the ground and author of all beings. Soul (ψυχή) is the object of psychology, world (totality of nature – κόσμος) is the object of cosmology, God (θεός) is the object of theology.

The metaphysical questions concerning soul, world, and God aim to define the *essence* of these, not just their empirically contingent characteristics. For traditional metaphysics, however, non-empirical knowledge is rational knowledge, i.e. knowledge proceeding from pure reason alone. Pure thought proceeds from concepts alone, independently of experience. Understood in this sense, the three above-mentioned disciplines together make up *genuine* metaphysics: rational psychology, rational cosmology, rational theology.

To inquire into the essence of metaphysics means to determine its inner possibility, thus marking it off against what does not properly belong to it, drawing boundaries and limits – κρίνειν. Criticism in the Kantian sense means determining the essence of metaphysics, i.e. determining the capacity of pure reason for a total knowledge of beings. Now it was Kant's innermost conviction that metaphysics, as questioning in the three indicated directions, is a 'natural disposition'[101] of man, such that meta-physical questions 'arise from the nature of universal human reason'.[102] Man's 'pure reason' 'projects' these questions 'which it is impelled by its own need to answer as best it can'.[103] So the problems arise as to whether, and in what degree, these questions are answerable, how they belong to the ground of human nature, why they are asked, and what kind of need they respond to. In what way are these questions grounded in universal human nature? How does Kant justify his assertion? He does so simply by alluding to human nature itself. However uncomfortable this circum-stance may be for earlier and contemporary interpretation of Kant, no sleight of hand can alter it or diminish its significance: Kant sees the grounding of metaphysics precisely as a return to human nature. The method of Kant's grounding, as well as its validity, thus ultimately depends on the primordiality, appropriateness, and completeness of his interpretation of man in relation to the foundation of metaphysics.

The requisite question concerning man can be neither psychological nor epistemological, nor can it be a phenomenology of consciousness and experience, nor anthropology. The specific character of this interpretation of man can be adequately defined only on the basis of a prior and simultaneous radical clarification of the task it serves: the task of meta-physics itself. One cannot eagerly busy oneself with epistemology or the phenomenology of consciousness or anthropology, and then later, from time to time, concern oneself with metaphysics. Despite the assurance with which Kant carries out his 'critique' in the narrower sense, the ground of his foundation of metaphysics remains uncertain and indefin-ite. In any case – and this is now the crucial matter – Kant must ground the three directions and domains of questioning by returning to human nature. In other words, he does not interpret human nature radically from itself, but already sees it from the perspective of the three indicated domains which have been made self-evident to him by the tradition. Only in this way does he turn to human nature.

What is involved here is a particular approach to man, namely that of Christianity. This is not in any way a philosophically necessary approach, but on the other hand it does not follow that (as is commonly believed nowadays) the essence of man can be left undefined. The problem of man poses difficulties which are still hardly beginning to dawn on us. Kant says that human nature, as determined through reason, 'projects' the questions concerning God, world, and soul. What is specific about these questions? What does reason have 'in mind' with these questions? The question of the immortality of the soul represents the soul in the completeness of its unity, simplicity, and indestructibility, thus in the totality of its being and essence. In asking about the world, reason is concerned with the totality of present beings in its beginning and end. The question of God as author of the world brings before us the ultimate totality of beings. In this representation of the totality, reason looks to the unity and completeness of what is representable and of that toward which man comports himself. For Kant, representations of the general nature (what-ness) of things are *concepts*. However, concepts which represent the totality belong specifically to reason, which is the faculty or power of representing something in its origin and outcome, i.e. in its 'principles'. Reason unifies these principles through concepts of reason, or as Kant calls them, 'ideas'. According to Kant, the idea is 'the concept provided by reason – of the form of the whole – insofar as the concept determines *a priori* not only the scope of its manifold content, but also the positions which the parts occupy relatively to one another'.[104] The ideas 'contain a certain completeness to which no possible empirical knowledge ever attains. In them reason aims only at a systematic unity, to which it seeks to approximate the unity that is empirically possible, without ever completely reaching it.'[105]

With the three traditional areas of metaphysical questioning in mind, Kant attempts to ground, from the nature of man, three basic directions of representation by ideas. Every idea has the general characteristic of representing something. Representation always relates to something. The manifold of all possible relations of representations can be reduced to three basic kinds: 'The relations which are to be found in all our representations are (1) relation to the subject; (2) relation to objects, either as appearances or as objects of thought in general'.[106] Accordingly, ideas can be created: (1) in respect of the representation of the subject, (2) in respect of the representation of the manifold of objects in appearance, (3) in respect of the representation of all things whatsoever. From these three basic kinds of possible re-presenting there emerge three classes of ideas as representations of something in regard to its totality. The *first* uncovers the unconditioned totality and unity of the subject, the *second* uncovers the unity and totality of the manifold of appearances (which we

143

now know to be a succession of conditions and conditioned), the *third* uncovers the absolute unity of the condition of all objects of thought whatsoever. In immediate connection with this derivation of three possible kinds of representation by ideas Kant mentions the three traditional disciplines of *metaphysica specialis*.

§ 22. Causality through Freedom. Freedom as Cosmological Idea

a) The Problem of Freedom as Originating from the Problem of World. Freedom as a Distinctive Mode of Natural Causality

We said that *the first way to the question of freedom is by way of the problem of the possibility of experience as the question of the possibility of metaphysics*. This latter, as the genuine and proper question, encompasses the three indicated disciplines. The *problem of freedom* must therefore *belong* in one of these disciplines. Which discipline (class of ideas) is this?

We are acquainted with freedom as the basic condition and character of the ethically acting person, thus of the genuine subject in the subjectivity and I-ness of man. It is rational psychology which concerns itself with the 'thinking subject' as represented by ideas. Freedom is properly speaking freedom of the will as a faculty of the soul. Since freedom is a *'psychological concept'*, the idea of freedom will be encountered in the *psychologia rationalis*. Yet we seek for it there in vain. One might thus be tempted to think that ultimately man is *not genuinely free* at all, that in the end freedom belongs *exclusively to the highest* essence of all essence, i.e. God. Freedom would then be a *theological* idea belonging in the *theologia rationalis*. But here also we seek for it in vain. Instead, freedom belongs where we least expect it: it is a *cosmological* idea. The problem of freedom *arises in the context of the problem of world*, understanding 'world' in Kant's sense as the 'totality of appearances' (nature and cosmos), thus the totality of present beings as accessible to finite human knowledge.

It is crucially important to see where the idea of freedom is situated within genuine metaphysics. Thus Kant says, in a note to the third section of Book One of the Transcendental Dialectic ('System of Transcendental Ideas'): 'Metaphysics has as the proper object of its inquiries three ideas only: *God, freedom, and immortality*'.[107] It is clear, therefore, not only that Kant understands the metaphysical problem of freedom as a cosmological problem, but that the idea of freedom itself has priority vis-à-vis the other cosmological ideas.

We must now show more precisely how the *problem of freedom arises from and as the problem of world*. One thing may be assumed in advance: if freedom belongs in the context of the problem of world, if world is the totality of appearances in their succession, and if the experientially accessible unity of appearances is determined by natural causality, then *freedom is forced into close connection with natural causality*. This is so even if *freedom is understood as a specific species of causality distinct from natural causality*. For when something is defined by distinguishing it from something else, the latter itself plays a determinative role in the definition. In brief, we can say that freedom is a *distinctive mode of natural causality*. If this were not so, there would be no possibility of conceiving it as a cosmological idea, i.e. as an idea essentially related to the totality of nature.

Ideas are concepts of pure reason, i.e. they are representations governed by the fundamental principle of reason in its capacity as 'the principle of unconditioned unity'.[108] Reason applies this principle in each of the three areas of representation. In the case of the representation of objects as appearances, reason demands the representation of the absolute totality of the synthesis of appearances, i.e. the representation of the unconditioned completeness of the unity of that which is present. When we consider reason in this representational activity, 'we are presented with a new phenomenon of human reason'. This is a natural 'conflict or antinomy of pure reason',[109] a rift in what pure reason as such must necessarily posit. So it is precisely when the principle of reason manifests itself and exhibits its character as principle that 'there emerge various forms of opposition and dissension'.[110]

In view of these statements by Kant, it is just blindness and lack of understanding to enthuse over a pure absolute reason, overlooking the fact that what Kant's concept of reason announces is precisely the deepest finitude of man, i.e. reason is not at all, as it is taken to be by superficial and external interpretations, a mark of infinity. In its representing (i.e. in its concepts) reason is only *seemingly* superior to the understanding as the genuine faculty of concepts. The situation is really the other way around: the representing of reason is an illegitimate transgression of the essential finitude of understanding, thus a *finitization*, 'dissension',[111] as in other cases illegitimate representing signifies transgression of limits and immoderation, thus is a mark of finitude. Nor does this transgression become a mark of infinity by being *necessary to human nature as such*. Instead, this only proves that finitude is essential to man rather than being something contingent or arbitrary which just happens to attach to him.

Kant emphasizes that it is only *from the understanding* that pure transcendental concepts can arise: 'Reason does not really generate any concept. The most it can do is to free a *concept of understanding* from the unavoidable limitations of possible experience, and so to endeavour to extend it beyond the limits of the empirical, though still, indeed, in terms of its relation to the empirical'.[112] Seeking to overcome limits, however, is a long way from *overcoming finitude*. On the contrary, genuine finitude can exist only if human knowledge is essentially subject to these limits, and if the attempt to transgress them results in the breakdown of reason! We conclude not only that pure reason is finite, but that the concepts of reason (the ideas) do not immediately relate to accessible beings as such. Rather, in accordance with their origin, the concepts of reason immediately relate only to the understanding, 'solely in order to prescribe to the understanding its direction towards a certain unity'.[113] In the domain of experience (knowledge of objects as appearances) the employment of the understanding is announced in the principles of experience. To these principles there belong the Analogies, as the laws of the unity of the contexture (synthesis) of the manifold of appearances.

b) The Idea of Freedom as 'Transcendental Concept of Nature': Absolute Natural Causality

What does it mean for reason to apply its 'principle of unconditioned unity'[114] to the determinations of the understanding? What appears in appearance is the multiplicity of that which is present in the contexture of its being-present. The latter involves occurrences, alteration, the succession of events, i.e. a specifically directed contexture of conditions and conditioned. In its demand for absolute totality, reason insists on going back from one condition to another until it arrives at *the unconditioned*. Thus the principle of reason is 'that *if the conditioned is given, the entire sum of conditions, and consequently the absolutely unconditioned* (through which alone the conditioned has been possible) *is also given*'.[115] When reason represents the completeness of the sequence of conditions, it proceeds backward in the direction of conditions and not forward in the direction of consequences, 'because for the complete comprehension of what is given in appearance we need consider only the *grounds*, not the *consequences*'.[116]

Incidentally, while this applies to the processes of corporeal *nature*, it does not apply in *history*, for a historical occurrence is understood essentially from its consequences. The consequences of a historical event cannot be understood merely as following on in time. This is because the historical past is not defined through its position in the bygone, but through its future. What is here determinative is not just anything occurring subsequent to a historical event, but *the future in its possibility*. Thus the history of the present is a contradiction in terms. Kant's lack of attention to (and at bottom, his ignorance of) this differently constituted dimension of beings is indirect evidence for his taking the domain of appearances simply as the *domain of present things*, i.e. nature in the broad sense.

'The cosmological ideas deal, therefore, with the totality of the regressive synthesis proceeding *in antecedentia*, not *in consequentia*.'[117] During our discussion of the principle of causality we saw that, in its dynamical meaning, this relates to events, i.e. the sequential occurrence of appearances. Thus what reason refers to here is precisely the unity and completeness of this sequence. The contexture of the sequence (the relation of the conditioned to the condition) is defined by the conditioned having been caused, i.e. by the causation of the conditions, through the causality which allows a sequence of appearances to follow on. A representation of the unconditioned unity of this sequence, of the causal relationship, will ascend to something unconditioned, thus representing 'the absolute completeness in the origination of an appearance'.[118] The representation by reason of an *unconditioned causality* is the representation of a causation which returns not just to something prior as its own particular cause, but to the absolute beginning of the sequence. This is a representation of 'an originary action',[119] of an action effective from itself, a *free* action. The concept of reason of this unconditioned causality, which seeks to represent the given and givable unity of appearances in its completeness, is related to something which *a priori* makes possible the totality of appearances, i.e. something transcendental. It is a representation of freedom in the *transcendental* sense: the *idea of transcendental freedom*. *Freedom as a kind of causality* is related to the *possible totality of sequences of appearances in general*. The idea of freedom is the representation of something dynamical, something unconditioned and pertaining to the completeness of the contexture of the being-present of appearances, i.e. a *'transcendental concept of nature'*.[120]

We have thus traversed, albeit somewhat roughly, Kant's first way to freedom. This way reflects neither historical influences on Kant nor his private considerations, but rather *the substantive connection between the idea of freedom and the problem of the possibility of finite knowledge*. At the same time, this way to freedom shows how, and as what, freedom is posited. Freedom is nothing other than *absolute natural causality*, or as Kant himself fittingly says, it is a concept of nature that transcends all possible experience.[121] Freedom does not thereby lose the character of a concept of nature, but retains this, precisely as broadened out and raised up to the unconditioned.

§ 23. The Two Kinds of Causality and the Antithetic of Pure Reason in the Third Antinomy

The concept that is properly represented in the idea of transcendental freedom, i.e. the concept of causality, is produced by the understanding and belongs to the essential determinations of nature as such. What the representing of reason accomplishes is only a broadening out to the unconditioned. This broadening out, however, brings to light *an antagonism within reason itself*. The cosmological idea of the absolute completeness of the origin of an appearance,[122] when unfolded in the form of propositions, produces a conflict between doctrine and counter-doctrine, leading to a concept which Kant grasps as transcendental freedom. The conflicting doctrines pertain not just to any arbitrary questions, but to questions 'which human reason must necessarily encounter in its progress'.[123] Each of the conflicting doctrines involves 'a natural and unavoidable illusion'. Each, even after close examination, seems to bear the clear stamp of truth. Since they are opposed to one another substantively, while making equally justified claims to truth, they stand in permanent and necessary antagonism. It is the aim of the *transcendental antithetic* to exhibit this antagonism as essential to human reason itself. Kant calls these conflicting doctrines 'pseudo-rational';[124] they can be neither confirmed nor refuted by experience. Pure human reason remains 'unavoidably subject' to their antagonism.[125] Each doctrine can be supported on grounds equally valid and necessary to those which support its opposite.[126]

The inner dissension of pure reason leading to the transcendental idea of freedom is treated by Kant under the heading of 'the Third Antinomy'

This is the antinomy in reason's concept of the unconditioned totality of the origin of an appearance. It thus concerns the *representation of the completeness of all appearances in respect of their origin*, i.e. in respect of their causal conditionedness. This kind of representation leads to the following two statements:[127]

1. 'Causality in accordance with laws of nature is not the only causality from which the appearances in the world can one and all be derived. To explain these appearances it is necessary to assume that there is also another causality, that of freedom.'
2. 'There is no freedom; everything in the world takes place solely in accordance with laws of nature.'

The second statement, which Kant calls the 'Antithesis', contradicts the first, which he calls the 'Thesis'. Kant provides proofs for each of the two statements, proofs which are meant to show that both are equally true and equally grounded in pure reason. Following the proofs, Kant makes 'Observations' on the Thesis and Antithesis respectively. The *proofs* are *indirect*, i.e. they begin by assuming the opposite of what is maintained in the statement under consideration.

a) The Thesis of the Third Antinomy.
The Possibility of Causality through Freedom (Transcendental Freedom)
Alongside the Causality of Nature in the Explanation of the Appearances of the World as Universal Ontological Problem

If there is no other kind of causality besides natural causality, then everything that occurs presupposes a prior state from which it inevitably follows according to a law. Now this *prior* state must itself be something that arose in time and thus previously *was not*. For otherwise, i.e. if this prior state had always been, its consequences would also have always been. The causation of an occurrence is always itself something occurring and as such refers back to something still earlier. Every beginning is 'only relative'[128] to what preceded it. There is thus *no first beginning* in the series of causes.

'But the law of nature is just this, that nothing takes place without a cause sufficiently determined *a priori*.'[129] But just this law of natural causality leads to no first beginning, to no sufficiently determining cause. The law of causality contradicts itself in what it demands and implies.

149

Thus, in respect of the necessary representation of the completeness of the origin of appearances, natural causality cannot be the only causality. It is necessary to assume another kind of causality whose causation is such that the cause is no longer determined by anything prior. If it is *itself* to initiate a sequence of appearances governed by natural laws, the causation of the cause must owe its existence to itself. Such causation, such absolute origination from itself, is *absolute spontaneity*, i.e. the *transcendental freedom* which goes beyond the series of natural causes. The sequence of appearances can never be complete without this.

In his 'Observation' on the Thesis, Kant gives a more precise characterization of the concept of freedom, at the same time analysing what the proof of the Thesis implies for the being of the world, and indicating how he understands the 'first beginning' – through freedom – of a determinate sequence.

To be sure, the concept of transcendental freedom 'does not by any means constitute the whole content of the psychological concept of that name, which is mainly empirical'.[130] What is the meaning of this distinction between the *transcendental* and the *psychological* concept of freedom? In the psychological concept there is represented a soul, a faculty of the soul, namely will. The latter is a specific being which we do not encounter in the mere representation of a present being; it must, instead, be *given to us*. On the other hand, the transcendental concept of freedom arises in connection with the question of the completeness of appearances (present beings in general) irrespective of their content. Transcendental freedom is a *universal* ontological concept, psychological freedom a *regional* one. However, the universal ontological concept is as such necessarily implicated in the regional concept, and constitutes the genuine difficulty in the psychological concept of freedom. Thus Kant says: 'What has always so greatly embarrassed speculative reason in dealing with the question of freedom of the will, is its strictly *transcendental* aspect. The problem, properly viewed, is solely this: whether we must admit a power of *spontaneously* beginning a series of successive things or states.'[131] In brief, the *problem of freedom*, and of the freedom of the will in particular, is really a *universal ontological problem within the ontology of the being-present of that which is present*, and does not relate specifically to will-governed or spiritual being. It is by no means the case that Kant posits being-free as characteristic of something essentially spiritual, and then treats this within the horizon of being-present. Instead, the being-present of that which is present, itself and as such, leads to the problem of *'free action'*. We shall come back to this all-important thesis of Kant.

We can already see that with the fundamental transformation of the ontological problem the problem of freedom also changes. For Kant, the only problem is whether to accept absolute spontaneity within, and in relation to, the being of that which is present in its totality (world). How such a causality is possible can no more be grasped than can the possibility of natural causality. For also in this latter case we must be content to establish *that* it is necessary as the condition of the possibility of experience and its objects.

In his 'Observation' on the Thesis, Kant raises the further question of what is proved in the proof. What is presented is only the necessity, for the comprehensibility of the world as totality of appearances, of an absolute beginning, i.e. of a world-origin out of freedom. Once brought into being, however, the world remains governed by natural causality. In the meantime, since the power of spontaneously beginning a temporal series has been demonstrated (although how this occurs remains unknown) 'it is now also permissible for us to admit within the course of the world different series . . . as beginning of themselves'. It is possible, that is, to admit present things, substances, which have the 'power of acting out of freedom'.[132]

This proof, in other words, allows for the possibility of freely acting beings within the domain of present occurrences. Again, nothing is decided here as to the human or non-human status of such beings. Rather, in accordance with the universal ontological concept of action, what is implied is only that something *can* begin quite spontaneously within the course of present occurrences. This self-origination does not have to be an absolute beginning 'according to time', i.e. it does not exclude the possibility that something occurred prior to it, without, however, *necessitating* it. If, for example, I now freely rise from my chair, this is the absolute origination – causally but not temporally – of a series of events in the world. 'For this resolution and act of mine do not form part of the succession of purely natural effects.'[133]

In concluding, Kant makes a historical reference to the philosophers of antiquity, who also (with some exceptions) explained the world by going beyond the sequence of natural causes to a first mover. Above all it was Aristotle, with the πρῶτον κινοῦν ἀκίνητον, who proceeded in this way. To be sure, the movement of this unmoved mover does not reduce to, indeed has nothing whatever to do with, absolute spontaneity, self-origination, κινεῖ ὡς ἐρώμενον. This is precisely a confirmation of the requirements of reason, as expressed in representing an unconditioned completeness of the origin of appearances.

It is vitally important to see that the Thesis and its proof are quite in accordance with the principles of pure reason and do not involve anything forced or artificial. Kant thus wants to say that the content of the Thesis, together with its mode of proof, is attested and affirmed in the most diverse modifications by common human reason. The same applies to the Antithesis, which asserts the opposite upon equally sound grounds.

b) The Antithesis of the Third Antinomy.
The Exclusion of Freedom from the Causality of the World-Process

'Antithesis: There is no freedom; everything in the world takes place solely in accordance with laws of nature.'[134] Here too the proof is indirect, i.e. it begins by assuming the truth of its opposite, the Thesis. If the proof of the Antithesis now proves the truth of the Thesis' opposite, the antagonism between the two, as equally true and provable, will be evident.

Proof of the Antithesis: 'If there is freedom in the transcendental sense, as a special kind of causality', then causality itself, as letting-follow-on, absolutely begins. For clearly, there would be nothing that could further determine it according to constant laws. This causation itself, as occurring action, is a being. But if there is no lawfulness governing this being, and if lawfulness belongs necessarily to the essence of appearances (that which is present), then transcendental freedom involves a causation which can never be present, 'an empty thought-entity'.[135] Therefore, since transcendental freedom is contrary to the law of causality, nothing exists but nature. If freedom were to enter into the causality of the world-process, this would not amount to a different causality, but to complete lawlessness, and nature as such would cease to be. On the other hand, if freedom were a kind of lawfulness, it would be nothing else than precisely nature. There is, consequently, no such thing as freedom. Everything that occurs is determined by the all-encompassing power of nature.

The truth of the Antithesis places cognition under the constant burden of having to seek ever higher for the beginning. At the same time, however, the illusion of freedom is overcome, and knowledge can comfortably bear its burden by safeguarding the constant and lawful unity of experience. Freedom, on the other hand, while it is indeed liberation from compulsion, also liberates from the guideline of all rules. For as an absolute beginning, freedom demolishes the law of the determination of occurrences, i.e. the determining return to prior states.

In his 'Observation' on the Antithesis, Kant shows how a proponent of the all-embracing power of nature would defend this view against the doctrine of freedom. Since the unity of experience at all times makes necessary the permanence of substance, i.e. since substances have always existed in the world, there is no difficulty in accepting that change has likewise always existed, thus that there is no first beginning. To be sure, the possibility of such an infinite regress cannot be made comprehensible. But such incomprehensibility is no reason for dismissing this 'enigma in nature'. For in this case 'alteration' too would have to be rejected, as even its possibility would be 'offensive'.[136] 'For were you not assured by experience that alteration actually occurs, you would never be able to excogitate *a priori* the possibility of such a ceaseless sequence of being and not-being.'[137]

c) The Special Character of the Cosmological Ideas in the Question of the Possibility of Genuine Metaphysics. Reason's Interest in Resolving the Antinomy

So Thesis and Antithesis are equally necessary, equally true, and equally provable. Their antagonism is a dissension within reason itself, a dissension which cannot be simply torn out of human nature and abolished. What is called for is a more thorough investigation of its origin. Before Kant pursues this course of inquiry, which aims at resolving rather than removing the antinomy, he raises the following questions. What attitude do we as human beings take to this internal dissension of reason as it constantly confronts us? Do we remain uninvolved? Do our interests favour one side, and if so which?[138] By our 'interests' Kant does not mean arbitrary needs and wishes, but what human beings take an interest in *qua* humans, i.e. what pertains to being-human as such. The pure concepts of reason, i.e. the ideas (soul, world, God), present 'glimpses of those ultimate ends [immortality, freedom, God] towards which all the endeavours of reason must ultimately converge'.[139]

The conflict just presented pertains quite generally to all present beings. To these beings there belongs the individual human as a present item of the world-totality. For an individual person, the dispute about whether a present being can by itself initiate a sequence of events becomes the question of 'whether I am free in my actions or, like other beings, am led by the hand of nature and fate'.[140] Am I free, or is everything compelled by natural necessity? Deciding in favour of the Thesis is a decision for *freedom*, but not freedom as mere lack of compulsion. Rather, we decide for freedom as the condition of the possibility of responsibility and thus of morality. So a certain *moral* interest is exhibited in deciding for the Thesis.[141] At the same time, however, a *speculative* interest is involved, i.e. to the degree that we want a satisfying answer (not obtainable on the side of the Antithesis) to the question concerning the totality of that which is present. While general theoretical and practical interests naturally favour the Thesis, the Antithesis does not enjoy such popularity. The Antithesis demands a restless search for ever-receding causes. It does not hold out the possibility of cognition arriving at a fixed point of rest, but man remains 'always with one foot in the air'.[142] Thus the ground of the Antithesis, just because it is really no ground at all, because it cannot guarantee anything primary and originary, cannot serve to erect a complete edifice of knowledge.[143] Now since 'human reason is by nature architectonic',[144] i.e. regards all knowledge as belonging to a system, 'the architectonic interest of reason . . . forms a natural recommendation for the assertions of the Thesis'.[145] This means that the main direction of metaphysical questioning, as arising from the 'natural disposition' of man, is given by the Thesis. Seen objectively, however, this does not give the Thesis greater credibility than the Antithesis, but only indicates that human reason is incapable, initially at least, of an unprejudiced evaluation of its own inner dissension. The connection of the Thesis with the general interest of human beings only indicates that if human beings 'were summoned to action, this play of the merely speculative reason' between Thesis and Antithesis 'would disappear like a dream', and human beings 'would choose their principles exclusively in accordance with practical interests'.[146] On the other hand, 'no one can be blamed for, much less be prohibited from, presenting for trial the two contending parties'.[147] Not only does pure reason harbour this dissension within itself, but the differing attitudes to this dissension can make valid points against one another.

The context of our problem requires that we must here dispense with any thorough examination of the antinomies as developed by Kant. More specifically, we shall not be concerned with the question of whether these antinomies are necessary as such, or whether they are only made necessary by Kant's approach to reason and human existence. Instead, we shall inquire into the problem's primordial rootedness in the essence of human existence. What interests us is solely the position of the problem of freedom within metaphysics, and how *the first way to freedom can be brought into unity with the second way.*

The problem of freedom belongs to the problem of world. The problematic arises as the antinomy of a cosmological idea, of reason's knowledge of the absolute totality of the originating sequence of an appearance. However, the cosmological idea of freedom thereby takes on a distinctive and privileged status (vis-à-vis the psychological and theological ideas) such that the task of resolving its inner dissension cannot be avoided. There is an obvious temptation thereto, for one could pronounce it 'impudent boasting' and 'extravagant self-conceit'[148] to want to solve all problems, insisting that these ultimate questions of reason call instead for a more modest attitude. However, although this may be true in respect of the psychological and theological ideas, it does not apply to the cosmological ideas, i.e. their antagonism must be resolved. Why is this so? The object of the cosmological ideas is the totality of appearances. To be sure, this completeness of that which is present in its being-present is never empirically given. But on the other hand, what is thematically intended in the cosmological ideas – cosmos, nature – is precisely the possible object of experience. These ideas must presuppose the object as given, and the questions which flow from these ideas relate precisely to the completeness of the synthesis of experience. We are acquainted with the object itself. What is given here as known must also provide the measure for evaluating the ideas and the way their objects are given. The cosmological ideas cannot be carried through, i.e. the totality as such cannot be given and intuitively presented, but the representing of the totality, for and from any given thing, is always possible. It could be that these ideas, in the way they arise and create contradictions, do not hold fast to that to which they relate as cosmological ideas (appearances), and especially not to the manner in which the object of these ideas is given. If we reflect on the matter, however, we can discover the key to the resolution and origination of their antagonism. Were this antagonism to rest on an illusion, it would resolve itself in such a way that what the ideas represent could be drawn positively into the possibility of experience. If the antagonism continues nevertheless, some way must be found for overcoming it. In regard to the problem of freedom, this means that freedom as a cosmological idea does not remain as the counter-concept to natural causality. Instead, their antagonism is resolved in such a way that the possible unity of the two – causality from freedom and natural causality – is at least not unthinkable.

But quite apart from the prospect of a possible resolution of the antagonism, it is already a matter of basic significance that Kant, in the Antithetic, sets these arguments of reason against one another. He calls this the sceptical method, which, however, does not mean scepticism, nor addiction to doubt, even less despair at the possibility of truth. Instead, it is σκέψις in the genuine meaning of the word – simply attentive looking at the fact of opposition, such that both sides of the argument come into view and sharply display their mutual antagonism. Only in this way can the antagonism be resolved, i.e. only thus can its possible false presuppositions come to light.[149]

§ 24. Preparatory (Negative) Determinations Towards Resolution of the Third Antinomy

a) The Delusion of Common Reason in the Handling of Its Principle

The transcendental concept of freedom originates within an idea-formation whereby reason applies its principle of necessary representation. This idea-formation pertains to the multiplicity of objects as a sequence of synthesis and as ever-progressing from conditioned to condition. Seen in this light freedom would be unconditioned causality. What principle does reason apply? If the conditioned is given, the whole series of its conditions is also given.

Hearing this principle, we feel that something is wrong, although we are unable to specify precisely what this is. We only have the intimation that the principle somehow involves a delusion. In what sense is this so? The principle speaks of condition and conditioned, of the relation between condition and conditioned. But it speaks of more, namely of the relation of the givenness of the conditioned to the givenness of the condition in the whole sequence, of the condition of the givenness of the whole sequence of conditions. There is much here that does not occur to us, at least not in its full content, when we simply enunciate the principle. Nevertheless, we believe ourselves capable of immediately understanding and applying this principle. We, that is common reason, believe this. So what does this commonness consist in? The common is the indifferent, i.e. all things are thrown together and treated as equivalent, however different they may actually be. Since commonness takes things for what they are not, this is already delusion and falsification.

How does reason make this principle common or indifferent? We first said quite generally that this principle speaks of conditioned and condition. The concept of conditioned already refers to a condition, more precisely, to a series of conditions. This applies irrespective of what is given as conditioned, indeed irrespective of whether anything is given at all, i.e. it is a matter of cognitive determinations as such, of the λόγος. It is a *purely logical postulate*. However, precisely because it is a purely logical postulate it can say nothing factical about the relationship between a given conditioned and its condition. In no way does the logical postulate imply that if something conditioned is given, so also is its whole series of conditions. The relationship between condition and conditioned is fundamentally different to the relationship between the givenness of something conditioned and the givenness of its conditions; the former is a logical-conceptual relationship which exists only in thought, the latter is an ontical-factical relationship within the temporal occurrence of experience. This fundamental difference is the first thing that common reason overlooks and levels out.

This levelling-out goes further. What does it mean for common reason to apply the principle to the *givenness* of the conditioned? Something conditioned is given, i.e. some being or other exists. If this being exists as conditioned, then what conditions it also exists, i.e. the complete series of conditions and the unconditioned itself must certainly exist. In speaking of givenness, the *what* and *where* and *how* of this givenness remain uninterrogated. It is simply taken for granted that the speaker (the human being) is acquainted with things as they are and is thus in a position to decide over what is conditioned and conditioning. Such talk of the givenness of something conditioned and of condition not only remains indefinite, but makes it appear self-evident that human beings know the things (beings) unconditionally, i.e. as they are in themselves. Common reason does not see that for beings to be given to us, for us to arrive [*erlangen*] at knowledge of beings, we must have already reached [*langen*] them and encountered them as beings. Beings are given to us only as self-showing, only as appearances. This letting-give is subject to definite conditions, including those which enable us to have an accepting representation, i.e. an intuition. What enables accepting belongs to the essence of accepting. If accepting is intuition, then what enables accepting must also have the character of intuition. That which enables is earlier and prior to what is enabled. The enabling intuiting must intuit in advance that which it is to represent.

This letting-give of appearances stands under definite conditions, namely that appearances are encountered in space and time. The latter are not things in themselves which could also be present next to, and simultaneously with, things within space and time. Rather, they are modes of human representation, of such a sort that everything we encounter shows itself within space and time. All relations attaching to the beings we encounter are therefore predetermined as temporal relations. This also applies to the relation between the encountered givenness of the conditioned and the givenness of the conditions. That is, if the conditioned is given in and as appearance, this does not mean that the unity of the temporal relations of the conditioned to its condition is already co-given. Rather, this series is only ever given successively in time. Consequently, the principle cannot claim that the whole series of conditions is given along with the conditioned, i.e. is actually present in its totality. It can claim only that the givenness of something conditioned implies the necessity of a series of conditions leading up to it. So we see the common procedure of reason in the conception and employment of this principle.

In order to once again briefly exhibit this levelling out of differences, let us consider the principle in its function as first premise of an argument, i.e. of the argument by which reason comes to its cosmological ideas, one of which is the idea of freedom. If the conditioned is given, so the whole series of its conditions, the unconditioned, is also given. Now the conditioned is given as something that originates (follows on) from something else. So the unconditioned of such a series is also given, the absolutely originary causation, i.e. freedom. Common reason takes the purely ontological relationship between concepts as equivalent to the ontical relationship between the givenness of an actually existing conditioned and its condition. The existing being is thereby taken as a thing-in-itself, i.e. without attending to the conditions of its possible givenness. Precisely this being is now taken as appearance – admittedly, without being recognized as meaning this – in the minor premise of the argument. What is falsely attributed to things-in-themselves is now transferred, with equal fallaciousness, to appearances. Provided only that the common procedure of reason has become transparent to itself, this conclusion can be seen as blatantly incorrect. Finally, the commonness of reason consists in the fact that it not only maintains itself within this indifference as something self-evident, but that it thus hinders itself from coming to self-transparency. So Kant can say that common reason, as it employs this principle in the formation of cosmological ideas, operates within a 'quite natural illusion'[150] which as such leads to the antinomies. The principle, however, is foundational for the proofs of both Thesis and Antithesis. So by clarifying the illusion at the basis of both statements, their proofs are found to involve an 'error'.[151] The claim of both to be actually provable and proven must accordingly be rejected.

b) The Distinction Between Appearance (Finite Knowledge) and Thing-in-Itself (Infinite Knowledge) as the Key to Resolving the Problem of the Antinomies

However, it has not yet been shown that the Thesis and Antithesis are substantively in error in what they claim as their respective conclusions. It is quite possible for a statement to be true even though the proofs advanced for it are invalid. If this were the case in regard to the Thesis and Antithesis, their antagonism would continue just as before.[152] The dispute can only be resolved by showing that they are really quarrelling about nothing. A particular illusion has made them accept a reality where none is to be found, so that the antagonism amounts to nothing. The question must be raised as to the character of this antagonism between Thesis and Antithesis. What kind of opposition do the antinomies involve?

To decide this, we shall keep to the Third Antinomy (the only one we have thus far treated), but bring it into a form that more clearly exhibits the antagonism. The Thesis asserts freedom as unconditioned causality, as the primordial origin subject to no further conditions. We can thus take the Thesis as saying that the ordered series of causes, considered in its totality, is finite. Clearly then, the Antithesis would say that the series of the regressive synthesis of conditions is infinite. The Thesis maintains that nature is finite, the Antithesis that nature is infinite. This kind of opposition is called a simple contradiction. To understand the antagonism in this way (i.e. in accordance with common reason) presupposes that nature is a thing-in-itself, i.e. that nature is given to us absolutely and is known absolutely. This presupposition overlooks the fact that as the fundamental concept of appearances, nature cannot possess absolute existence. Since nature is not being-in-itself it cannot be said to be either finite or infinite. The presupposition of both Thesis and Antithesis is false. Once this false presupposition is uncovered, the supposedly genuine contradiction becomes a mere apparent antagonism, i.e. a dialectical opposition. Both Thesis and Antithesis are based on an illusion, and indeed, as we saw, on an illusion necessary to common reason.[153]

The antagonism is removed by pointing to its false presupposition, namely that appearances are taken as things-in-themselves. This distinction is necessary if pure reason is to obtain self-transparency with regard to its own genuine possibilities. However, this distinction between appearance and thing-in-itself is nothing else than the distinction between finite and infinite knowledge. The problem of pure reason must therefore be recognized as the problem of finite knowledge. This also means that the finitude of human nature must be defined from and in the essence of knowledge. But it is the task of the first – positive and fundamental – part of the *Critique of Pure Reason* to delineate the finitude of knowledge in its essence. If, therefore, the antinomies can only be resolved on the basis of the indicated distinction between appearance and thing-in-itself, the doctrine of antinomies, for Kant, is indirect proof for what he had to establish positively in the transcendental aesthetic. This is unambiguously stated by Kant himself, in this way making plain the basic tendency the *Critique of Pure Reason*. We can now understand why the problem of the antinomies was the crucial impetus for this work. For the solution of this problem requires reflecting on the distinction between appearance and thing-in-itself, between finite and infinite knowledge. More precisely, the problem of the antinomies was what first led Kant to discover this distinction, and to hold fast to it as the centre of all further metaphysical problematics.

To be sure, in Kant's critical discussion of the *metaphysica specialis* we see the same fundamental attitude as in his critical consideration of the *metaphysica generalis* (ontology). The finitude of man is not decided upon, and is not made thematic, in connection with the problem of the foundations of metaphysics as such. In the doctrine of the antinomies, for example, Kant contents himself, quite properly given his immediate purposes, with exhibiting the antagonism, and then resolving it by reference to the natural illusion residing in human nature. Natural reason is common reason because it levels out essential differences, i.e. does not let them emerge as differences. This commonness belongs to the essence of human reason. Not only was it necessary to show this more comprehensively and primordially, but above all this natural commonness had to be exhibited as an essential moment of finitude. It was a matter of showing what this commonness genuinely consists in and why it belongs to natural reason. Our way of interpreting the employment of the principle of reason already provides a direction here. What is the significance of this erasure of the differences between the logical, ontical, and ontological, such that these are all understood, with equally indefiniteness, as 'being'?[154]

§ 25. The Positive Resolution of the Third Antinomy. Freedom as the Causality of Reason: Transcendental Idea of an Unconditioned Causality. Character and Limits of the Problem of Freedom within the Problem of the Antinomies

a) The Resolution of the Problem of the Antinomies as Going Beyond the Problem of Finite Knowledge to the Problem of Human Finitude as Such

Let us once again consider *the problem of freedom as it emerges within the problem of the antinomies*. If we follow Kant's *first way to freedom*, we encounter this within the problem of the antinomies. This is the form of the problem of world as the basic question of the critical resolution of the traditional metaphysical discipline of rational cosmology. Within the problem of the antinomies, i.e. within the antagonism between Thesis and Antithesis, there is a necessary reference to freedom, and indeed in opposing senses: on the one hand freedom exists alongside and in nature, on the other hand there is only nature and freedom does not exist. The antagonism cannot be resolved by placing the truth wholly on either side. A decision is only possible by way of a resolution of the antagonism, i.e. by showing that the origin of the conflict is such that no such decision can be demanded. At the same time, this origin is such that it can continue to walk abroad in human nature.

The resolution of the antagonism, through the consideration of origins, proceeds in two stages. First, it is shown that the principle is deceptive in the way it functions to generate the conflicting statements. That is, what applies to purely logical connections is taken as applicable to purely ontical connections, which in turn are conceived now in the sense of absolute knowledge, now in the sense of finite knowledge. Not only is the principle of proof for both Thesis and Antithesis deceptive in this sense, but the substantive opposition of the statements does not amount to anything, i.e. it is an illusory opposition. Secondly, closer consideration of the opposition reveals that it is not a genuine contradiction. For both statements – that nature is infinite, that nature is finite – attribute to

161

nature something it is not. They say more than what is necessary for contradiction: it is thus an illusory dialectical contradiction.

The key to resolving the difficulty is the *distinction between appearance and thing-in-itself, a distinction that itself involves the problem of the finitude of knowledge*. This becomes a problem in connection with the definition of accessible beings and the condition of the possibility of their accessibility.

But what is signified by the undifferentiated character of both? Is this just an error of traditional metaphysics, or is it something essential? If metaphysical questioning belongs to the nature of man, then so also does *this specific delusion* (according to Kant, necessarily). What is it in human nature that produces this delusion? We have already indicated what it is: the *mode of the understanding of being*, i.e. its undifferentiatedness. From where does this originate, and why does it occur? Can its necessity be seen from the understanding of being itself? In what way is it necessary? It is a matter of *bringing the finitude of man to light beyond the mere finitude of his knowledge*. This finitude must be exhibited, not in order to ascertain its boundaries and limits, but in order to awaken the inner resolve and composure wherein and within which everything essential begins and abides.

If the *Critique of Pure Reason* takes the basic problem of the foundation of metaphysics to concern the finitude of man, then a comprehensive and penetrating consideration of this book will inevitably need to focus on the problem of finitude. But, it will be said, we are concerned here with the problem of freedom. What has our discussion of the antinomies taught us about this problem? Has what we are seeking, namely *the systematic position of the problem of freedom within the context of the grounding of metaphysics*, become any more clear? If the antagonism between Thesis and Antithesis is resolved in the manner indicated, this is only a negative result, demonstrating the inner nullity and invalidity of the purported opposition. In this case, however, the problem of freedom as it arises in the antinomies would itself be null and void. Does this problem in fact disappear along with the resolution of the antinomies?

We cannot get beyond the point that *freedom is posited in the sense of a transcendental concept of nature*. This is the bare result, but it is not what we actually seek from an authentic understanding of the problem. The problem concerns the resolution of the antagonism between natural causality and the causality of freedom. To be sure, the resolution of this antagonism initially has a negative meaning, but it must lead to something positive, i.e. to the possibility of the *unity* of the two opposing sides. Why is this so?

Kant would answer that this is because unity is a basic principle of human reason as such, and further, because the cosmological ideas relate specifically to experience, which itself presents a lawful unity. Only by reaching a positive unity can we grasp the metaphysical core of the problem of the antinomies and thus the problem of freedom. This has been the goal of our discussions, which have not been concerned to provide a complete historical report of the *Critique of Pure Reason*.

The negative character of Kant's consideration of the antinomies must now be transformed into something positive. This means that the mere critique of the principle in its employment by common reason must make way for a consideration of its correct form, i.e. such that the cosmological ideas, in their specific relatedness to the unity of experience, can lay claim to a *positive function* within the total problem of the possibility of experience.

Common reason misrecognizes the character of the principle by taking it to assert something about things-in-themselves. On the other hand, it became clear that what the principle demands is only the continuous return from the givenness of the conditioned to the givenness of a condition. This, however, does not mean settling on something absolutely unconditioned as given and givable. The principle says nothing concerning the essential structure and constitution of nature. It is not a constitutive principle like the Analogies of Experience,[155] but only gives a rule for the knowledge of nature in accordance with the idea of completeness. It is only a *regulative principle*. In Kantian terminology: the principle does not anticipate or predetermine what the object is as such, but merely postulates what must occur in the regression. Now the question arises as to the implications of this regulative validity (which is the only kind of validity possessed by the principle) for the positive resolution of the antinomies. This does not involve an ontical interpretation of the totality, but an ontological postulate pertaining to the totality of experiential knowledge. A positive resolution of the inner antagonism of reason will have the task of disclosing the sense of the possible unity of the opposing elements. Therefore, the question concerns the possibility or otherwise of reason's unification of natural necessity with the causality of freedom.

What is the ultimate origin and motivation of this problem concerning the unity of nature and freedom? Is this problem basically determined by a purely speculative interest in the ultimate harmony of knowledge, or is there some other interest behind it? However, in posing the question of a possible positive resolution of the antagonism, we can no longer proceed from, or remain within, either of the two alternatives, i.e. that every effect within the world issues from either nature or freedom. With this either/or, every bridge towards unification is already broken. For the problem of the unification of nature and freedom to even be posed, we must entertain the possibility that one and the same world-event may be determined by *both* natural causality and the causality of freedom. But if one and the same event is to proceed from two fundamentally different kinds of causality, one and the same effect must be causally determinable in different relations. Thus *the possibility of the unification of the two causalities in relation to one and the same effect depends on whether an effect can permit a double relation to causality*, i.e. on whether the effect can be understood in terms of both natural causality and the causality of freedom.

b) The Displacement of the Problem of the Resolution of the Antinomies.
The Question Concerning a Causation for Appearances Outside the Appearances and Conditions of Time.
The Resolution of the Third Antinomy in Looking Towards Man as Ethically Acting Person

After all this, we remark at once that the present problem *must undergo a displacement in its factical implementation*. This is because the simultaneity of the two causalities is such that natural causality still retains the upper hand. Natural causality is already demonstrated in its reality, i.e. as necessarily belonging to the essential content of nature – which does not mean, however, that a nature must necessarily actually exist. Since the validity of the principle of natural causality is incontrovertibly established by Kant himself in the Analogies of Experience, the unification of natural causality with the causality of freedom cannot occur through compromising the closed causality of nature. Instead, the question concerning the possibility of unification can only be about whether, despite the lawfulness of nature, 'freedom can also occur'.[156] We see that natural causality and unity of the manifold of appearances, of the being-present of that which is present, remains the decisive instance. So ultimately the question concerning the unification of the two causalities is about whether freedom can be 'saved' in the face of another causality which is already immovably established.[157]

For Kant, therefore, the problem is whether effects (appearances) can be seen in two different ways, such that this difference *corresponds to the difference between two causes in their causation.* In other words, do appearances necessarily have causes which are appearances, or do appearances exist which are related to causes that are not themselves appearances? If this is possible, then there are *causes* which *in their causation are outside the sequence of appearances.* However, since sequences of appearances are themselves causally determined, and indeed precisely in respect of causation, through temporal succession, thus through a temporal relation, the problem is as follows. Can an intra-temporal being, as well as having intra-temporal causes, also have other causes, which themselves, and *in their causation, are extra-temporal*?

Kant himself admits that, presented in this abstract way, the problem is 'extremely subtle and obscure', but adds that it will become clear 'in the course of its application'.[158] He means that the problem cannot be clarified at a general ontological level, but only by reference to particular domains of beings. What this shows is that *the problem of the resolution of the causal antinomies steers toward a quite specific being.* The question concerning the possible unification of natural causality with the causality of freedom is to be discussed in relation to this particular being, which is none other than *man as ethically acting person.* It is important to notice, however, that Kant does not want to disprove the antagonism between the two kinds of causality by appealing to the factically existing entity possessing the mode of being of man. On the contrary, he wants to present the *possibility* of a unification of the two causalities in a purely hypothetical-constructive general ontological reflection, and then on this basis to show the possibility of the unification of nature with freedom, thus the metaphysical possibility of man as a world-entity.

Once again, it is all important to see the problems, the method and direction of questioning, and not just the content of the questions. The approach and direction of the problem, and the field of its solution, are not formal and external to the content, but these alone determine whether the genuine substantiality in the content is philosophical. If one fails to see this, then Kant's philosophy will be indistinguishable from the most commonplace discussions of freedom of the will. It is characteristic of all vulgar conceptions of philosophy to see only material for learning and knowing.

We are now in a position to review – not in an empty and general manner, but on the basis of our concrete discussions – the specific character of Kant's first way to freedom. What is to be demonstrated about freedom? Within which horizon does the discussion operate?

What emerges from all this for the inner content of the problem of freedom?

The first thing to be said here is that the existence and possibility of freedom is not to be proved or shown. Rather, *the resolution of the antinomies is concerned only to demonstrate the possibility of the unification of freedom and nature*. In this task, *nature is taken as the authoritative instance*: it is a matter of 'saving' freedom in relation to nature. This problem of resolution determines the *genuine character and limits of the problem of freedom*. For this reason we shall not hear anything substantively new in these discussions of Kant, but we must attend to the kind of problematic at work. In any case, since Kant undertakes the resolution of the antagonism *with a view to man*, we have the opportunity for more concretely grasping the essence of a causality of freedom, and for characterizing the causation of this kind of cause. This means that previously obtained concepts such as causation and action will receive a more precise determination.

The importance of the resolution of precisely this Third Antinomy is indicated by its more extensive treatment in Kant's text, where the discussion is divided into three sections. The first has a preparatory character, and is concerned at a quite general level with the antagonism in 'the idea of totality in the derivation of cosmical events from their causes'.[159] The next section is headed: 'Possibility of causality through freedom, in harmony with the universal law of natural necessity'.[160]

Kant's procedure is to begin by asking how a being must be if it is to be simultaneously and unitarily determinable through natural causality and causality from freedom. How is the unity of causality to be conceived in this case? In particular, how is the causal character of freedom to be more precisely defined? Kant goes on to give a construction for the resolution of the antinomies, and says himself of this section: 'I have thought it advisable to give this outline sketch of the solution of our transcendental problem, so that we may be the better enabled to survey the course which reason has to adopt in arriving at the solution'.[161] Only now does he provide a concrete treatment of the same problem by way of an application to man. This does not involve appealing to man as the ground of proof for his construction. Instead, the opposite is the case: the discussion of the problem in relation to man is simply an intuitive presentation. Thus Kant heads the final section: 'Explanation of the cosmological idea of freedom in its connection with universal natural necessity'.[162] Only if this reference to man signifies nothing more than an explanatory confirmation does it become completely clear that the unity of natural causality and causality from freedom, as concretely-factually presented in man, is *merely an instance of the universal cosmologically determined unification of both causalities*. This means not only that freedom is posited as a concept of nature, but that the unity of the concrete human being as a rational-sensory entity is metaphysically prescribed from the cosmological problematic. If we use the term 'Existence' [*Existenz*] to designate the being of man in his totality and authenticity, then it emerges that the *problem of man is drawn into the universal ontological problem.* More precisely, *the metaphysical-ontological problem of Existence does not break through, but is held back in the universal and self-evident ontological problematic of traditional metaphysics.* Thus what is possibly not-nature in the ontological constitution of human beings is *also* defined in the same way as nature, i.e. through *causality.* That causality is thereby modified does not alter the fact that causality remains the fundamental ontological characteristic. Kant's critique is not and cannot be radical, for he does not pose the question of being in a fundamental way. This means that the problem of freedom, however central for Kant, is unable to occupy the crucial position within the problematic of metaphysics.

c) Empirical and Intelligible Character.
The Intelligible Character as the Mode of Causation of Causality from Freedom.
The Double Character of Appearance and the Possibility of Two Fundamentally Different Causalities in Relation to the Appearance as Effect

We must now briefly present the course of *Kant's positive resolution of the Third Antinomy,* which is, however, the genuine *metaphysical resolution of the problem of freedom as a problem of world.* In so doing, we pay particular attention to certain additional determinations relating to causality as such. Let us recall the universal ontological concept of action:[163] 'The relation of the subject of causality to the effect'. In general ontological terms, this means the object in relation to the subject. Now Kant says that 'every efficient cause must have a character'.[164] In this context 'character' means law of causality, necessary rule of the 'how' of causation of the cause. The character governs the kind of connections between actions and thus also between effects. As the 'how' of causation the character clearly determines the relation of the subject of causation to its effect, and this is precisely action.

Now Kant distinguishes two characters, the *empirical* and the *intelligible*. It is of the utmost importance to understand the terminology here, especially so because this is by no means unambiguous and consistent. This is no accident. Let us begin with the first so-called 'empirical' character – ἐμπειρία, experience. Something is empirical if it belongs to experience. For Kant, this means accessible through experience, whereby we must not forget that the foundation of finite experience is sensory intuition, sensibility. The essence of experience consists in receptivity, in receiving acceptance. To be noted here is that not every accepting intuiting is receiving. There is also an accepting which accepts what it gives itself, a self-giving accepting, i.e. pure intuition. When something is called 'empirical' it is conceived in relation to its mode of knowability. The *empirical character is that lawfulness of causation which is empirically accessible in experience*, as appearance. It is causation in its 'how' as belonging to appearance, i.e. the causality of nature.

The *intelligible character* – we can already guess – is *the mode of causation of causality from freedom*. This is, to be sure, correct as regards content, but it does not amount to real understanding. Intelligible is seemingly the counter-concept to empirical. But looked at more closely, intelligible cannot at all be this counter-concept. 'Empirical' is properly ascribed to a way of knowing objects, whereas 'intelligible' applies to the objects themselves. Accordingly, Kant says in his work *De mundi sensibilis atque intelligibilis forma et principiis* (1770) § 3: 'Objectum sensualitatis est sensibile; quod autem nihil continet, nisi per intelligentiam cognoscendum, est intelligibile. Prius scholis veterum *Phaenomenon*, posterius *Noumenon* audiebat' (The object of sensibility is the sensible; that which contains nothing save what must be known through intelligence, is the intelligible. The former was called, in the schools of the ancients, *phenomenon*; the latter, *noumenon*.)[165]

From this two points are clear. First, since intelligibility pertains to objects, to say that something is intelligible means that it belongs in a particular domain of objects. To be sure, these objects are characterized through their mode of becoming-known: *intelligentia, intellectus*. The way in which intelligible objects are known is purely intellectual. Secondly, the counter-concept to intelligible is not 'empirical' but rather 'sensible'. Now it is important to note that Kant refers to the empirical as the sensible and vice versa. Likewise, he refers to the intellectual as the intelligible and vice versa, as e.g. in our passage from the *Critique of Pure Reason* where he speaks of intelligible causality as intellectual.

The distinction between empirical and intelligible operates at quite different levels. The first pertains to the way in which objects are apprehended, the second to the object itself, albeit in respect of its possible knowability. But there is another, purely substantive reason for Kant's displeasing terminology, connected with the way he resolves the overarching problem of the two causalities and their unity. When Kant deliberately plays on the ambiguity of the expressions 'intelligible' and 'intellectual', this is not to obscure anything but to bring out the peculiar knotting together of contextures. He does not himself unravel these knots, because he does not see any possibility of doing so. The conscious ambiguity in Kant's employment of 'intelligible' and 'intellectual' in relation to the causality of freedom is due to the circumstance that this kind of causation is not accessible exclusively to pure intelligence independently of sense, but is itself, in its mode of being (intelligence), something intellectual, something which has the character of understanding: 'Whatever in an object of the senses is not itself appearance, I entitle intelligible'.[166] 'Objects, insofar as they can be represented merely by the understanding, and to which none of our sensible intuitions can refer, are termed "intelligible". But as some possible intuition must correspond to every object, we would have to think an understanding that intuits things immediately; but of such we have not the least concept, nor of beings of the understanding to which it should be applied'.[167] The intelligible character is therefore the mode of causation of a cause which can be understood (if at all) only through the understanding, independently of sensibility.

What leads Kant to this distinction between the empirical and intelligible is precisely the general problem of a possible unification of the two causalities. Such unification requires that one and the same effect, at one and the same time, is causally determined in different respects. Is such an effect at all possible? The giving of an effect is always something which shows itself in experience, as appearance. So the problem is whether an appearance can stand in two fundamentally different relations. As existing in time, every appearance stands in an obvious relation to other appearances which precede and follow it in time. Yet this is not the only possible kind of relation which can apply to appearances. The appearance, that which appears, is the being itself. To be sure, but this is so only insofar as the being shows itself for human knowledge. What it is in itself, for absolute knowledge, remains unknown to us. However, already in this not-knowing we intend and think something we do not know: not the appearance, but the unknown X, the transcendental object which must underlie the appearances. Of this X, then, we say that 'it' appears, albeit not as it is in itself.[168] While the object X is utterly empty, it is still, in its emptiness, not sensible but intelligible. It is negatively intelligible and unknown in any further aspect. The X is the intelligible object. It is what is intelligible about the object (this in a universal ontological sense). But the X is not in itself a separate object of knowledge. Thus Kant says: 'So there is nothing to prevent us from ascribing to this transcendental object, besides the quality in terms of which it appears, a *causality* which is not appearance, although its *effect* is to be met with in appearance'.[169] But what is not appearance is intelligible. In accordance with this *double relation of appearance* as such, it can stand in relation to other appearances, can be the effect of appearances, and *at the same time be related to intelligible causes*.

From the *essence of appearance* there is deduced the *possibility of this double relation*, and thus the possibility of the applicability of two fundamentally different causalities to one and the same event as effect. The essential double character of every appearance, such that not only is it connected with other appearances but is also the appearance of something which appears (X), involves the fundamental possibility of a relation to both the empirical and the non-empirical. These two fundamentally different relations as such provide the possibility for two fundamentally different relations of causation in the sense of the empirical and intelligible characters. The possibility of the unification of both causalities is thus proven in principle. To be sure, the appeal to human beings still remains invalidated.

d) The Causality of Reason.
Freedom as Intelligible Causality: Transcendental Idea of an Unconditioned Causality.
The Application of the Universal Ontological (Cosmological) Problematic to Man as World-Entity

Before Kant brings this result to bear on the human being, he attempts, still at a quite general level, to more precisely exhibit the structural con-texture of the unity of both causalities. Clearly, the relatedness of one and the same effect to both kinds of causality cannot be a matter of one com-ing into play after the other, for the intelligible is distinguished precisely by its extra-temporal character. On the other hand, the intelligible must have a relationship to the empirical, for they come together in the one effect. Must the causation of the cause (which cause is itself appearance, i.e. empirical) therefore in turn be appearance, or is it impossible for this causation to itself be the effect of an intelligible causality? In this case the causation of the empirical cause would be determined in its action by something intelligible. We are already aware of the ambiguity of the expression. The intelligible itself possesses the character of the understanding, and the intelligible ground determines 'thought [and action] in the pure understanding'.[170] In brief, just as an appearance always remains related to something (X) that never appears, so the intelligible can be the non-appearing transcendental cause of the empirical and thus be the cause of one and the same appearance as effect. What appears can also be determined by what does not appear, i.e. by what the appearing is an appearance *of*. From the perspective of appearance, however, the intelligible cause begins from and of itself, thus making possible an originary action.[171] In one of the extant 'Reflections', Kant says that the two kinds of causality are 'present in all beings, but only in will do we notice the second'.[172] 'On the other hand we cannot attribute any causality to the intelligibility of the body, for its appearances do not testify to any intelligence; thus we cannot ascribe any freedom to its *substrato intelligibili*, and we do not know it through any predicate.'[173]

We can conclude two things from these remarks. First, that the distinction between the two causalities functions at a universal ontological level and applies to all beings. Not only humans or angels are 'intelligences', but so is every being whatever, i.e. insofar as it can be related to absolute knowledge (pure intelligence). Material things too are intelligent, a circumstance that has nothing to do with spirits or goblins, the representations of which are precisely perceptual, only falsely absolutized as objects of absolute knowledge. Yet the only intelligences we can notice are those of the will, i.e. those intelligences that we ourselves are. This means that, in regard to our own self, there is the possibility of 'noticing' our being-in-itself in a formally 'absolute' sense.

It would be a very superficial way of thinking to conclude that, since knowledge of things-in-themselves pertains to absolute as opposed to merely finite knowledge, we ourselves are infinite beings. Instead, it is necessary to hold fast to the primary sense of absolute knowing as the knowing which actually produces its object rather than encountering it ready-made. In a certain sense, we ourselves create our action and factical being. But this is not absolutely so, for we do not give ourselves our there-being [*Da-sein*] through our own decision, but always encounter it as a fact, i.e. we are at the same time appearances to ourselves. As beings we are conditioned, which does not at all fit with the essence of infinity. Still, it is this knowledge of one's own willing as an 'I will', and of the 'I am' in this 'I will', that moves Kant to speak here of knowing something that does not appear but rather forms itself.

These considerations have led us into the region where Kant applies his general metaphysical reflections. We should remember, however, that Kant has had this region all the while in view. For man is not, for us human beings, just an arbitrary world-entity among others, but is precisely what is pre-given for us to be. But, following Kant, we must first attempt to define this being quite generally as a world-entity, i.e. in cosmological rather than moral terms. This means taking man just as one possible kind of present being and obtaining fundamental knowledge of man at this level of reflection. After analysing the universal trans- cendental cosmological construction of the possibility of the unity of nature and freedom, Kant says: 'Let us apply this [this aforementioned fundamental knowledge] to experience. Man is one of the appearances of the sensible world'.[174] As appearance man must have an empirical character 'like all other things in nature'.[175] Since all natural things are appearances, they are always determined by appearances. In so far as appearances show themselves only in and for sensibility, the occurrence of natural things is conditioned by sense. Also in the case of 'lifeless or merely animal nature we find no ground for thinking that any faculty is conditioned otherwise than in a merely sensible manner. Man, however, who knows all the rest of nature through the senses, knows himself also through pure apperception'.[176] Man is a special kind of natural thing by virtue of the fact that he knows himself. More precisely, it is not self-knowledge as such, not self-consciousness in the formal sense, that distinguishes man, but his particular kind of self-knowledge 'through pure apperception'. 'Pure' here does not indicate any deficiency or restriction but something positive and superior, i.e. as opposed to 'empirical apperception'.

What does Kant mean with this? The concept of apperception plays a major role in the *Critique of Pure Reason*, and it is tempting to define it through the context of its treatment there. We remark at once, however, that the interpretation of this concept, especially in Neo-Kantianism, is hopelessly confused. This could not have occurred if the crucial signifi cance of our passage had been recognized. Although Kant does not here discuss the meaning and function of apperception for the founding of a universal metaphysics, he gives the crucial and most universal description of its essence. 'Pure apperception' means 'actions and inner determinations which [man] cannot regard as impressions of the senses'.[177] Pure apperception as action involves a causality, a determining letting-follow such that what gets determined is not just received and accepted but originates from itself. Pure apperception then means giving oneself to oneself, and indeed 'simply' in existence [*im Dasein*],[178] not in what I am in myself [*nicht in dem, was ich an sich bin*]. I cannot know myself in *what* I am, but I can know *that* I am, i.e. I can know my existence absolutely in its 'that'. This is because I always already form, in all thinking and determining, the 'I'-being as the 'I think'. I am absolutely given to myself only in the act of this determining, and never prior to this as something present which determines. The interpretation and conception of the 'I' depends on the essence of 'I-ness' [*Ichheit*].

Pure apperception is an action which is non-receptive, i.e. it involves a different relation between cause and effect. It is a determination from itself rather than from something else. Such a non-empirical and non-receptive *intelligible faculty* is *reason*. But this means that reason is itself a kind of causality.

In what way then does it become evident that reason has a causality? In these actions of the 'I think' which we ourselves enact (in this kind of effecting), we provide rules for the 'acting forces'. This provision of rules is a kind of determining. What we stipulate for our action has in each case an 'ought' character. ' "Ought" expresses a kind of necessity and of connection with grounds which is found nowhere else in the whole of nature.'[179] Connection with grounds means a relation determined by a ground as such, a grounding, defining, causing in the broad sense. Insofar as reason is determined through the ought, 'it frames for itself with perfect spontaneity an order of its own according to ideas',[180] i.e. opposed to the order of the lawfulness of appearances. The ought cannot itself occur, but is given as such for reason, i.e. represented as universally determining. To represent something 'universally' means to represent it in concepts. What is universally represented, the ought as rule, is a concept. Thus the ground of the determination of action is the concept: 'The "ought" expresses a possible action the ground of which cannot be anything but a mere concept; whereas in the case of a merely natural action the ground must always be an appearance'.[181]

The *essence of the causality of reason* has thus been clarified. Its action is an effecting, as determined by a prior representation of what is to take place, and as intrinsically related to willing. In the mode of fulfilled enactment, such ought-governed action belongs within the order of appearances. Where, as with man, action occurs in unity with nature, reason possesses an empirical as well as an intelligible character. The empirical character is 'only the sensible schema' of the intelligible character. In regard to the latter there is no before and after. 'Reason is present in all the actions of men at all times and under all circumstances, and is always the same; but it is not itself in time, and does not fall into any new state in which it was not before. In respect to new states, it is *determining, not determinable*.'[182] 'Reason is the abiding condition of all those actions of the will under [the guise of which] man appears.'[183] 'Reason in its causality is not subject to any conditions of appearance or of time.'[184] Since appearances are not things-in-themselves, neither are they causes in themselves. Only reason is a 'cause in itself', pure causality so to speak. The elucidation of the universal metaphysical construction of the possible unity of nature and freedom shows that there is indeed a world-entity in which this unity factically exists, i.e. in man as a rational living being.

Kant is concerned merely with the metaphysical possibility of the unity of natural causality and the causality of freedom. What does 'possibility' mean here? It means thinkability. But how is something shown to be thinkable? By being thought without contradiction? To be sure, but mere logical thinkability, mere freedom from contradictions, is not an adequate criterion for metaphysical possibility. The essential *universal metaphysical ground of the possibility of the unity of the two causalities* lies in the fact that *appearances are determinable as both intelligible and sensible*. In respect of the particular appearance (world-entity) which is man, this means: 'Man, who in this way regards himself as intelligence, puts himself in a different order of things and in a relationship to determining grounds of an altogether different kind when he thinks of himself as an intelligence with a will and thus as endowed with causality, compared with that other order of things and that other set of determining grounds which become relevant when he perceives himself as a phenomenon in the world of sense (as he really is also) and submits his causality to external determination according to natural laws.'[185]

We have arrived at the goal of the first way to freedom. What have we learnt from our reflections? *Freedom is a non-empirical (intelligible) kind of causality*. As a *causality of reason*, freedom can come into *unity with the causality of nature.* With this conception of the result we remain within the *limits of a purely cosmological consideration of beings* wherein man, the being whom we know to be free, is just one being among others and as such has no priority over other beings. Indeed, man does not even provide the primary and crucial motive for the problem of freedom, which arises from the thematic task of a knowledge of the totality of appearances (world), as the *transcendental idea of unconditioned causality.* We now come to Kant's second way to freedom.

Notes

1 P. Jordan, 'Kausalität und Statistik in der modernen Physik', in *Die Naturwissenschaften* XV (1927), p. 105 ff.
2 M. Born, 'Quantenmechanik und Statistik', in *Die Naturwissenschaften* XV (1927), p. 239.
3 P. Jordan, 'Kausalität und Statistik in der modernen Physik', p. 105.
4 CPR A 177 f.
5 CPR A 189 ff., B 232 ff.
6 CPR A 189.
7 CPR B 232.
8 CPR A 189.
9 CPR B 232.
10 CPR A 31, B 47.
11 CPR A 183, B 226.
12 CPR A 144, B 183.
13 CPR A 41, B 58.
14 CPR A 182, B 226.
15 CPR A 177, B 219.
16 CPR A 182.
17 CPR B 224.
18 CPR A 211.
19 CPR B 256.
20 CPR B 218.
21 CPR B 218.
22 CPR B 219.
23 CPR A 194, B 239.
24 CPR B 219.
25 CPR B 219.
26 CPR A 216, B 263.
27 CPR A 215, B 262.

28 CPR B 219.

29 CPR B 225.

30 CPR B 233, cf. B 257.

31 Time – temporality – finitude – human existence. Cf. Heidegger, *Kant and the Problem of Metaphysics*, translated by James S. Churchill, Bloomington, Indiana University Press, 1962.

32 CPR A 188 f., B 232.

33 CPR A 217, B 264.

34 CPR A 217, B 264.

35 CPR A 215, B 262.

36 CPR A 215, B 262.

37 CPR A 145, B 184–5. Cf. Heidegger, *Kant and the Problem of Metaphysics*, § 22.

38 Time in this sense is not primordial time. Cf. Heidegger, *Being and Time*, translated by John Macquarrie and Edward Robinson, Basil Blackwell, Oxford, 1962, §79–81.

39 *Critique of Practical Reason*, p. 209 (V, 186).

40 See above, pp. 29 ff. on the various meanings of 'is' (what-being, that-being; *essentia*, *existentia*).

41 CPR A 182.

42 CPR A 185, B 228.

43 CPR A 184, B 227.

44 CPR A 184, B 227.

45 CPR A 184, B 227.

46 CPR A 185, B 228.

47 CPR A 184, B 227.

48 CPR A 186, B 229.

49 CPR A 179 f., B 222.

50 CPR A 213, B 259 f.

51 CPR A 187, B 230.

52 CPR A 80, B 106.

53 CPR A 73, B 98.

54 CPR A 187, B 230.

55 CPR A 187, B 230 f.

56 CPR A 188, B 231.

57 CPR A 189, B 232.

58 CPR A 189.

59 CPR B 232.

60 CPR B 232 f.

61 CPR B 233.

62 CPR B 232.

63 CPR A 201, B 246.

64 CPR A 206, B 251.

65 CPR A 193, B 238.
66 CPR A 197, B 242.
67 CPR A 192, B 237.
68 CPR A 192 f., B 238.
69 CPR A 192, B 237.
70 CPR A 192, B 237.
71 CPR A 200, B 245.
72 CPR A 200, B 245.
73 Cf. CPR A 198 ff., B 243 ff.
74 CPR A 202, B 247.
75 CPR A 544, B 572.
76 CPR A 213, B 259 f.
77 *Prolegomena to Any Future Metaphysics*, p. 84 (IV, 344).
78 *Critique of Practical Reason*, p. 157 (V, 47).
79 *Prolegomena*, p. 84 (IV, 344).
80 *Critique of Practical Reason*, p. 175 (V, 118).
81 *Critique of Practical Reason*, p. 121 note (V, 10).
82 *Critique of Practical Reason*, p. 201 (V, 170).
83 *Critique of Practical Reason*, pp. 120–21, Preface (V, 9).
84 *Critique of Practical Reason*, p. 209 (V, 185).
85 *Critique of Practical Reason*, p. 196 (V, 160).
86 *Critique of Practical Reason*, p. 118, Preface (V, 4).
87 CPR A 202, B 247.
88 CPR A 202, B 247 f.
89 CPR A 203, B 248.
90 See Kant's example of a ball making a hollow in a cushion, CPR A 203, B 248 f.
91 CPR A 800, B 828.
92 CPR A 314, B 371.
93 *Critique of Judgement* § 43.
94 CPR A 547, B 575.
95 *Prolegomena* § 53, p. 85 note (IV, 344).
96 *Prolegomena* § 53, p. 84 (IV, 343).
97 CPR A 205, B 250.
98 See above pp. 123 ff.
99 *Prolegomena*, p. 3 (IV, 258).
100 CPR A 544, B 572.
101 CPR B 21.
102 CPR B 22.
103 CPR B 22.
104 CPR A 832, B 860.
105 CPR A 567 f., B 595 f.

106 CPR A 333 f., B 390 f.
107 CPR A 337, B 395 note. The usual list is God, world, soul. Instead of world there now appears freedom; 'soul': immortality.
108 CPR A 407, B 433.
109 CPR A 407, B 434.
110 CPR A 407, B 434.
111 CPR A 464, B 492.
112 CPR A 409, B 435 f.
113 CPR A 326, B 383.
114 CPR A 407, B 433.
115 CPR A 409, B 436.
116 CPR A 411, B 438.
117 CPR A 411, B 438.
118 CPR A 415, B 443.
119 Cf. CPR A 544, B 572.
120 Cf. CPR A 420, B 448.
121 CPR A 420, B 447 f. See also A 327, B 384; A 496, B 525.
122 CPR A 413, B 443.
123 CPR A 422, B 449.
124 CPR A 421, B 449.
125 CPR A 421, B 449.
126 Cf. CPR A 420 ff., B 448 ff.
127 CPR A 444 ff., B 472 ff.
128 Cf. CPR A 444, B 472.
129 CPR A 446, B 474.
130 CPR A 448, B 476.
131 CPR A 449, B 477.
132 CPR A 450, B 478.
133 CPR A 450, B 478.
134 CPR A 445, B 475.
135 CPR A 447, B 475.
136 CPR A 451, B 479.
137 CPR A 451, B 479.
138 CPR A 465, B 493.
139 CPR A 463, B 491.
140 CPR A 463, B 491.
141 Cf. CPR A 466, B 494.
142 CPR A 467, B 495.
143 Cf. CPR A 474, B 502.
144 CPR A 474, B 502.
145 CPR A 475, B 503.
146 CPR A 475, B 503.

147 CPR A 475 f., B 503 f.
148 CPR A 476, B 504.
149 Cf. CPR A 507, B 535.
150 CPR A 500, B 528.
151 CPR A 501, B 529.
152 CPR A 501, B 529.
153 CPR A 506, B 534.
154 See above p. 86. The 'indifference' of the understanding of being, 'undif-ferentiatedness', was one of the eight characteristics we enumerated.
155 These also are only regulative. They are not constitutive but they are still genuine principles. 'Not constitutive' is ambiguous: 1. saying nothing at all about the objects as such, 2. saying nothing about their what-content, rather something about their mode of presence. Constitutive: 1. concerning what-content, 2. concerning presence. The analogies are constitutive in the second sense.
156 CPR A 536, B 564.
157 Cf. CPR A 536, B 564.
158 CPR A 537, B 565.
159 CPR A 532 ff., B 560 ff.
160 CPR A 538 ff., B 566 ff.
161 CPR A 542, B 570.
162 CPR A 542, B 570.
163 See above pp. 136 ff.
164 CPR A 539, B 567.
165 *Dissertation on the Form and Principles of the Sensible and Intelligible World*, p. 44.
166 CPR A 538, B 566; cf. B 312.
167 *Prolegomena*, p. 59 note (IV, 317); cf. CPR B 306.
168 On the concept of appearance in general, see CPR A 249 ff., especially A 251 f. On the negative and positive senses of noumenon see B 307.
169 CPR A 538, B 566 f.
170 CPR A 545, B 573.
171 CPR A 544, B 572.
172 *Reflexionen Kants zur Kritik der reinen Vernunft*. Hg. Benno Erdmann, Leipzig 1884, no. 1404.
173 *Reflexionen*, no. 1531.
174 CPR A 546, B 574.
175 CPR A 546, B 574.
176 CPR A 546, B 574.
177 CPR A 546, B 574.
178 Cf. CPR B 157 ff.
179 CPR A 547, B 575.
180 CPR A 548, B 576.

181 CPR A 547 f., B 575 f.
182 CPR A 556, B 584.
183 CPR A 553, B 581.
184 CPR A 556, B 584.
185 *Foundations of the Metaphysics of Morals*, p. 111 (IV, 457).

2

The Second Way to Freedom in the Kantian System.
Practical Freedom as Specific to Man as a Rational Being

In thus going over to Kant's second way, this is something external: we give the impression that the two ways run independently alongside each other and that we are now jumping in unmediated fashion from the first to the second. In a certain sense this is so and in another sense not. For precisely the direction of the first way not only makes it clear that the idea of freedom arises in the course of reason's inner dissension in its thinking of the world, but also allows us to see – albeit from a very restricted perspective – a freedom which is quite *differently* situated and impossible to reach from the first way itself. This is the freedom of man. To be sure, we emphasized that from the perspective of the first way human freedom is just one case of cosmological freedom. But the question remains as to whether this is the only possible way of seeing freedom, or whether another perspective is possible, indeed necessary. If this is so then the second way turns out to be imperative. But further, if there is a second way to freedom, and to the freedom of man as such, and if man remains a particular being within the world, then what the first way to freedom establishes also holds for the second. In fact, Kant himself explicitly maintains that the content of the cosmological problem of freedom is just what is genuinely problematical in the problem of freedom. It is thus clear that, although the second way must be considered in its own terms, the results of the first way are not irrelevant to it. The second way is considerably shorter, which does not mean that the problems posed therein are any easier to master.

§ 26. The Essence of Man as a Being of Sense and Reason. The Distinction Between Transcendental and Practical Freedom

a) The Essence of Man (Humanity) as Person (Personality). Personality and Self-Responsibility

The second way aims at freedom not as a possible kind of causality in the world but as the *specific characteristic of man as a rational being*. Insofar as man, as belonging to the world, falls under the idea of freedom discovered along the first way, the freedom of man is also already noticed there, but it is not made thematic as a specific characteristic. For that to occur, man must be considered otherwise than in the cosmological discussion, i.e. man must be considered precisely in respect of what distinguishes him. Now what is distinctive to man is his *personality*. Kant employs this expression in a definite terminological meaning. We say, for example, that at a social gathering various 'personalities' were present, meaning people who 'are something', or of whom it is in any case said that they 'are somebody'. Kant does not use the word in this sense, indeed he does not use it in the plural at all. For Kant, the personality is that which constitutes the essence of the person as person, the *being a person*. This essence can be referred to only in the singular. In corresponding fashion, animality refers to what is specific to animals, and humanity refers to what is specific to human beings rather than to all humans taken collectively.

In what does the personality of a person consist? We can understand this if we consider the personality as distinct from the humanity and animality of man.[1] All these elements go together to define the full essence of man. To be sure, the traditional definition of man recognizes only two elements: *homo animale rationale*, man as the animal endowed with reason. It is thus animality which characterizes man as a *living* being. Reason is the second moment, but this does not make up the content of what Kant calls humanity. It is, rather, *humanity* that characterizes man as both a living and a rational being. The relation to animality is contained in the concept of humanity. In a certain sense, Kant's understanding of humanity is given by the traditional definition. But humanity in this specific sense does not exhaust the essence of man, which is realized and genuinely defined only in personality. This makes man not just a rational being but a being capable of *accountability*. Such a being must be capable of *self-responsibility*. The *essence of person*, the *personality*, consists in self-responsibility. Kant expressly emphasizes that the definition of man as rational animal does not suffice, for a being can be rational without being capable of acting on behalf of itself, of being practical for itself. Reason could be purely theoretical, such that man's actions were guided by reason, but with his impulses stemming entirely from sensibility, i.e. from his animality. The essence of man, if this is not exhaustively defined by his humanity, consists precisely in his going beyond himself, as person, in personality. Thus Kant defines 'personality' as 'that which elevates man above himself as part of the world of sense'.[2] The essence of man consists of more than just his humanity as the unity of reason and sensibility. Genuine being-human, the essence of humanity itself, resides in the person. So Kant also employs the expression 'humanity' as the formal term for the total and proper essence of man, speaking of the 'humanity in his person'.[3]

If we understand man not as a sensory world-entity, not cosmologically, but rather in his personality, what we have in view is a self-responsible being. *Self-responsibility* is the *fundamental kind of being* determining distinctively *human* action, i.e. *ethical praxis*. How do we encounter freedom here, when we take man according to his being a person, his personality?

b) The Two Ways to Freedom and the Distinction between Transcendental and Practical Freedom.
Possibility and Actuality of Freedom

Just as was the case in regard to Kant's first way to freedom, an understanding of his second way depends on paying close attention to the nature of the problematic and not just to the enunciated content. We would fall into the latter error were we to content ourselves with establishing that the first way treats freedom in the context of the totality of nature, thus as a concept of theoretical philosophy, while the second way treats freedom as a concept of practical philosophy, viewing the human being as a responsible autonomous acting practical nature, i.e. as person.

In the first way, the concept of freedom arises in connection with the question as to how the totality of appearances can itself be determined. Such a question is 'transcendental' in Kant's sense, i.e. it is directed to the conditions of the possibility of knowing objects as such. Thus the concept of freedom in Kant's first way is the concept of *transcendental freedom*. On the other hand, the concept of freedom in his second way, the concept oriented to ethical praxis, is what Kant calls '*practical freedom*'. After all our discussions, we understand these distinctions and expressions in a more definite and lively manner than was possible at the beginning of the lecture course, where we introduced Kant's two concepts of freedom merely through examples. But we still do not understand what is specific to Kant's second way, i.e. we still do not understand the problematic which lies hidden under the heading 'practical freedom'. As long as we are lacking in this understanding, we shall also be unable to grasp the problematic of the first way. This is so in spite of the fact that the first way appears to be independent of the second, but apparently not vice versa. Kant himself emphasizes in the *Foundations of the Metaphysics of Morals* that 'speculative philosophy' (i.e. the treatment of the problem of the Antinomies) 'clears the way for practical philosophy'.[4]

How are we to obtain a better understanding of the specific problematic of the second way? Can the first way give us a guideline here, assuming that we keep in view not just the results of the first way but also and primarily its problematic? The first way asked after freedom by inquiring into the possibility of its unity with the causality of nature. So there it is a question merely of the possibility of freedom, not of actual freedom or of the freedom which actually exists in man. Accordingly, the problem of the second way will be to discuss and demonstrate actually existing freedom as the freedom of the ethically acting human being. The *first way* treats the *possible freedom of a present being in general*, the *second* treats the *actual freedom* of a specific present being, i.e. of *the human being as person*.

§ 27. The Actuality of Human (Practical) Freedom

a) Freedom as Fact.
The Factuality (Actuality) of Practical Freedom in Ethical Praxis and the Problem of Its 'Experience'.
The Practical Reality of Freedom

How can the actual freedom of the person become a problem? When something actual becomes as such a problem, i.e. becomes questionable, what has to be decided is whether it is actual or not. In the end, such a question can only be settled if the actuality in question is exhibited and made accessible. It is a matter, therefore, of exhibiting freedom as a fact in human beings. Formally speaking, this is the same kind of task as showing that human beings eat meat. To be sure, not all humans do eat meat; there are some exceptions. It is the same in the case of freedom, for it often happens that people who could act freely do not do so in fact, e.g. because of some mental state that renders them unaccountable for their actions. It is only in and from experience that we can decide about the actual practical freedom of human beings. Accordingly, the concept of practical freedom is an 'empirical concept'. But Kant denies this: 'This [practical] freedom is not an empirical concept.'[5] 'We could not prove freedom to be actual in ourselves and in human nature.'[6] Practical freedom cannot be proved 'as something actual'. This means, then, that the actuality of practical freedom is not a problem; as with cosmological freedom we can inquire only into its *possibility*. But its possibility has precisely been decided by the first way to freedom. Since this first way shows that the freedom of a world-entity is possible in nature, the possibility of the freedom of the person in the context of the animal nature of man is also demonstrated. It is impossible to demonstrate practical freedom as something actual; to demonstrate the possibility of practical freedom is unnecessary. The second way to freedom thus loses all point and sense. But if there is indeed a second way to freedom, where Kant treats of a practical freedom unconsidered in the first way, the question arises as to *the sense in which practical freedom at all becomes a problem*.

We are surrounded by great difficulties. What appears, as long as we merely read off results and establish opinions, to be a smooth and obvious distinction between cosmological and practical freedom, proves thoroughly dubious as soon as we remember that philosophizing is here going on. Not only do we not know how the actual freedom of man is to be determined, we do not even know how to inquire into this. Only one negative point is initially clear, namely that practical freedom, according to Kant's own unambiguous statement, is not an empirical concept. However, this statement runs up against Kant's contrary claim, in the *Critique of Judgement*, that practical freedom is a 'fact'.[7] To be sure, the latter statement comes five years (1790) after the first (1785). Freedom as a fact, thus as experienceable, and practical freedom as not an empirical concept. Can these be reconciled?

The easiest solution in such cases is to say that the philosopher has changed his standpoint. Such things do happen, and Kant's philosophy is rich in 'overturnings'. These, however, cannot be comprehended by the disastrous method of the common understanding which wants to hold up different results against each other. By contrast, a genuine and substantively necessary overturning is always a sign of inner continuity and thus can be grasped only from the whole problematic. When confronted by opposing statements we must always exert ourselves to understand the underlying problem. It will then emerge that no change of standpoint in fact occurs.

We want to define the problem of practical freedom by answering the question of whether Kant's conflicting statements concerning practical freedom can be reconciled. That is, we want to indicate *how the actual freedom of man* – as distinct from the possibility of a world-entity's freedom in general – *can be interrogated*.

Freedom is not an empirical concept of experience, yet freedom is a fact. What is a fact? Kant distinguishes three kinds of 'knowable things': 'matters of opinion', 'matters of fact', 'matters of faith'.[8] *Res facti* (facts) are 'objects for concepts whose *objective* reality [among present objects] . . . can be proved'.[9] If we can demonstrate what we represent as occurring among present objects, i.e. as belonging to the being-present of objects, then it (e.g. a house) is a fact. Its reality is objective. What is real in a representation is its what-content. Demonstrating that something belongs among the objects that can be encountered as present involves presenting in an intuition what was initially just conceptually represented: the presentation of the universal *thought* in an immediate representing of a corresponding *present individual thing*.

The kind of intuitive presentation most familiar to us is *experience*, whether one's own or as mediated by others. But intuitive presentation can also occur through pure reason, and indeed 'from the theoretical or practical data of the same'.[10] In any case, the proof of the objectivity of the real must always be intuitive presentation, i.e. bringing something to givenness. There are different ways of giving. Here Kant maintains that there are data of both theoretical and practical reason. Earlier, during our preparation for the problem of the Antinomies, we heard of peculiar representations, the ideas, which conceive of a totality and of unconditionedness beyond anything experienceable. In principle, therefore, an idea cannot be intuitively presented. Experience always gives too little. But freedom is an idea: by freedom we understand *unconditioned causality*. Now Kant says: 'It is very remarkable, however, that even an idea of reason is to be found among the matters of fact: the idea of *freedom*.'[11] So this thesis claims that what we represent conceptually under freedom can be presented in a corresponding intuition. Clearly, *this* intuition of what is thought in the idea of freedom cannot be experience. For it belongs to the essence of an idea to go beyond all experience, i.e. not to be intuitively presentable in experience. But Kant explicitly says that there are intuitive presentations other than those of experience. So facts do not exist *only* in the domain of the experience of present natural things. *Freedom can very well be a fact without being an empirical concept.* The two assertions, that freedom is a fact, and that freedom is not an empirical concept, are by no means inconsistent with one another. However, it still remains unclear how this *non-experientially demonstrable factuality (actuality)* of freedom is to be understood, especially since Kant says that the idea of freedom is exhibited in experience. To the *new concept of factuality* there corresponds a *new concept of experience*.

One could give the whole problem a twist that would lead to a simple solution. One could point out that Kant does not say that freedom is a fact, but rather that 'the idea of freedom' is a fact. This means that it is a fact that we have the idea of freedom, that in our representing, as a contexture of occurrences of mental acts, there also occurs the act of representing freedom. This representing is a fact which says nothing about the actuality of what is represented. The representing and thinking of practical freedom can always be exhibited through psychological experience. However, such an interpretation of Kant would be quite erroneous. Kant does indeed say that the idea of freedom is a fact, but this means precisely that what is conceptually represented (objectively intended) in this idea can be intuitively presented as actual. Kant explicitly says of the idea of freedom: 'Among all the ideas of pure reason this is the only one whose object is a matter of fact, and must be included among the *scibilia*'.[12]

The *problem of actual freedom* is thus to *demonstrate its actuality*. But this is something different to pointing out, from experience, some actual case of being-free. It means *demonstrating the kind of actuality of freedom* and its mode of intuitive validation. Freedom is a fact, i.e. the *factuality of this fact* is precisely the crucial problem. When Kant says that 'we could not prove freedom to be actual in ourselves and in human nature',[13] this means only that freedom cannot be experienced in the manner of a natural thing. The reality of a natural thing is in every case objective, i.e. its what-content can be found in the actual objects of spatio-temporal experience. If freedom is not like this, yet is still factual, the reality of freedom must be capable of intuitive presentation in a mode other than that applicable for natural things. The reality of freedom requires another kind of actuality than that exhibited by natural objects, i.e. the reality of freedom is *not an objective reality*. Alternatively, if one conceives actuality (as Kant does here) as objective actuality, one could say that the objectivity of freedom differs from the objectivity of natural things. *The factuality corresponding to the idea of freedom is that of praxis.* We experience the reality of freedom in practical will-governed action. *Freedom possesses practical reality*, i.e. its objective reality is practical in respect of its objectivity. We can now understand Kant's statement that 'among the matters of fact' there is also 'the idea of freedom, whose reality, as a specific kind of causality . . . can be established in actual actions, hence in experience, through practical laws of pure reason'.[14] Here we have at the same time an indication of the direction in which the problem of actual freedom, that is, of the actuality of freedom, is to be sought. The reality of the idea of freedom, what is represented in the concept of the essence of freedom, can be exhibited as actual 'through practical laws of pure reason'.

To summarize. The second way poses the problem of actual freedom, i.e. the *question concerning the actuality of freedom*. Answering this question involves determining the mode of possible knowledge of actual freedom: the *problem of the specific essence of the 'experience' of freedom in will-governed action*. The first way inquires into the possibility of a unity between freedom and nature; the second way inquires into freedom's *kind of actuality*, i.e. in Kant's terms, into the way in which the idea of freedom can be demonstrated as actual in its reality. It can be demonstrated through the practical laws of pure reason, so its reality is practical. In its essential content, freedom belongs in the actuality of the practical. To demonstrate the reality of freedom means finding grounds to prove 'that freedom does in fact belong to the human will (and thus to the will of all rational beings)'.[15] Once again, this sounds as if freedom can be demonstrated empirically as something present. After what has been said, however, we can see that the problem concerns the way in which the actuality (factuality) of freedom is to be understood. Clearly, this question needs to be answered before actually existing freedom can itself become a problem. If we can succeed in showing how the factuality of freedom is to be understood, this will give a preliminary indication of the nature of that 'experience' which makes actual freedom accessible as such.

Practical action is the way of being of the person. Experience of practical freedom is experience of the person as person. Personality is the proper essence of man. Experience of the person is at the same time the essential experience of man, the mode of knowing which reveals man in his proper actuality. To be sure, Kant does not speak of the 'experience' of the person as such. Yet while Kant reserves the term 'experience' for the disclosure of natural things, the former way of speaking is entirely consonant with his general problematic. Since Kant did not proceed any further, the problem of the factuality of freedom has become surrounded by difficulties and misunderstandings. These have in no way been overcome today, indeed they have not even been squarely faced. The philosophy of value in particular represents a total distortion of the genuinely Kantian problem.

b) The Essence of Pure Reason as Practical.
Pure Practical Reason as Pure Will

Kant's thesis concerning the actuality of freedom runs as follows: *the objective reality of freedom can be demonstrated only through practical laws of pure reason.* This thesis lays down the genuine task of the second way and also the specific problematic. The factuality of freedom can be demonstrated only from and in the factuality of the practical lawfulness of pure reason. In brief, the fact of freedom is accessible only in the understanding of the *facticity of freedom.* The facticity of freedom can be demonstrated and clarified only from the *facticity of pure reason as practical.* So the question becomes: *what is the essence of pure reason as practical?* Further, *what kind of factuality belongs to the essence of pure practical reason?* The essence of something is what prescribes its mode of factuality (actuality).

In moving from the first to the second way, we said that the latter aims at the freedom of man as a rational being. But what is distinctive to man is his personality, the essence of which is self-responsibility. The authentic essence of the humanity of man, thus also the essence of pure reason as practical, must be understood from self-responsibility. We have already quoted Kant's thesis and the task contained therein: to demonstrate the objective reality of freedom solely through the practical laws of pure reason. We are now asking: what is the essence of pure reason as practical? This involves the general question of the nature of practical reason as such. What do 'practical' and 'praxis' mean? Praxis means action. But we know that action as such is the relation of a subject of causality to the effect. Praxis is the particular kind of action made possible by a *will,* i.e. such that the relation of the subject of the causation, the determining instance, to the effect, occurs through will. The will is 'a power to act according to concepts'. A concept is the representation of something, being able and willing to act according to what is thus represented. For example, the determining instance may be the representation of the scientific education of man. What is represented in this representation can determine an action. An effect that is determined in this way is will-governed, i.e. praxis. According to Kant's way of speaking, an action can also be caused by a machine, but since the machine and its parts do not act through willing, there is in this case no effecting through concepts.

Will is the power of acting in the sense of praxis. However, to will there belongs this determining representation of something. Conceptual representing is a matter of the understanding. Insofar as what is represented functions as determining instance, as principle, representing involves the capacity for relating to principles, i.e. reason. Will and reason belong together as a representing that determines an effect within praxis. *Will is nothing other than practical reason and vice versa*. Practical reason is will, i.e. *a capacity to effect according to the representation of something as principle*. Kant often speaks of 'practical reason' or of 'the will of a rational being'.[16] Reason is practical as 'a cause determining the will'.[17] Will is 'causality through reason',[18] i.e. reason in its practical employment, practical reason. So 'practical knowledge' has to do exclusively with 'the determining ground of the will'.[19]

We are inquiring into the essence of pure practical reason. When we speak of practical reason we are not considering reason in its relation to objects; instead, we have to do with a will. We are considering reason in its relation to the 'will and its causality',[20] i.e. we are asking about how reason determines the will. But what does it mean to say that *pure* reason is practical? Pure reason is a representing of something. What is represented in pure reason does not derive from experience and is not directed toward experience. If I represent to myself human beings possessing a specific kind of education, and if what I thus represent determines my action, then this action is *will-governed*, practical, but not through pure reason. For here the determining instance, this representation of a specific kind of education, is obtained through experience of actually present human beings with definite characteristics. What determines the will are the experienceable beings that are to be brought forth. The will is not determined *a priori* independently of experience, i.e. it is not purely determined will.

When is a will determined *a priori*? When is practical reason *practical as pure reason*? When it is not determined by that which is to be effected, nor by the representation of such, but by . . . by what then? Is there anything that could determine the will other than the representation of a desired effect? What is brought about by the will is always something actual and empirical. The will is 'a faculty ... either of bringing forth objects corresponding to representations, or of determining itself, i.e. its causality to effect such objects'.[21] Will is the capacity to determine one's causality, to determine oneself in one's causation. In what way determine? Either through something represented that is to be brought forth (effected), or otherwise what? What other possibilities of determination does the will possess? Now if will can determine its own causation, it has the possibility of determining itself in its causation through itself. What does this mean? As the capacity to bring about something corresponding to representations, the will is itself representing the possible determining ground for its willing. Will-governed determining is intrinsically 'addressed' to itself. In will-governed representing, therefore, willing is always and necessarily co-represented. The willing as such can thus be represented as the determining instance. If this occurs, willing as such is the determining instance of the will. In this case willing takes its determining ground not from somewhere else but *from itself*. And what does willing take from itself? It takes itself, in its essence.

The will is the determining instance for itself. It determines itself from what it *is* itself in its essence. The essence of the will is thus the determining instance for willing. Such a willing is determined solely through itself, not through anything experienceable, i.e. empirical. Such a will is *pure will*. *Pure will is pure reason* which, for itself alone, determines itself to will-governed action, i.e. to praxis. *Pure will is pure reason which is practical only for itself.* We can now understand the statement with which Kant opens the thematic discussion in the *Foundations of the Metaphysics of Morals*: 'Nothing in the world – indeed nothing even beyond the world – can possibly be conceived which could be called good without qualification except a *good will*.'[22] What is good without qualification is what is to be highly valued in itself: 'The good will is not good because of what it effects or accomplishes or because of its adequacy to achieve some proposed end; it is good only because of its willing, i.e. it is good of itself.'[23] *Qua* will, i.e. insofar as it only wills willing, a good will is absolutely good. *Qua* absolutely good, a good will is a pure will.

We have now presented *the essence of pure practical reason as pure will*. And yet we are still not adequately prepared for understanding Kant's thesis that the objective reality of freedom can be demonstrated only through practical laws of pure reason.[24] What are these laws of pure practical reason? How do we arrive at these laws? They belong to pure practical reason, thus to the pure will. What does the pure will have to do with laws, and what is the law of the pure will, the fundamental law of pure practical reason?

c) The Actuality of Pure Practical Reason in the Moral Law

Pure will is that willing which is determined solely by the essence of will as such. Pure willing is the willing of one's own essence as will. The determining instance for pure will, the causation for this itself, resides in its own essence insofar as this is represented as determining, i.e. is willed purely. But the causation, the causality of something, is always the law of the existence of something. In Kant's words, this means that 'the concept of causality always contains a relation to a law which determines the existence of the many in their relation to one another'.[25] The law of pure will does not pertain to this or that representable effect but is the law for the existence of the will, i.e. the will is the willing itself. Pure will, however, i.e. the essence of the will as determinatively representing pure willing, is the mode of law-giving. Everything that determines contains nothing other than the mode and form of the will's pure willing in and for itself. This mode as pure, the form of the how, is the mode of law-giving for willing. When this alone is determining, then the law of pure will is nothing else than the form of law-giving for a pure will.

It thus emerges that the *basic law of the pure will, of pure practical reason,* is nothing else than the *form of law-giving*. This is the meaning of the statement that the basic law of ethics is a formal law. 'Formal' is the counter-concept to 'material'. If these expressions are understood in the vulgar sense, i.e. if their genuine metaphysical meaning is not recognized, 'formal' will have connotations of emptiness and indefiniteness. A formal ethical law will then be something empty, i.e. saying nothing about what I should materially do. An ethics based upon a formal law would necessarily fail, for actual practical ethical action always requires definite decisions. Such an ethic remains stuck in formalism. Instead of this, various attempts (Max Scheler, Nicolai Hartmann) are today made to construct a *material ethic of value*. But this interpretation, in rejecting Kant's ethics as formalistic, totally misunderstands the crucial problem in the concept of 'the formal'. This is because the factuality of pure practical reason does not become a central problem. The law of pure will is formal but not empty. Instead, the form of the law is precisely the decisive, proper, and determining instance in relation to the law.

What is genuinely law-giving for willing is the actual pure willing itself and nothing else. Unless pure willing, as the genuinely actual of all ethical action, actually wills itself, a material table of values – however finely structured and comprehensive – remains a pure phantom with no binding force. This willing of itself is allegedly empty, but at bottom it is precisely this which is most concrete in the lawfulness of ethical action. The ethicality of action does not consist in realizing so-called values, but in the actual willing to take responsibility, in the decision to exist within this responsibility.

Yet to will the essence of willing – is this not in fact an empty willing? What kind of will is it which purely wills itself? Such a will determines its own willing unconditionally. It cannot help but be in harmony with itself, its pure essence, i.e. it cannot but be good. And a will that cannot but be good is a perfectly good will, or as Kant says, a holy, divine will.

However, where the pure will does not unconditionally obey its own essence, but rather, as in the case of a finite being possessing sensibility, can and does become determined by other motives, the pure law-giving of the will has the character of a command or imperative, i.e. of a 'you ought'. To the holy willing (to the necessarily good will) the law is simply what it in any case wills. But to the contingently good will the law is the 'ought' of pure willing. What 'ought to be' is pure willing, i.e. the willing that does not aim at something else attainable by willing. The law of the will does not say 'you ought' in the conditional sense, e.g. you ought to be truthful if you wish to be respected in human society. Instead, the law speaks unconditionally: you ought to act in such and such a way, with no ifs and buts. Now in logic a statement of the form 'if-then' is called 'hypothetical' (ὑπόθεσις, presupposition), while a simple 'is' statement is called 'categorical'. An ought which is subject to conditions is a hypothetical imperative, but the ought demanded by pure willing is a categorical imperative. Thus *the fundamental law of a finite pure willing, i.e. of a pure practical reason, is a categorical imperative*. How then does it run?, so we ask quite involuntarily. But it is not at all permissible to ask this now. Why not? Let us once again reflect upon our task and upon what we have achieved thus far. We are concerned to understand the thesis that the objective reality of freedom can only be demonstrated through the practical laws of pure reason. We have discovered the fundamental law of pure practical reason, and have thus attained the necessary basis for demonstrating the factuality of freedom in Kant's sense.

Have we really arrived at the fundamental law of pure practical reason? Could we have obtained this at all? How have we proceeded thus far? We have discussed what belongs to the idea of a pure will as such, i.e. what pure practical reason is as such. Further, we have discussed the necessary character of the law of a pure will insofar as finite will is simultaneously determined through sensibility. We have seen that the law must be a categorical imperative. But we have not yet demonstrated that a law which has the form of the categorical imperative actually exists. We have not even shown that finite pure practical reason actually exists.

d) The Categorical Imperative.
On the Question of Its Actuality and 'Universal Validity'

After all this it will be said that, while the actual existence of finite pure practical reason has admittedly not been demonstrated, such demonstration is in any case unnecessary. Man just 'is' a finite rational being. Whether man is the only such being remains unknown and is irrelevant to our purposes. It is enough that one such being, i.e. man, factually exists. Or is this also in need of demonstration? We cannot see how we human beings are supposed to provide a factual proof that we factually exist. The demand for such a proof is senseless. But granted this, does it follow that we exist, or that our existence is self-evident? And if we do assume this as self-evident, does it follow that a pure practical reason exists? This is open to doubt. Not only do we not know whether the existence of man implies the existence of a pure will, we do not even know what the factual existence of a pure will is supposed to be. For in the end, the factuality of a pure will, i.e. existence in and as pure will, is something totally different from the being-present of man as a world-entity. So the factuality of the fundamental law of pure practical reason, and thus also of a categorical imperative, is of a nature all its own.

The possibility of proving the factuality of practical freedom depends on demonstrating the fact of a pure practical reason. Freedom 'is revealed by the moral law'.[26] Thus the latter must itself first be revealed as actual. If the factuality of freedom is shown by its actuality, then the *possibility* of freedom is also established. What is actual must be possible. If the actuality of freedom has a nature all its own, so also must the possibility of freedom. In regard to the first way to freedom this means that the possibility of practical freedom cannot be immediately equated with the possibility of transcendental freedom. The specific problem of the second way is thus noticeably sharpened. Our previous construction of the idea of a pure will, of a complete, necessary and contingently pure will, and of the kind of lawfulness (categorical imperative) belonging to this, still does not prove the *factuality of a pure practical reason*. We know only that this factuality has a nature all its own, which does not coincide with the being-present of human beings. What kind of factuality is it then? How is the specific factuality of pure will, of pure reason as practical, to be demonstrated? Do we not first require a sufficiently comprehensive elucidation of the essence of this specific kind of factuality? Or is the most obvious method simply to assert the factual existence of a pure will, treating the question of the essence of this fact, i.e. the facticity of the human being as existing person, as a matter for subsequent investigation?

To demonstrate the factual existence of pure practical reason it is not unconditionally necessary to possess a well-formed and comprehensively grounded concept of the facticity of this fact. On the other hand, it is not at all possible to undertake the demonstration of the factuality of pure will in man without a prior preconceptual understanding of the essence of this factuality. It is a matter of showing that, in man, pure reason alone is practical for itself, that pure reason determines the will without regard to a desired effect, and that pure reason practically wills a pure will. It is a matter of showing that man actually knows himself to be under the obligation of a pure willing.

If man in himself actually wills a pure will (e.g. wills to speak the truth) this means that his willing is governed only by the representation of a pure willing. The representing of the laws of practical action is undertaken by reason. When pure will, not this or that empirically determined will, is represented as regulative, this is a law-giving from pure reason. Then it is reason which determines action practically, purely from itself. The binding character of the pure will is not dependent on contingent factors but is universally valid. As Kant says, it is an objectively conditioned and not a subjectively conditioned law. The purity of willing raises the will of the individual up beyond the contingency of his particular circumstances. The purity of willing grounds the possibility of the universal validity of the law of the will. The reverse does not apply, i.e. the purity of willing is not a consequence of the universality of the law. If this willing of the pure will transcends the contingency of empirical action, this does not amount to becoming lost in the empty abstraction of a valid form of lawfulness, such that what one is to do remains totally indeterminate. Rather, this transcending is the coming into operation of genuine concrete willing, concrete because it wills willing and nothing else besides. On the other hand, when someone subjects himself to a law valid only for his particular subjective will, this subjective principle is a 'maxim'. 'Tell someone, for instance, that in his youth he should work and save in order not to want in his old age – that is a correct and important precept of the will. One easily sees, however, that the will is thereby directed to something else.'[27]

The pure will, since it is not conditioned by specific subjective aims, is an objective law and not a maxim. On the other hand, if we act in such a way that the determining ground of our willing, i.e. our maxims, can always at the same time determine *every willing as such*, then we act according to the objective fundamental law of our will. Thus the objective fundamental law of pure practical reason, having the character of an unconditional command (categorical imperative) runs as follows: 'So act that the maxim of your will could always hold at the same time as the principle of a universal legislation.'[28]

Let us repeat our guiding question: how does pure reason actually prove itself as practical? It does so by virtue of the categorical imperative demonstrating its factuality. How does this occur? By the proof of *the factuality of the consciousness of this fundamental law of reason*. But what does this now mean? This is the *decisive point for the understanding of the whole problem*. Kant says that we become conscious of the moral law 'as soon as we construct maxims for the will'.[29] The categorical imperative impresses itself upon us from itself. The fact of this law is 'undeniable'.[30] 'The common understanding' can see it 'without instruction'.[31] 'This principle needs no search and no invention, having long been in the reason of all men and embodied in their being. It is the principle of *ethics*.'[32]

These statements, especially the last, sound very peculiar, and are highly susceptible of misunderstanding. The categorical imperative as undeniable and immediately evident to the commonest reason? As a fact embodied in the essence of man? So something that is always present and that we can confirm at any time, just like our nose and ears? And present to the commonest reason? If this were so, we would not need to approach it in such a speculative way and by means of a special method.

Let us examine Kant's claim. If we observe ourselves in a completely unprejudiced way, without any assistance from philosophy, do we discover the categorical imperative as a fact within us? Do we discover as a fact the demand: 'So act that the maxim of your will could always hold at the same time as the principle of a universal legislation'. We discover nothing of the sort. Instead, we find that this principle has its origin in philosophical thought, indeed in a specific philosophical system. At best, we can discover the reason that precisely *Kant* came up with this categorical imperative. Indeed, this explanation from the history of ideas has long been available, usually as a way of making the matter itself intelligible. The categorical imperative of pure practical reason belongs to the Age of Enlightenment, to the time of the Prussia of Frederick the Great. Expressed in contemporary terms: the categorical imperative is a specific sociologically determined philosophico-ethico ideology, i.e. by no means is it the most general law of action for all rational beings as maintained by Kant. We dispense here with any discussion of how much an intellectual-historical sociological explanation can contribute to the substantive understanding of a philosophical problematic. We can easily admit that the Enlightenment, the Prussian state and so forth, influenced both Kant's concrete existence and his philosophical work. We must even emphasize that it would be unnatural if the situation were otherwise.

§ 28. The Consciousness of Human Freedom and Its Actuality

a) Pure Will and Actuality.
The Specific Character of Will-governed Actuality as Fact

Has all this provided us with an understanding of the matter at hand? Or does this talk about intellectual history and sociology prove only that we have not understood anything at all, that we are not even in possession of the most elementary conditions for such an understanding? If this is so, then just one thing is initially clear, namely that it is not the province of everyday understanding and vulgar philosophical discussion to decide in what way the categorical imperative is a fact, nor to decide what it means for this fact to be accessible to the common understanding. Indeed our examination has confirmed the contrary. We do not discover any trace of this fact, and we could never do so by proceeding in this way. This is because, in this kind of immediate self-observation, or in the phenomenological searching out of our consciousness for the presence of the categorical imperative, we have from the very beginning gone astray concerning the kind of factuality characteristic of this fact.

Kant nowhere maintains that the fact of the categorical imperative simply occurs within us like nerves and veins, but with the difference that it is spiritual rather than material. Instead, Kant says that 'it is the moral law, of which we become immediately conscious as soon as we construct maxims of the will'.[33] Thus the experience of the principle of pure will is subject to the condition 'as soon as we construct maxims of the will', i.e. as soon as we actually will, as soon as we become conscious of the motive of action and make decisions about it. The condition of the possibility of the experience of the law as fact is that we betake ourselves into the specific region of such facts, i.e. that we actually will. Actually willing does not mean wishing to will, thinking that one wills, but rather: at all times, here and now, willing.

But willing what precisely? Again, this seductive question already leads us astray from actual willing. The question looks as if one is making an effort to actually will, for one is seeking something that can be willed. But in this way willing is closed off to precisely the one who at that moment is supposed to will. Willing what? Everyone who actually wills knows: *to actually will is to will nothing else but the ought of one's existence.*

Only in this kind of willing is that actual within which the fact of the ethical law is actually a fact. This actuality of the ought is the actuality of our will in a double sense. First, it is the actuality that gives what is actual only through and in our will. Secondly and following on from this, it is the actuality that is proper to our will as will. The factuality of this fact does not stand over against us but belongs with us ourselves such that we *are claimed* for the possibility of this actuality, not just in this or that way, but in our *essence*. When Kant says that even the commonest understanding can assure itself of the fact of the categorical imperative he does not mean that this common understanding, which in the domain of theory falls prey to illusion and to the deceptive employment of principles, is the proper faculty for apprehending the fact of the ethical law. What he means is that theoretical or philosophical knowledge is not relevant to this sphere, i.e. that here the will alone decides. Knowledge of the determining ground of action belongs to willing as effecting through representation of what is willed. Actual willing is always clear about its determining grounds. Actual willing is a specific kind of actual knowing and understanding. It is a kind of knowing that cannot be replaced by anything else, least of all through (e.g. psychological) knowledge of human beings.

As soon as we actually will we see that human reason, as Kant says 'incorruptible and self-constrained, in every action confronts the maxim of the will with the pure will, i.e. with itself regarded as *a priori* practical'.[34] In actual willing we experience that the essence of willing, the will that wills on behalf of itself, demands to be willed. Whether the willing factically succeeds or not is a secondary question; it is sufficient that the fact of the ought announces itself in the actual willing. In actual willing we bring ourselves into the situation where we have to decide on the determining grounds of our action. But, one will say, this only transfers the problem to actual willing. Only when willing is actual does pure practical reason possess actuality. Just as with a chair: only when it gets built can it be present. However, this again falls into the error of measuring the actuality of the will against that of a present thing.

Even when we avoid decisions, even when we dissemble to ourselves about the motives for our actions, we have actually *decided* to turn away from the ought. Indeed, precisely in this turning away do we experience the fact of the ought most vividly. In this not-willing as a specific kind of willing there lurks a definite knowledge of the ought, i.e. *that* we ought and *what* we ought. The actuality of willing does not begin where an act of will is present, and by no means ceases where we do not earnestly will. This not-earnestly-willing, this letting things go their own way, is perhaps even the most frequent mode of the actuality of the will, for which reason we so easily overlook it, and go astray within it.

It should now be clear that we can never encounter the fact of the ought by analysing and observing our own action and willing in the manner of physical occurrences. *The actuality of willing only exists in the willing of this actuality.* In so doing, we experience the fact that pure reason alone is practical for itself, i.e. that the pure will, as the essence of the will, announces itself as the will's determining ground. To be sure, one might say, this fact of an unconditional obligation may well exist, and if so is obviously connected with what we call 'conscience'. It could also be conceded that this fact represents a specific kind of factuality quite different from that pertaining to present things, for which reason it would be senseless to ask whether conscience and the like is or is not present. Or to want to prove through ethnological research that particular peoples do not possess a conscience, have no word for this, and so forth. As if ethnology could prove anything of the kind, as if it would say anything either for or against the factuality of conscience if it could be established that this conscience does not exist everywhere and at all times.

Yet even if we do not fall prey to such misinterpretations, it does not follow that the fundamental law of pure practical reason must be understood in terms of the formula of the Kantian categorical imperative. Indeed it is not the formula that is important; it is not at all intended that whoever acts in a moral way must expressly hold to the formula. Rather, the formula is only one among many possible philosophical interpretations; in fact we find a number of different interpretations in Kant himself. But irrespective of the possible diversity of formulas and directions of interpretation, they all refer to one essential and decisive thing about the facticity of the fact of man in the authenticity of his essence. It is this alone that concerns us here.

As long as we hang on mere words, taking the Kantian philosophy, likewise every other great and genuine philosophy, as an interesting historical standpoint, as long as we do not resolutely enter into the occurrence of philosophy by means of a philosophizing controversy, everything remains closed to us. At best we shall discover some interesting points of view, but without understanding why so much conceptual work was needed to put them forward. If true controversy takes place, however, it becomes irrelevant whether the categorical imperative is formulated by Kant or someone else. To be sure, controversy does not mean what the common understanding assumes, i.e. criticizing and contradicting. Instead, it is a bringing back of the other, and thereby also of oneself, to what is primary and originary, to that which, as the essential, is itself the common, and thus not needful of any subsequent alliance. *Philosophical controversy is interpretation as destruction.*

b) The Fact of the Ethical Law and the Consciousness of the Freedom of the Will

In order that the Kantian interpretation of the essence of the moral law may not appear so strange, I would like to briefly discuss *one* more formulation of the categorical imperative. It is to be found in the *Foundations of the Metaphysics of Morals,* and runs: 'Act so that you treat humanity, whether in your own person or in that of another, always as an end and never as a means only'.[35] The end of human action is humanity. What does 'end' [*Zweck*] mean? We know this, without having previously discussed the concept of end. An end is what is represented in advance as the determining ground for the actualization of an object. The end has the character of the determining instance. What should never be a means but only an end, is that which cannot be determining for the sake of something else, i.e. what determines the will as end: 'the humanity in the person', the essence of man as personality. Thus the categorical imperative says: before anything else, in all your actions, always act in your essence. The essence of person is this self-responsibility: to bind oneself to oneself, but not egotistically, i.e. not in relation to the accidental 'I'. To be in the mode of self-responsibility, to answer only to the essence of one's self. To give this priority in everything, to will the ought of pure willing.

Sophistry creeps in here all too quickly and easily, attempting to open a theoretical speculative discussion about the essence of man, claiming that we do not know this, or at least, that there is no general agreement on the subject. In this way one postpones actual willing and acting to a time when theoretical agreement has been reached, i.e. to a time that is never given to the temporality of man; one evades precisely that which alone actuates the actuality of man and forms his essentiality. In other words, we first occupy ourselves with a programme, then gather together those who represent it and attach themselves to it. We then wonder why we never achieve unity and commonality, i.e. power of existence. As if this were something that could be achieved subsequently and from the outside. We do not grasp that actual essential willing already in itself brings about mutual understanding, and this through the mystery of the actual willing of the individual.

What is crucial for understanding the moral law, therefore, is not that we come to know any formula, or that some value is held up before us. It is not a matter of a table of values hovering over us, as if individual human beings were only realizers of the law in the same way that individual tables realize the essence of tablehood. It is not a formula and rule that we come to understand, but the character of the specific actuality of action, i.e. what is and becomes actual in and as action. However, Kant remains a long way from explicitly making this factuality as such into a central metaphysical problem, i.e. from bringing its conceptual articulation over into the essence of man and thus arriving at the threshold of a fundamentally different problematic. This is one of the reasons that Kant's decisive insights have remained without effect for the philosophical problematic as such.

Despite all this, it remains true that Kant experienced, albeit within the indicated limits, the *specificity of will-governed actuality as fact*, and defined the problematic of practical reason from this experience. *The factuality of the fact of pure practical reason is always and only given by us ourselves* in our resolve *to* pure willing or *against* this, or again, in confusion and indecision by mixing together willing and not-willing. This factuality of willing is itself only accessible through a knowledge that arises from such willing and not-willing, or better, that already consists precisely in this. The actuality of the pure will does not mark out a domain of objects which at first stand indifferently over against us, only subsequently to be willed or not-willed. Rather, willing or not-willing is what first allows this actuality *to occur* and in its own way *to be*.

This pure willing is the praxis in and through which the fundamental law of pure practical reason has actuality. The pure will is not a mental occurrence that perceives the value of an independently existing law and directs our behaviour accordingly, but itself *constitutes the factuality* of the law of pure practical reason. Only because, and insofar as, the pure will wills, does the law exist.

We are now in a position to understand the factuality of a pure practical reason and its law. We understand that, here in this domain, the existence of facts means that the fact of pure reason and its law is provable and proven. Only now are we adequately prepared for the task contained in the main thesis: to present the objective reality, i.e. practical reality, the specific factuality of freedom, solely through the factuality of the law of pure practical reason.

What course must this proof take? If we ask in this way we do not understand the problem. Is it therefore beside the point to engage in long-winded discussions concerning the mode of proof? Should we simply set to work and carry through the proof? This also is a misunderstanding of the problem. For the proof has already been given. This is the most essential thing to grasp for a real understanding of the whole problem of practical freedom and its objective reality.

I said earlier that the proof of the factuality of freedom is short, namely so short that when the task of this proof is grasped, the proof is not at all necessary – at any rate if by proof we understand the theoretical demonstration of a present freedom from the prior demonstration of the presence of the practical law. The proof of the practical reality of freedom consists in nothing else than in understanding that freedom exists only as the actual willing of the pure ought. The actualization and actuality of practical freedom consists in nothing else than actual willing letting its own essence determine itself. We can now derive the *essence of freedom* from the character of the factuality of the fact of practical freedom: *practical freedom is self-legislation, pure will, autonomy*. Freedom now reveals itself as *the condition of the possibility of the factuality of pure practical reason*. Practical freedom as autonomy is self-responsibility, which is the essence of the personality of the human person, the authentic essence, the humanity of man.

So we now see: pure will – pure practical reason – the lawfulness of the fundamental law of factical action – self-responsibility – personality – freedom. All these necessarily belong together. We can now see the specific conditioning relations between practical reason and freedom. Practical reason and its law is 'the condition . . . under which freedom [as autonomy] can be known',[36] i.e. *the law is the ground of the possibility of knowledge of freedom (ratio cognoscendi)*. On the other hand, freedom is the ground of the possibility of the being of the law and of practical reason, the *ratio essendi* of the moral law. 'For had not the moral law already been distinctly thought in our reason, we would never have been justified in assuming anything like freedom, even though it is not self-contradictory. But if there were no freedom, the moral law would never have been encountered in us.'[37] 'Freedom and unconditional practical law reciprocally imply one another. I do not here ask whether they are actually different, instead of an unconditional law being merely the self-consciousness of a pure practical reason, and thus identical with the positive concept of freedom.'[38] Although Kant does not ask this here, at this particular point, the task of the whole analytic of practical reason is precisely to show 'this fact to be inextricably bound up with the consciousness of freedom of the will, and actually to be identical with it'.[39]

Notes

1 Cf. Kant, *Religion Within the Limits of Reason Alone*, translated by Theodore M. Greene and Hoyt H. Hudson, Harper and Row, New York, 1934, Book One, Section II (VI, 164).

2 *Critique of Practical Reason*, p. 193 (V, 86).

3 *Critique of Practical Reason*, p. 194 (V, 88).

4 *Foundations of the Metaphysics of Morals*, p. 111 (IV, 457).

5 *Foundations*, pp. 110–11 (IV, 455).

6 *Foundations*, pp. 103–4 (IV, 448).

7 *Critique of Judgement*, § 91, p. 362 (V, 469).

8 *Critique of Judgement*, § 91, p. 360 (V, 467).

9 *Critique of Judgement*, § 91, p. 361 (V, 468).

10 *Critique of Judgement*, § 91, p. 362 (V, 469).

11 *Critique of Judgement*, § 91, p. 362 (V, 469).

12 *Critique of Judgement*, § 91, p. 362 (V, 469).

13 *Foundations*, pp. 103–4 (IV, 448).

14 *Critique of Judgement*, § 91, p. 362 (V, 469).

15 *Critique of Practical Reason*, p. 129 (V, 16).

16 *Foundations*, p. 103 (IV, 448).

17 *Foundations*, p. 114 note (IV, 460).

18 *Foundations*, p. 115 (IV, 461).

19 *Critique of Practical Reason*, p. 146 (V, 35).

20 *Critique of Practical Reason*, p. 143 (V, 32).

21 *Critique of Practical Reason*, p. 128 (V, 15).

22 *Foundations*, p. 55 (IV, 393).

23 *Foundations*, p. 56 (IV, 394).

24 Cf. *Critique of Judgement*, § 91, p. 362 (V, 469); cf. above p. 185.

25 *Critique of Practical Reason*, p. 196 (V, 90).

26 *Critique of Practical Reason*, p. 119 (V, 5).

27 *Critique of Practical Reason*, p. 131 (V, 20).

28 *Critique of Practical Reason*, p. 142 (V, 31).

29 *Critique of Practical Reason*, p. 141 (V, 30).

30 *Critique of Practical Reason*, p. 143 (V, 32).

31 *Critique of Practical Reason*, p. 148 (V, 36).

32 *Critique of Practical Reason*, p. 210 (V, 105).

33 *Critique of Practical Reason*, p. 141 (V, 30).

34 *Critique of Practical Reason*, p. 143 (V, 32).

35 *Foundations*, p. 87 (IV, 429).

36 *Critique of Practical Reason*, p. 119 note (V, 5).

37 *Critique of Practical Reason*, p. 119 note (V, 5).

38 *Critique of Practical Reason*, p. 140 (V, 29).

39 *Critique of Practical Reason*, p. 152 (V, 42).

CONCLUSION

The Proper Ontological Dimension of Freedom.
The Rootedness of the Question of Being in the Question Concerning the Essence of Human Freedom.
Freedom as the Ground of Causality

___

§ 29. The Limits of the Kantian Discussion of Freedom. Kant's Binding of the Problem of Freedom to the Problem of Causality

We have arrived at the goal of Kant's second way to freedom. It was necessary to travel along both roads in order to really experience their utter distinctiveness, and thus to obtain a feeling for the whole weight of the problem of freedom.

The interpretation of the Kantian problem of freedom was necessary because we recognized that, in the metaphysical tradition, the question of freedom concerns a particular kind of causality. Kant treats the problem of causality as such, as well as the problem of freedom as a particular kind of causality, in a more radical manner than anyone else. Once the problem of freedom is understood in a metaphysical sense, controversy with Kant is not only unavoidable, but must stand in the forefront. Once freedom is understood as a metaphysical problem, the question is already raised as to whether freedom is a kind of causality, or whether, on the contrary, causality is a problem of freedom.

What if the latter were the case? As a category, causality is a basic character of the being of beings. If we consider that the being of beings is proximally comprehended as constant presence – and this involves producedness, producing, finishing in the broad sense of actualizing – it is clear that precisely *causality*, in the traditional sense of the being of beings, in common understanding as in traditional metaphysics, is the *fundamental category of being as being-present*. If *causality is a problem of freedom* and not vice versa then the *problem of being in general* is in itself a *problem of freedom*. However, the problem of being, as we showed in our preliminary considerations, is the fundamental problem of philosophy as such. Thus *the question concerning the essence of human freedom is the fundamental question of philosophy, in which is rooted even the question of being*. But this is the thesis we already discussed at the end of our preliminary considerations, and in the transition to the problem of freedom as causality. The problem of freedom as causality has now been discussed. But it has not been shown that causality is a problem of freedom, i.e. that the question of being is built into the problem of freedom. Our basic thesis has not been established.

This is indeed the situation. And yet, if we have really understood, we have grasped something essential, namely that there is something very specific and unique about the actuality of freedom, thus about the problematic that aims at it and especially about the proofs which can here be carried out. The basic thesis, which we have seemingly forced into philosophy by violent means, is not a statement that can be theoretically proven by the limited methods of a science. For it says nothing at all about anything present. To be sure, it says something about essence. But essence is not capable of straightforward examination. Essence remains closed off to us as long as we ourselves do not become essential in our essence.

What we originally sought was a simple characterization of Kant's two ways to freedom. We said that the first way concerns the *possibility* of freedom, the second way the *actuality* of freedom. Then we rejected this characterization. Now that we have familiarized ourselves with both ways we may take it up again, for properly understood it permits a crucial concentration of the whole problem. The *actuality* of practical freedom is indeed the problem of the second way. Yet the actuality of this actual freedom does not become a problem such that the essence of this specific being, i.e. of the being announced in the will-governed action of the human person, is genuinely interrogated. The actuality of freedom is not interrogated in a properly metaphysical sense, not *as a problem of being*.

The *possibility* of freedom is the problem of the first way, but only in the specific *form* of an inquiry into the possibility of the unity of freedom and natural causality. This makes it look as if the possibility of freedom is a problem only insofar as freedom is a kind of causality. Once freedom is conceived in this fashion, the question of its possibility can concern nothing else but the compatibility of this causality with natural causality.

However, the possibility of freedom precisely does not become a problem such that the specific being of the beings to be unified through the two causalities is genuinely interrogated. *Both ways neglect the question of the ontological character of what is placed in question as possible and actual.* The possibility as also the actuality of freedom as freedom remains undefined, likewise (although this alone is constantly under discussion) the relation between the actuality of freedom and its possibility.

§ 30. Freedom as the Condition of the Possibility of the Manifestness of the Being of Beings, i.e. of the Understanding of Being

The questionworthiness of the two ways and their unity is obscured by the fact that in both cases the problem is considered in terms of the category of causality, but without making causality itself problematic through a radical discussion of the ontological problem it involves. What would have to occur for causality (still in the Kantian sense at first) to become a problem? For Kant, causality is a character of the objectivity of objects. Objects are the beings as accessible through the theoretical experience of finite human nature. The categories are determinations of the being of such beings, determinations which allow them to show themselves in their being. But beings can only show themselves as *objects* if the appearance of beings, and that which at bottom makes this possible, i.e. the understanding of being, has the character of letting-stand-over-against. Letting something stand-over-against as something given, basically the manifestness of beings in the binding character of their so- and that-being, is only possible where the comportment to beings, whether in theoretical or practical knowledge, already acknowledges this binding character. But the latter amounts to an originary self-binding, or, in Kantian terms, the giving of a law unto oneself. The letting-be-encountered of beings, comportment to beings in each and every mode of manifestness, is only possible where freedom *exists. Freedom is the condition of the possibility of the manifestness of the being of beings, of the understanding of being*.

Causality, however, is *one* ontological determination of beings among others. *Causality is grounded in freedom. The problem of causality is a problem of freedom and not vice versa.* The question concerning the essence of freedom is the *fundamental problem* of philosophy, even if the *leading question* thereof consists in the question of being.

This fundamental thesis and its proof is not the concern of a theoretical scientific discussion, but of a grasping which always and necessarily includes the one who does the grasping, claiming him in the root of his existence, and so that he may become essential in the actual willing of his ownmost essence.

If actual being-free and willing from the ground of essence determines the fundamental philosophical stance, and thus the content of philosophy, this confirms Kant's statement on philosophy in the *Foundations of the Metaphysics of Morals*: 'Here we see philosophy brought to what is, in fact, a precarious position, which should be made fast even though it is supported by nothing in either heaven or earth. Here philosophy must show its purity, as the absolute sustainer of its laws, and not as the herald of those which an inplanted sense or who knows what tutelary nature whispers to it.'[1]

Note

1 *Foundations of the Metaphysics of Morals*, p. 84 (IV, 425).

Editor's Afterword to the German Edition of July 1981

The text presented here as Volume 31 of Martin Heidegger's *Collected Works* is that of the four-hour-per-week Freiburg lecture course from the summer semester of 1930 (beginning on April 29). The basis of this edition is the lecture manuscript, together with a copy made by Fritz Heidegger which was collated with the manuscript. The copy has been supplemented by a number of marginal comments and insertions from the manuscript, not originally included by Fritz Heidegger.

With few exceptions, citations from books and articles have been verified from Martin Heidegger's private copies, whose marginalia point to their employment in preparing the lectures. Bibliographical information is provided on the occasion of the first citation.

The lecture manuscript, which with two exceptions lacks internal headings, was comprehensively subdivided according to Heidegger's instructions for editing his *Collected Works*. The headings 'Causality and Freedom' and 'The Second Analogy' were employed in the main text as well as for two appendices and a separate summary. For the rest, headings and sub-headings were derived from important passages of text.

Comparison with the two accessible lecture transcripts of Helene Weiß and Hermann Ochsner showed that a lengthy discussion of the ὂν ὡς ἀληθές (Aristotle, *Metaphysics* Θ 10), the result of questions from Heidegger's audience, is missing from the copy. In the manuscript there is merely a reference to a corresponding appendix. This appendix was discovered among the handwritten *Nachlaß* in the separate folder 'Aristotle, *Metaphysics* Θ', with a copy likewise originating from Fritz

Heidegger. Martin Heidegger had worked these up in the course of the present lectures. Apparently he also drew from this appendix in the lecture course (two semesters later, i.e. summer semester 1931) 'Aristotle, *Metaphysics* Θ 10', later leaving it in the folder.

The copy of the appendix was likewise collated with the manuscript, and, together with additional material which had not been copied, inserted in the manuscript at the point clearly indicated by Martin Heidegger. The appendix supplements Heidegger's interpretation of the Greek understanding of Being (οὐσία) in terms of actuality, what-being, and the being of movement. Through the interpretation of Chapter Θ of Aristotle's *Metaphysics*, Heidegger attempts to show that 'presence' functions as the implicit horizon of the Greek interpretation of being not only for being as actuality, what-being, and being-moved, but also for being in the sense of true-being (truth, ἀλήθεια). The prevailing interpretation of this Chapter Θ 10 by classical philology necessitates a discussion of this chapter's placement in Book Θ. The connection between the textual question and the substantive question (ὄν ὡς ἀληθές as κυριώτατα ὄν) requires Heidegger to engage with the theses of Jaeger and Schwegler.

The lecture course, subtitled 'Introduction to Philosophy' by Heidegger himself, offers a penetrating introduction to the general problematic of Heidegger's main work, *Being and Time*. Part One treats the question of human freedom, which is unfolded from the fundamental question of philosophy (being and time) as worked up from the guiding question of metaphysics (τί τὸ ὄν). The 'going-after-the-whole' clearly implied by this question of freedom is interrogated in respect of the philosophical claim to 'go-to-the-roots', i.e. in respect of its character as challenge. This way of unfolding the problem of freedom means (Part Two of the lecture course) that Kant's concepts of transcendental and practical freedom, and their connection to causality, cannot be adequately discussed as 'problems' of a 'practical philosophy' in the sense of one particular philosophical discipline among others. Instead, they must be treated in terms of the ontological dimension exhibited in Part One (and again taken up in the Conclusion), i.e. by conceiving freedom as the condition of the possibility of the manifestness of the being of beings. Only in this ontological dimension does philosophy – especially in the discussion of human freedom – demonstrate its going-after-the-whole as a challenge in the sense of a going-to-the-root.

For extensive and crucial assistance in editing this volume, I am deeply indebted to Dr Hermann Heidegger and Prof. F.-W. von Hermann. Further thanks are due to Dr Luise Michaelson and Mr Hans-Helmuth Gander for their meticulous proof corrections.

Hartmut Tietjen
Glottertal, July 1981

English–German Glossary

absence: *Abwesenheit*
accessible: *zugänglich*; accessibility: *Zugänglichkeit*
accidental: *zufällig*; the accidental: *das Zufällige*
accountability: *Zurechnung*
act: *Tat*
action: *Handlung*
activity: *Tätigkeit*
actual: *wirklich*; actuality: *Wirklichkeit*; the actual: *das Wirkliche*
actualization: *Verwirklichung*; actualize: *verwirklichen*
administrator: *Verwalter*
alteration: *Veränderung*
animality: *Tierheit*
announce itself: *sich bekunden*
appearance: *Erscheinung*
apprehension: *Apprehension*
appropriate: *sich zueignen*
assertion: *Aussage*; assertoric truth: *Satzwahrheit, Aussagewahrheit*
authentic (genuine): *eigentlich*
awakening: *Erwachen*

being-present (presence): *Vorhandensein*
being-true: *Wahrsein*
beingness: *Seiendheit*
bygone: *das Gewesene*

causality: *Kausalität*
causation: *Ursachesein*
cause: *Ursache*
challenge: *Angriff*
change: *Wechsel, Umschlag*
commonness: *Gemeinheit*
comport: *sich verhalten*
comportment: *Verhalten*
concept: *Begriff*
condition: *Bedingung*
confusion (helplessness): *Ratlosigkeit*
connection: *Verknüpfung, Zusammenhang*
conscience: *Gewissen*
consciousness: *Bewußtsein*
constancy: *Beständigkeit*
constant presence: *beständige Anwesenheit*
context (contexture): *Zusammenhang*
contingency: *Zufälligkeit*
criticism: *Kritik*

Dasein (existence, human existence, there-being): *Dasein, Da-sein*
deconcealed: *entborgen*
deconcealment: *Entborgenheit*
deed: *Tathandlung*
distortion: *Verstelltheit*
divided: *gegliedert*
dividedness: *Gegliedertheit*
division (structuration): *Gliederung*
duration: *Dauer*

effect: *Wirkung*
empirical concept: *Erfahrungsbegriff*
enable: *ermöglichen*
enablement: *Ermöglichung*
enactment: *Wirkungsvollzug*
encounter: *begegnen*
end (aim): *Zweck*
essence: *Wesen*; essentiality: *Wesentlichkeit*
essencehood: *Wesenheit*

eternal: *ewig*
eternity: *Ewigkeit*
ethical: *sittlich*
ethics: *Sittlichkeit*
event: *Begebenheit*
existence: *Dasein; Existenz*
experience: *Erfahrung*

fact: *Tatsache*
factical: *faktisch*
facticity: *Faktizität*
factuality: *Tatsächlichkeit*
faculty (power): *Vermögen*
final: *endgültig;* finality: *Endgültigkeit*
finitization: *Verendlichung*
finitude: *Endlichkeit*
follow on: *folgen*
forgetting: *Vergessenheit*
freedom: *Freiheit*
fundamental law: *Grundgesetz*

genuine (authentic): *eigentlich*
given: *gegeben*
God: *Gott*
guideline: *Leitfaden*

historical: *geschichtlich*
history: *Geschichte*
hold oneself: *sich halten*
human: *menschlich*
humanity: *Menschheit*

idea: *Idee*
idea-formation: *Ideenbildung*
illuminate: *erhellen*
illumination (brightness): *Helle*
individualization: *Vereinzelung*
individualize: *vereinzeln*
infinity: *Unendlichkeit*

intention: *Absicht*
intra-temporal, the: *das Innerzeitige*
intra-temporality: *Innerzeitigkeit*
intuition: *Anschauung*

knowledge: *Erkenntnis*

leading question: *Leitfrage*
living being: *Lebewesen*

man: *Mensch*
manifest: *offenbar*
manifestness: *Offenbarkeit*
materiality: *Stofflichkeit*
modifications: *Abwandlungen*
multiplicity: *Mannigfaltigkeit*

occur: *geschehen*
occurrence: *Geschehen, Geschehnis*
occurrence of Being: *Seinsgeschehnis*
originary: *anfänglich*
ought: *sollen*; the ought: *das Sollen*
ownmost: *eigen*

past: *Vergangenheit*
perceive: *wahrnehmen*
perception: *Wahrnehmung*
permanence: *Beharrlichkeit*
person: *Person*; being a person: *Personsein*
personality: *Persönlichkeit*
power (faculty): *Vermögen*
preconceptual: *vorbegrifflich*
presence: *Vorhandensein, Vorhandenheit* (both = being-present);
    Anwesenheit; *Gegenwart*
present: *vorhanden*
presentation: *Darstellung*
pre-understanding: *Vorverständnis*
primal activity: *Urhandlung*
primordial: *ürsprunglich*

principle: *Grundsatz*
process: *Vorgang*
producedness: *Hergestelltheit*
producing: *Herstellen*
project: *aufwerfen*
proper: *eigentlich*

questionability: *Fraglichkeit*
questionable: *fraglich*
questionworthiness: *Fragwürdigkeit*

rational being: *Vernunftwesen*
reality: *Realität*; the real: *das Reale*
reason: *Vernunft*
reasonable (rational): *vernünftige*
receiving acceptance: *empfangendes Hinnehmen*
reflection: *Besinnung*
relatedness: *Bezogenheit*
relation (relationship): *Beziehung, Verhältnis*
relationality: *Verhältnishaftigkeit*
represent: *vorstellen*
representation: *Vorstellung*
running ahead: *Vorangehen*

science: *Wissenschaft*
scientific: *wissenschaftlich*
self-abidingness: *Beisichselbstsein*
self-determination: *Selbstbestimmung*
self-legislation: *Selbstgeseztgebung*
self-responsibility: *Selbstverantwortlichkeit*
sensibility: *Sinnlichkeit*
sensory: *sinnlich*
sequence (series, succession): *Reihe, Abfolge*
simplex: *das Einfache*
simultaneity: *Zugleichsein, Simultaneität*
so-being: *Sosein*
state (condition): *Zustand*
steadfast silence: *Stillhalten*
structuration: *Gliederung*

217

substance: *Substanz*
substantiality: *Substanzialität*
substantive content: *Sachgehalt*
substantive context: *Sachzusammenhang*
succession: *Abfolge, Nacheinander*
summation: *Inbegriff*

temporal: *zeitlich*
temporal determination: *Zeitbestimmung*
temporal relations: *Zeitverhältnisse*
temporal succession: *Zeitfolge*
temporality: *Zeitlichkeit*
there-being: *Da-sein*
there-standingness: *Da-stehendheit*
thought: *Denken*
time: *Zeit*
transform: *verwandeln*
transformation: *Verwandlung*

ultimate: *letzte*
unconditioned: *unbedingt;* the unconditioned: *das Unbedingte*
uncoveredness: *Entdecktheit*
uncovering: *entdeckend*
un-deconcealment: *Un-entborgenheit*
understanding: *Verstand*
understanding of Being: *Seinsverständnis*
undifferentiated character: *Unterscheidungslosigkeit*
unfolding: *Entfaltung*
unhiddenness: *Unverborgenheit*
unveiling: *enthüllend*

vulgar: *vulgär*

what-being: *Wassein*
what-content: *Wasgehalt*
will: *Wille*
willing: *das Wollen*
will-governed: *willentlich*
world: *Welt*
world-entity: *Weltwesen*

Greek–English Glossary

ἀγαθός: good
ἀδιαίρετος: indivisible
ἀλήθεια: truth
ἀληθεύειν: to uncover
ἀληθης: true, deconcealed
ἀπλοῦν: simple
ἀπουσία: absence
ἀρχή: principle
ἀσύνθετος: non-composite

διάνοια: thought
δύναμις: possibility, potentiality

εἶδος: look, form
εἶναι: being
ἐνέργεια: actuality
ἐπιστήμη: knowledge
ἔργον: work

θεωρία: contemplation

ἰδέα: idea

κατηγορίαι: categories

λόγος: speech, discourse

νοῦς: intellect, mind

οὐσία: being, substance

παρουσία: presence
πράγματα: things
πρᾶξις: praxis, practice

συγκείμενος: composite
συμβεβηκός: accidental

ὕλη: matter
ὑποκείμενον: what underlies
ὑπομένον: what stays the same

ψεῦδης: false, distorted

Question what you thought before

Continuum Impacts - books that change the way we think

AESTHETIC THEORY - Theodor Adorno 0826476910
I AND THOU - Martin Buber 0826476937
ANTI-OEDIPUS - Gilles Deleuze & Félix Guattari 0826476953
A THOUSAND PLATEAUS - Gilles Deleuze & Félix Guattari 0826476945
DISSEMINATION - Jacques Derrida 0826476961
BERLIN ALEXANDERPLATZ - Alfred Döblin 0826477895
PEDAGOGY OF HOPE - Paolo Freire 0826477909
MARX'S CONCEPT OF MAN - Erich Fromm 0826477917
TRUTH AND METHOD - Hans-Georg Gadamer 082647697X
THE ESSENCE OF TRUTH - Martin Heidegger 0826477046
JAZZ WRITINGS - Philip Larkin 0826476996
LIBIDINAL ECONOMY - Jean-François Lyotard 0826477003
DECONSTRUCTION AND CRITICISM - Harold Bloom et al 0826476929
DIFFERENCE AND REPETITION - Gilles Deleuze 0826477151
THE LOGIC OF SENSE - Gilles Deleuze 082647716X
GOD IS NEW EACH MOMENT - Edward Schillebeeckx 0826477011
THE DOCTRINE OF RECONCILIATION - Karl Barth 0826477925
CRITICISM AND TRUTH - Roland Barthes 0826477070
ON NIETZSCHE - George Bataille 0826477089
THE CONFLICT OF INTERPRETATIONS - Paul Ricoeur 0826477097
POSITIONS - Jacques Derrida 0826477119
ECLIPSE OF REASON - Max Horkheimer 0826477933
AN ETHICS OF SEXUAL DIFFERENCE - Luce Irigaray 0826477127
LITERATURE, POLITICS
AND CULTURE IN POSTWAR BRITAIN - Alan Sinfield 082647702X
CINEMA 1 - Gilles Deleuze 0826477054
CINEMA 2 - Gilles Deleuze 0826477062
AN INTRODUCTION TO PHILOSOPHY - Jacques Maritain 0826477178
MORAL MAN AND IMMORAL SOCIETY - Reinhld Niebuhr 0826477143
EDUCATION FOR CRITICAL CONSCIOUSNESS - Paolo Freire 082647795X
DISCOURSE ON FREE WILL -
Desiderius Erasmus & Martin Luther 0826477941
VIOLENCE AND THE SACRED - René Girard 0826477186
NIETZSCHE AND THE VICIOUS CIRCLE - Pierre Klossowski 0826477194

Continuum Impacts
CHANGING MINDS

www.continuumbooks.com